Java EE 8 High Performance

Master techniques such as memory optimization, caching, concurrency, and multithreading to achieve maximum performance from your enterprise applications

Romain Manni-Bucau

BIRMINGHAM - MUMBAI

Java EE 8 High Performance

Copyright © 2018 Packt Publishing

Commissioning Editor: Richa Tripathi
Acquisition Editor: Aiswarya Narayanan
Content Development Editor: Vikas Tiwari
Technical Editor: Diwakar Shukla
Copy Editor: Muktikant Garimella
Project Coordinator: Ulhas Kambali
Proofreader: Safis Editing
Indexer: Aishwarya Gangawane
Graphics: Tania Dutta
Production Coordinator: Shantanu Zagade

First published: January 2018

Production reference: 1250118

Published by Packt Publishing Ltd.
Livery Place
35 Livery Street
Birmingham
B3 2PB, UK.

ISBN 978-1-78847-306-4

www.packtpub.com

This book is dedicated to my family and closest ones, to all the wonderful people I met, to the people who inspire me everyday, Mark, David, Theresa, Jean-Louis, Jean-François, Jean-Baptiste, and to all my other Apache Software Foundation friends.

Finally I would like to dedicate this book to you, reminding you the quote assigned to Margaret Fuller:
"Today a reader, tomorrow a leader!"

mapt.io

Mapt is an online digital library that gives you full access to over 5,000 books and videos, as well as industry leading tools to help you plan your personal development and advance your career. For more information, please visit our website.

Why subscribe?

- Spend less time learning and more time coding with practical eBooks and Videos from over 4,000 industry professionals

- Improve your learning with Skill Plans built especially for you

- Get a free eBook or video every month

- Mapt is fully searchable

- Copy and paste, print, and bookmark content

PacktPub.com

Did you know that Packt offers eBook versions of every book published, with PDF and ePub files available? You can upgrade to the eBook version at www.PacktPub.com and as a print book customer, you are entitled to a discount on the eBook copy. Get in touch with us at service@packtpub.com for more details.

At www.PacktPub.com, you can also read a collection of free technical articles, sign up for a range of free newsletters, and receive exclusive discounts and offers on Packt books and eBooks.

Contributors

About the author

Romain Manni-Bucau is a senior software engineer who has been working in the Java EE space for 7 years and, more recently, with big data. He joined the Apache EE family in 2011 (TomEE, Johnzon, OpenWebBeans, BatchEE, OpenJPA, and Meecrowave). He mainly contributes to open source projects (CukeSpace, Arquillian, Apache Beam, and others) and aims to make development easy and efficient, letting people create what they have in mind without caring for the technical challenges. You can follow Romain on twitter at `@rmannibucau`.

About the reviewer

Luigi Fugaro has been a developer since he was a little child, doing experiments and trying out any new technologies—that is, video games! Growing up in the Java environment taught him how great and valuable the open source world is, but only when he worked at Red Hat he did get the the time and tools to really participate in this big family, the open source community. He has been working for Red Hat for 6 years as an EMEA Middleware Architect.

He has authored two books, *WildFly Cookbook* and *Mastering JBoss EAP 7*, both published by Packt.

Packt is searching for authors like you

If you're interested in becoming an author for Packt, please visit `authors.packtpub.com` and apply today. We have worked with thousands of developers and tech professionals, just like you, to help them share their insight with the global tech community. You can make a general application, apply for a specific hot topic that we are recruiting an author for, or submit your own idea.

Table of Contents

Preface

Java has been a mainstream technology for backend development for many years. Part of the reason behind this is its high stability in terms of APIs, hard backward-compatibility rules, offering a very stable and reliable backbone for any professional software, and its good performance.

The Java EE platform gives developers a flexible and powerful API that allows them to concentrate on the features more than on the technical challenges already solved by the platform. However, it doesn't mean that you should use it blindly and forget all about the work the container does for you; it would lead to a poorly behaving and unresponsive application.

When it comes to performance, Java EE is well-designed to let you get metrics, instrument your application, find any potential bottlenecks, enhance your application's performance to reach your expected Service Level Agreements (SLAs), and satisfy your customers and end users.

However, performance is often thought of as something we look at once the application is completely developed. This can be true for standalone applications, which are easy to optimize as they are self-contained. However, with the advent of microservices and distributed applications, you need to think of performance as a continuous process in order to avoid having to redevelop your application afterwards.

That is all this book is about—giving you the needed tools to be able to work on the performance of your Java EE application, ensure you benefit from the simplicity of the Java EE API without abusing of them and having bad surprises, ensure you think upfront of the whole application flow and not only on a subpart of the full system which can lead to local optimizations and global tragedies and finally, ensure you can continuously control your performances and thus work smoothly on them during all the development phase and succeed to deliver a high quality product.

Who this book is for

This books targets people who have to work with Java and Java EE applications, especially people working on performance topics in local or distributed environments and production or development environments.

This book assumes that you are, at least, familiar with Java 8 development and some Java EE concepts. You don't need to be a Java EE guru, but a basic understanding of things such as Java proxying and interception will help you get up to speed with the concepts covered in the book.

What this book covers

Chapter 1, *Money – The Quote Manager Application*, starts by explaining how to set up a basic environment to be able to follow the book's chapters. It also shows you how to develop a common Java EE 8 application, which you can use all along the chapters to easily test every topic.

Chapter 2, *Looking Under the Cover – What is This EE Thing?*, explains why we use a JavaEE 8 container and what it brings to the developers. It goes through some mainstream technologies, and shows the work done under the cover by the server and how it can impact the performance when not used the way it was designed to be.

Chapter 3, *Monitor Your Application*, targets the instrumentation of the application in several flavors. The high-level goal is to get the metrics of your application at every level and layer to ensure that you can clearly identify bottlenecks work on the performance of your application. It uses several techniques, more or less simple, and targets the different phases of work you can do on your application.

Chapter 4, *Application Optimization – Memory Management and Server Configuration*, targets the configuration you can use to optimize your application without modifying your code at all. It concentrates around JVM memory tuning, which can be very advanced with modern platforms, and Java EE server configuration, which can be worth having a look at.

Chapter 5, *Scale Up – Threading and Implications*, concentrates on the threading model that Java EE 8 offers. It starts by listing the thread pool you will work with, how you can define new thread pools specific to your application and integrating with the platform, and, finally, it opens the end of the chapter, talking about modern programming models in the Java EE 8 platform, which completely changes the way you use threads to be more reactive.

Chapter 6, *Be Lazy; Cache Your Data*, deals with the caching. It starts by explaining what caching is and how it is supposed to help you improve performance. Then, it explains how Java EE 8 helps you to rely on the cache at HTTP level and how it integrates with JCache specification to speed up your code drastically.

`Chapter 7`, *Be Fault-Tolerant*, helps you design and code distributed applications such as microservices to keep your performance under control and your application stable. The overall goal is to ensure that you don't get affected by services you rely on in a bad manner and that your service stays available irrespective of the state others are in. In other words, it helps you prevent a domino effect on your system if something goes wrong somewhere.

`Chapter 8`, *Loggers and Performances – A Trade-Off*, deals with loggers. This is surely the most common API used across all applications, but it can also viciously affect the performance, since a badly used or configured logger can be very significant to your performance figures. This chapter explains what a logging framework is and how to use it. It will help you avoid all these pitfalls.

`Chapter 9`, *Benchmarking Your Application*, is about dedicated benchmark projects or phases of your project. It explains which tools to use, what steps to go through so as to ensure your benchmark is useful, and how to get the most out of a benchmark.

`Chapter 10`, *Continuous Performance Evaluation*, goes through several solutions to make sure that you can evaluate the performance of your system in a continuous way. It aims to ensure you can get performance figures out of your system at each and every development stage and, used at the extreme, you can even get it for each pull request done on your project. This chapter goes through some tools and solutions, and explains how to enrich some existing frameworks with some glue code to go further and not stay blocked on the topic that is not yet that common but very important for applications with a defined SLA.

To get the most out of this book

1. A minimal knowledge of the Java technology is needed to follow this book
2. Some basic experience on performance investigation is nice to have
3. Some knowledge of distributed systems, although not mandatory, can help you to understand some parts
4. A computer where you can develop and run a Java application is highly encouraged even if not mandatory. A setup example is a machine with Linux or Windows, 1 GB (recommended 2 GB) of memory, a dual core CPU and at least 1 GB of available disk space.
5. Being able to use a console would greatly help

Download the example code files

You can download the example code files for this book from your account at `www.packtpub.com`. If you purchased this book elsewhere, you can visit `www.packtpub.com/support` and register to have the files emailed directly to you.

You can download the code files by following these steps:

1. Log in or register at `www.packtpub.com`.
2. Select the **SUPPORT** tab.
3. Click on **Code Downloads & Errata**.
4. Enter the name of the book in the **Search** box and follow the onscreen instructions.

Once the file is downloaded, please make sure that you unzip or extract the folder using the latest version of:

- WinRAR/7-Zip for Windows
- Zipeg/iZip/UnRarX for Mac
- 7-Zip/PeaZip for Linux

The code bundle for the book is also hosted on GitHub at `https://github.com/PacktPublishing/Java-EE-8-High-Performance`. We also have other code bundles from our rich catalog of books and videos available at `https://github.com/PacktPublishing/`. Check them out!

Download the color images

We also provide a PDF file that has color images of the screenshots/diagrams used in this book. You can download it here: `http://www.packtpub.com/sites/default/files/downloads/JavaEE8HighPerformance_ColorImages.pdf`.

Conventions used

There are a number of text conventions used throughout this book.

`CodeInText`: Indicates code words in text, database table names, folder names, filenames, file extensions, pathnames, dummy URLs, user input, and Twitter handles. Here is an example: "Most of this book will work with a web profile server, so we will package our application as `war`:"

A block of code is set as follows:

```
<packaging>war</packaging>
```

Any command-line input or output is written as follows:

```
$ export JAVA_HOME=/home/developer/jdk1.8.0_144
$ export MAVEN_HOME=/home/developer/apache-maven-3.5.0
```

Bold: Indicates a new term, an important word, or words that you see onscreen. For example, words in menus or dialog boxes appear in the text like this. Here is an example: "Select **System info** from the **Administration** panel."

Warnings or important notes appear like this.

Tips and tricks appear like this.

Get in touch

Feedback from our readers is always welcome.

General feedback: Email `feedback@packtpub.com` and mention the book title in the subject of your message. If you have questions about any aspect of this book, please email us at `questions@packtpub.com`.

Errata: Although we have taken every care to ensure the accuracy of our content, mistakes do happen. If you have found a mistake in this book, we would be grateful if you would report this to us. Please visit www.packtpub.com/submit-errata, selecting your book, clicking on the Errata Submission Form link, and entering the details.

Piracy: If you come across any illegal copies of our works in any form on the Internet, we would be grateful if you would provide us with the location address or website name. Please contact us at copyright@packtpub.com with a link to the material.

If you are interested in becoming an author: If there is a topic that you have expertise in and you are interested in either writing or contributing to a book, please visit authors.packtpub.com.

Reviews

Please leave a review. Once you have read and used this book, why not leave a review on the site that you purchased it from? Potential readers can then see and use your unbiased opinion to make purchase decisions, we at Packt can understand what you think about our products, and our authors can see your feedback on their book. Thank you!

For more information about Packt, please visit packtpub.com

1
Money – The Quote Manager Application

Before working on evaluating and enhancing the performance of your application, you need to indeed have an application. In this part, we will create a small application that we will use to illustrate every part of the book. This chapter doesn't intend to explain all the steps required to create a Java EE application. It will give you the overall steps and ensure that the references to the steps will be obvious later.

The use case of this application will be a microservice that provides a set of web services to manage stocks and shares. This chapter will, therefore, introduce you to the application environment:

- Application code structure
- Database setup
- Data persistence
- Exposing data over HTTP
- Deploying your application

Setting up the environment

Before starting with writing code, make sure that you have an environment ready to work with Java EE. We need a **Java Virtual Machine 8** (**JVM 8**) and, more particularly, the **Java Development Kit 8** (**JDK 8**). As a quick reminder, Java EE version *V* is based on **Java Standalone Edition** (**Java SE**) version *V* as well. You can download the JDK on the Oracle website (`http://www.oracle.com/technetwork/java/javase/downloads/jdk8-downloads-2133151.html`).

Alternatively, you can download the OpenJDK version of the JDK on the OpenJDK project website (`http://openjdk.java.net/install/`), but I recommend that you use the Oracle version. We will discuss this later in the book.

Don't forget to accept the license agreement and select the right distribution for your operating system (Windows, Linux, or macOS).

Now that we have a JDK, we need a tool to build our application and convert it into a format that we will be able to deploy in our Java EE server. This book will use Apache Maven (`https://maven.apache.org/`) to build the application. It can be downloaded on the Apache Maven download page (`https://maven.apache.org/download.cgi`). We need the binary distribution; Linux users have to select the `tar.gz` format while Windows users have to select the `.zip` archive.

At this point, we have everything we need to create our application. You will probably want to have an **Integrated Development Environment** (**IDE**), such as NetBeans (`https://netbeans.org/`), Eclipse (`https://eclipse.org/ide/`), or Intellij Idea (`https://www.jetbrains.com/idea/`). Since this book is more about performance than development, we won't go into much detail about IDEs. If you need one, just select the one you are the most familiar with.

To ensure that the environment is ready, we will set variables to define where to find the software without having to use the full path to the binary or script each time. `JAVA_HOME` will point to the folder you extracted from the JDK, and `MAVEN_HOME` will point to the folder you extracted from the Apache Maven archive. Here is an example for Linux (replace `export` with `set` for a DOS shell):

```
$ export JAVA_HOME=/home/developer/jdk1.8.0_144
$ export MAVEN_HOME=/home/developer/apache-maven-3.5.0
```

Now, we need to ensure that the JDK and Maven tools are available. For this, we add them to `PATH` on Linux and `Path` on Windows:

```
# On Linux
$ export PATH=$JAVA_HOME/bin:$MAVEN_HOME/bin:$PATH

# On Windows
$ set Path=%JAVA_HOME%\bin;%MAVEN_HOME%\bin;%Path%
```

You can validate your setup by executing the following command:

```
$ mvn -version
Maven home: /home/developer/apache-maven-3.5.0
Java version: 1.8.0_144, vendor: Oracle Corporation
Java home: /home/developer/jdk1.8.0_144/jre
Default locale: fr_FR, platform encoding: UTF-8
OS name: "linux", version: "4.10.0-32-generic", arch: "amd64", family:
"unix"
```

To run a Java EE application, we also need a container, such as GlassFish, WildFly, WebSphere Liberty Profile, or Apache TomEE. The deployment being specific and Java EE 8 being very recent, we will use GlassFish in this book.

Finally, to get everything ready, we will use a database. We will use MySQL as a very common case, but any other relational database will work as well. You can download MySQL from `https://dev.mysql.com/downloads/mysql/`, but most Linux distributions will have a package ready to install. For instance, on Ubuntu you can just execute the following line:

```
sudo apt install mysql-server
```

The application architecture

Our application will import some stock quotations daily; it will then expose them and allow you to update them through a web service.

To implement it, we will use a standard Java EE architecture:

- The persistence layer will use JPA 2.2 and store the data in a MySQL database.
- A service layer will implement the business logic and orchestrate the persistence layer. It will rely on the following:
  - **Java Transaction API (JTA)** 1.2 for transactionality
  - **Context and Dependency Injection** 2.0 (**CDI**) for **Inversion of Control (IoC)**
  - Bean Validation 2.0 for validations

- A front layer will expose a part of the service layer through HTTP. It will rely on the following:
    - JAX-RS 2.1 for stateless endpoints
    - WebSocket 1.1 for stateful communications
    - JSON-B 1.0 for marshalling/unmarshalling

Here is a picture summarizing this structure:

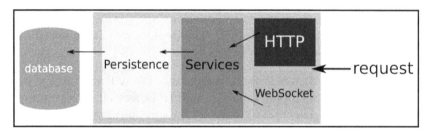

Application project highlights

To be able to create and run this application, we will need to set up a build tool. For this book, it will be Apache Maven; however, Gradle, Ant, or any other alternative will work perfectly as well. We will then identify some key parts of the application code and, finally, we will insert some data to ensure that our application is usable before investigating its performance.

The build

The only dependency Java EE requires is the Java EE API:

```
<dependency>
  <groupId>javax</groupId>
  <artifactId>javaee-api</artifactId>
  <version>${javaee-api.version}</version> <!-- 8.0 -->
  <scope>provided</scope>
</dependency>
```

If you prefer, you can indeed register all the individual specifications, but it will require more work to maintain the list with Java EE upgrades. For this reason, the bundle is often preferred.

Here, the point is to ensure that the API is provided, which means it will not be packaged in the deliverable and will inherit from the server API. The server providing the services associated with the API also provides the API with the right supported version and the right defaults matching the built-in implementations.

Since Java EE 6, there are two main flavors of Java EE: the web profile and the full profile. The web profile is a light version, with only half the specifications compared with the full profile, more or less. The web profile supports only web applications and, therefore, `war` files. Most of this book will work with a web profile server, so we will package our application as `war`:

```
<packaging>war</packaging>
```

Since we need Java 8, don't forget to configure the Java source and target version in the build. It can be done in different ways, but configuring `maven-compiler-plugin` as follows is an efficient one:

```
<plugin>
  <groupId>org.apache.maven.plugins</groupId>
  <artifactId>maven-compiler-plugin</artifactId>
  <version>3.6.1</version>
  <configuration>
    <source>1.8</source>
    <target>1.8</target>
  </configuration>
</plugin>
```

The persistence layer

Our data model will be simple: a *quote* will be linked to a *customer*. This means that a *customer* can see a set of *quotes*, and *quotes* can be seen by a set of customers. In terms of use cases, we want to be able to monetize our API and make the customers pay to access some quote prices. To do so, we will need a sort of whitelist of quotes per customer.

JPA uses a descriptor called `persistence.xml`, placed in the META-INF repository of resources (or WEB-INF), which defines how `EntityManager`, which is a class that allows the manipulation of our model, will be instantiated. Here is what it looks like for our application:

```
<persistence xmlns="http://xmlns.jcp.org/xml/ns/persistence"
             xmlns:xsi="http://www.w3.org/2001/XMLSchema-instance"
             xsi:schemaLocation="
http://xmlns.jcp.org/xml/ns/persistence
```

```
            http://xmlns.jcp.org/xml/ns/persistence/persistence_2_2.xsd"
            version="2.2">
  <persistence-unit name="quote">
    <class>com.github.rmannibucau.quote.manager.model.Customer</class>
    <class>com.github.rmannibucau.quote.manager.model.Quote</class>
    <exclude-unlisted-classes>true</exclude-unlisted-classes>
    <properties>
      <property name="avax.persistence.schema
      -generation.database.action" value="create"/>
    </properties>
  </persistence-unit>
</persistence>
```

The link between the database and the Java code is done through entities. An entity is a
plain old java object (**POJO**) that is decorated with the `javax.persistence` annotations.
They mainly define the mapping between the database and the Java model. For
instance, `@Id` marks a Java field that must match the database identifier.

Here is an example of our `Quote` entity:

```
@Entity
public class Quote {
    @Id
    @GeneratedValue
    private long id;

    private String name;

    private double value;

    @ManyToMany
    private Set<Customer> customers;

    // getters/setters
}
```

This simple model implicitly defines a *QUOTE* table with three columns, *ID*, *NAME*, and
VALUE (the casing can depend on the database), and a table to manage the relationship
with the *CUSTOMER* table, which is named `QUOTE_CUSTOMER` by default.

In the same spirit, our `Customer` entity just defines an identifier and name as columns and also the reverse relationship to the `Quote` entity:

```
@Entity
public class Customer {
    @Id
    @GeneratedValue
    private long id;

    private String name;

    @ManyToMany(mappedBy = "customers")
    private Set<Quote> quotes;

    // getters/setters
}
```

What is important here is to notice the relationships in the model. We will deal with this later on.

The service layer

The goal of the book being to discuss the performance and not how to write a Java EE application, we will not detail the whole service layer here. However, to ensure a common knowledge of what we are dealing with, we will illustrate the code with one service.

We are using JTA 1.2 with JPA 2.2 to establish a link between our database and the Java model. The `QuoteService` bean, responsible for managing the `Quote` persistence, can therefore look like the following:

```
@Transactional
@ApplicationScoped
public class QuoteService {
    @PersistenceContext
    private EntityManager entityManager;

    public Optional<Quote> findByName(final String name) {
        return entityManager.createQuery("select q from Quote q where
        q.name = :name", Quote.class)
                .setParameter("name", name)
                .getResultStream()
                .findFirst();
    }

    public Optional<Quote> findById(final long id) {
```

```
        return Optional.ofNullable(entityManager.find(Quote.class, id));
    }

    public long countAll() {
        return entityManager.createQuery("select count(q) from Quote
        q", Number.class)
                .getSingleResult()
                .longValue();
    }

    public Quote create(final Quote newQuote) {
        entityManager.persist(newQuote);
        entityManager.flush();
        return newQuote;
    }

    // ... other methods based on the same model
}
```

JPA may or may not be used in a transactional context, depending on the kind of operation you do. When you *read* data, you can often do it without any transaction until you need some lazy loading. However, when you *write* data (insert/update/delete entities), JPA requires a running transaction to be able to execute the action. This is to ensure consistency of data but also has some implications on the code. To respect that requirement, and have an active transaction, we use `@Transactional` on methods instead of relying on **Enterprise Java Bean 3.2** (**EJB 3.2**), so we can reuse the power of CDI (`@ApplicationScoped`, for instance, which will avoid creating a new instance per injection).

Our finders are very simple and directly use the `EntityManager` API. The only new thing Java 8 brings us in this code is the ability to wrap the result with `Optional` which offers a programmatic way to deal with the presence or absense of the entity instead of relying on a null check. Concretely, the caller can use our finder this way:

```
final int quoteCount = getCustomer().getCountFor("myquote");
final double quotesPrice = quoteService.findByName("myquote")
    .map(quote -> quote.getValue() * quoteCount)
    .orElse(0);
```

This kind of code hides the conditional branches behind a fluent API, which makes it more expressive and readable, while the lambdas stay small enough.

Finally, we used inline queries in this code, not static ones like in the `@NamedQuery` API.

The JAX-RS layer

If we step back one second and think about which stopover the application will execute, we can identify a few of them:

- HTTP communication handling
- Payload (un)marshalling
- Routing
- Service invocation

Because of the separation of concern principles, or simply for technical constraints between layers, it is very common to use a Data Transfer Object between the JAX-RS/front layer and the CDI/business layer. Of course, this statement can be applied to the business sub-layers as well, but in the case of this book, we will just do it in the JAX-RS layer. To make it obvious in the book, we will prefix the JAX-RS model with `Json`. Check out the following code snippet:

```
@JsonbPropertyOrder({"id", "name", "customerCount"})
public class JsonQuote {
    private long id;
    private String name;
    private double value;

    @JsonbProperty("customer_count")
    private long customerCount;

    // getters/setters
}
```

In this context, the front layer role is to delegate most of the logic to the service layer and convert the business model to the front model (it can almost be seen as a Java to JavaScript conversion for a lot of modern applications):

```
@Path("quote")
@RequestScoped
public class QuoteResource {
    @Inject
    private QuoteService quoteService;

    @GET
    @Path("{id}")
    public JsonQuote findById(@PathParam("id") final long id) {
        return quoteService.findById(id) // delegation to the business
        layer
                .map(quote -> { // the model conversion
```

```
            final JsonQuote json = new JsonQuote();
            json.setId(quote.getId());
            json.setName(quote.getName());
            json.setValue(quote.getValue());
    json.setCustomerCount(ofNullable(quote.getCustomers())
    .map(Collection::size).orElse(0));
            return json;
        })
        .orElseThrow(() -> new
        WebApplicationException(Response.Status.NO_CONTENT));
    }

    // other methods
}
```

 We set the JAX-RS `@ApplicationPath` to `/api` to ensure that our endpoints are deployed under the `/api` subcontext.

The WebSocket layer

Why use JAX-RS and WebSocket? Don't they serve the same purpose? Not exactly, in fact, it is becoming more and more common to use both in the same application even if WebSocket is still a bit recent.

JAX-RS (and, more generally, HTTP/1 and the brand new HTTP/2) is generally web application oriented. Understand that it is often used for applications with a user interface (which needs to be compatible with all browsers). It is also commonly used in environments where you cannot assume much about the network setup. More particularly, in environments where you cannot assume the network setup, the proxies will let WebSocket connections work properly (either preventing them completely or disconnecting them too early). The last common case where HTTP-based solutions make a lot of sense is to try to target a market where clients can be developed in any language (Java, Python, Ruby, Go, Node.js, and so on). The fact that the technology is today spreading all over the world and works well with stateless connections, makes it easier to get started with, and it is therefore more accessible than WebSocket, which requires some care from client developers.

However, WebSocket will fit cases where you have higher performance or reactivity constraints, a state to maintain in order to handle the business use case, or you simply want to push the information from the server without requiring a client operation (such as polling).

When you start using a connected protocol such as WebSocket, the first thing to define is your own communication protocol: the format of the message you send/receive and the order of the messages (if needed).

Our WebSocket layer will be responsible for enabling a client to quickly access the quote prices. Therefore, we will react on a client's request (it will contain the name of the quote that we want to get the price for) and we will respond with two pieces of information: whether we found the quote and the current price, if existing.

Then, you need to pick a format to prepare the content sent through the WebSocket over the wire. Here, the choice is often guided by a trade-off between the client (consumers of the service), the requirements, the performances, and the ease of implementation. In our case, we will consider that our clients can be written in Java as well as in JavaScript. That is why we will use JSON.

To summarize the protocol, here is a full communication round-trip, as shown in the following diagram:

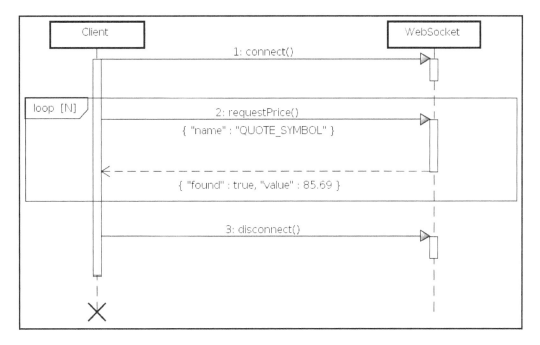

The communication protocol is based on a single message type in our case, so a full client/server communication looks like these steps:

1. The client will connect to the server.
2. The client will request the price of a quote N times, based on its symbol (name/identifier).
3. Assuming there is no I/O error or timeout, the client will trigger a disconnect, which will end the communication.

In terms of code, we need multiple bricks of Java EE and we need the following to put them together:

- The WebSocket API, obviously
- JSON-B (we could use JSON-P, but it is less friendly) for the Java to JSON conversion
- CDI, to link the WebSocket to the business layer

To start easy, we can modelize our payloads. Our request has only one `name` attribute, so JSON-B allows us to define it this way:

```
public class ValueRequest {
    private String name;

    // getter/setter
}
```

On the other side (that is, the response), we have to return a `value` attribute with the price of the quote and a `found` Boolean marking `value` as filled or not. Here again, JSON-B allows us to do a direct mapping of this model with a plain POJO:

```
public static class ValueResponse {
    private double value;
    private boolean found;

    // getters/setters
}
```

Now, we need to ensure that the WebSocket will be able to deserialize and serialize these objects as required. The specification defines `Encoder` and `Decoder` APIs for this purpose. Since we will back our implementation by JSON-B, we can directly implement it using the (I/O) stream flavors of these APIs (called `TextStream`). Actually, before doing so, we need to get a `Jsonb` instance. Considering that we have already created one and made it available in CDI, we can then simply inject the instance in our coders:

```
@Dependent
public class JsonEncoder implements Encoder.TextStream<Object> {
    @Inject
    private Jsonb jsonb;

    @Override
    public void encode(final Object o, final Writer writer) throws
EncodeException, IOException {
        jsonb.toJson(o, writer);
    }

    // other methods are no-op methods
}
```

The decoding side is now fast to develop, thanks to the JSON-B API, which fits this usage very well with its `fromJson()` API. We will just note that this side is specific to `ValueRequest`, since we need to specify the type to instantiate it (compared with the encoding side, which can determine it dynamically):

```
@Dependent
public class RequestDecoder implements Decoder.TextStream<ValueRequest> {
    @Inject
    private Jsonb jsonb;

    @Override
    public ValueRequest decode(final Reader reader) throws DecodeException,
IOException {
        return jsonb.fromJson(reader, ValueRequest.class);
    }

    // other methods are no-op methods
}
```

Now that we have a way to handle our messages, we need to bind our WebSocket endpoint and implement the `@OnMessage` method to find the price and send it back to the client relying on our business layer. In terms of implementation, we will react to a `ValueRequest` message, try to find the corresponding quote, fill the response payload, and send it back to the client:

```
@Dependent
@ServerEndpoint(
  value = "/quote",
  decoders = RequestDecoder.class,
  encoders = JsonEncoder.class)
  public class DirectQuoteSocket {
  @Inject
  private QuoteService quoteService;

  @OnMessage
  public void onMessage(final Session session, final ValueRequest request)
{
    final Optional<Quote> quote =
quoteService.findByName(request.getName());
      final ValueResponse response = new ValueResponse();
      if (quote.isPresent()) {
          response.setFound(true);
          response.setValue(quote.get().getValue()); // false
      }

      if (session.isOpen()) {
          try {
              session.getBasicRemote().sendObject(response);
              }
              catch (final EncodeException | IOException e) {
              throw new IllegalArgumentException(e);
          }
      }
    }
}
```

Provision some data

At this point, we have our application. Now, we need to ensure that it has some data and, then, move on to evaluating its performance.

Without delving too much into the business details, we will implement the provisioning in two passes:

- Find all the symbols to update
- For each symbol found, update the price in the database

To do so, we will use two public webservices:

- http://www.cboe.com/publish/ScheduledTask/MktData/cboesymboldir2.csv, to find a set of symbols
- https://query1.finance.yahoo.com/v10/finance/quoteSummary/{symbol}? modules=financialData, to find the current price of each quote

The first one is a plain CSV file, which we will parse without any library to keep things simple and because the format does not require special escaping/parsing. The second one will return a JSON payload, which we can read directly using the JAX-RS 2.1 client API.

Here is how we can retrieve our data:

```
private String[] getSymbols(final Client client) {
    try (final BufferedReader stream = new BufferedReader(
            new InputStreamReader(
                    client.target(symbolIndex)
                            .request(APPLICATION_OCTET_STREAM_TYPE)
                            .get(InputStream.class),
                    StandardCharsets.UTF_8))) {

        return stream.lines().skip(2/*comment+header*/)
                .map(line -> line.split(","))
                .filter(columns -> columns.length > 2 &&
!columns[1].isEmpty())
                .map(columns -> columns[1])
                .toArray(String[]::new);
    } catch (final IOException e) {
        throw new IllegalArgumentException("Can't connect to find symbols",
e);
    }
}
```

Note that we directly read a buffered reader backed by the HTTP response stream. Once the symbols are extracted, we can simply iterate over them and request the price of each quote:

```java
try {
    final Data data = client.target(financialData)
            .resolveTemplate("symbol", symbol)
            .request(APPLICATION_JSON_TYPE)
            .get(Data.class);

    if (!data.hasPrice()) {
        LOGGER.warning("Can't retrieve '" + symbol + "'");
        return;
    }

    final double value = data.getQuoteSummary().getResult().get(0)
        .getFinancialData().getCurrentPrice().getRaw();

    final Quote quote = quoteService.mutate(symbol, quoteOrEmpty ->
            quoteOrEmpty.map(q -> {
                q.setValue(value);
                return q;
            }).orElseGet(() -> {
                final Quote newQuote = new Quote();
                newQuote.setName(symbol);
                newQuote.setValue(value);
                quoteService.create(newQuote);
                return newQuote;
            }));

    LOGGER.info("Updated quote '" + quote.getName() + "'");
} catch (final WebApplicationException error) {
    LOGGER.info("Error getting '" + symbol + "': " + error.getMessage()
    + " (HTTP " + (error.getResponse() == null ? "-" :
    error.getResponse().getStatus()) + ")");
}
```

This piece of code sends an HTTP request, thanks to the JAX-RS client API and JSON-B, which unmarshalls a data model. Then, we use the obtained data to update our database quote if it already exists; otherwise, we use the data to create the database quote.

The code now needs to be wired to be executed. We have multiple options here:

- Execute it at startup
- Execute it regularly
- Execute it when an endpoint is called

In the context of this book, we will use the first two options. The startup is common for us, even if it is not as realistic, because once started, we will get some data. The second option will use an EJB 3.2 @Schedule, which will run hourly.

The startup implementation requires a simple CDI bean with a method calling the previous logic when @ApplicationScoped is created (at startup):

```
@ApplicationScoped
public class InitialProvisioning {
    @Inject
    private ProvisioningService provisioningService;

    public void onStart(@Observes @Initialized(ApplicationScoped.class)
final ServletContext context) {
        provisioningService.refresh();
    }
}
```

The scheduling is done, thanks to the Enterprise Java Bean @Schedule API, which allows us, in one annotation, to request the container to regularly execute a method:

```
@Singleton
@Lock(WRITE)
public class DataRefresher {
    @Inject
    private ProvisioningService provisioningService;

    @Schedule(hour = "*", persistent = false, info = "refresh-quotes")
    public void refresh() {
        provisioningService.refresh();
    }
}
```

 In a real application, you will probably want to configure the refresh frequency and use the TimerService API to trigger the execution based on the application configuration. In the same spirit, the startup execution could be ignored based on the configuration in order to have a faster startup.

Application summary

When working on the performance, it is always important to keep two things in mind:

- The application business (what the application does)
- The application technical stack (how the application was designed)

Even if the information you have about these two points is very high-level, ensure that you know them before working on the performance.

Let's do this exercise with our application and ensure that we know how to answer both the questions.

The application business

Our application is responsible for providing the quote prices to HTTP or WebSocket clients. With its model and customer/quote relationship, it can enable us to provide (or not provide) the price accessed by the customer if we add permissions or rules, for instance. What is important to see at this stage is that both the entities are in a relationship and that our application can visit this relationship for its business needs and trigger an implicit lazy loading of the relationship entities.

The data is injected into the system based on two external HTTP sources (CBOE and Yahoo). The first one provides a symbol dictionary of the quotes, and the second one, the prices.

The application design

Technically, the provisioning of the quote and prices is done asynchronously (not when a customer request is sent). It retrieves the data using a JAX-RS 2.1 client and inserts it as fast as possible into the database.

Access to the application is gained either through HTTP or WebSocket. In both cases, the application uses a JSON format for message exchange.

The application server

Java EE defines specifications and, therefore, you can find several different implementations. Each major vendor has its own server but, of course, for us and Java EE, a lot of servers are fully open source. As Java EE 8 is very recent, we will use GlassFish, which is the reference implementation and is therefore the first one to be compliant with the specification (it must be released with the specification). However, there are a lot of alternatives (such as Apache TomEE, Wildfly, Payara, Liberty Profile, and so on), which will probably follow in the coming months.

GlassFish can be downloaded from its website (`https://javaee.github.io/glassfish/ download`). We need the 5.x version to target Java EE 8, but due to its early release, a major part of this book will work with the previous versions.

If you want to integrate it with your development environment (and Maven), you can add the GlassFish repository to `pom.xml`, as follows:

```
<pluginRepository>
  <id>maven-java-net</id>
  <url>https://maven.java.net/content/groups/promoted/</url>
</pluginRepository>
```

Add the GlassFish plugin without forgetting to specify the version of the server in order to override the default one, which is now quite old:

```
<plugin> <!-- glassfish.version = 5.0 -->
  <groupId>org.glassfish.embedded</groupId>
  <artifactId>maven-embedded-glassfish-plugin</artifactId>
  <version>3.1.2.2</version>
  <configuration>
    <app>target/${project.build.finalName}</app>
    <port>9090</port>
    <contextRoot>${project.artifactId}</contextRoot>
  </configuration>
  <dependencies>
    <dependency>
      <groupId>org.glassfish.main.common</groupId>
      <artifactId>simple-glassfish-api</artifactId>
      <version>${glassfish.version}</version>
    </dependency>
    <dependency>
      <groupId>org.glassfish.main.extras</groupId>
      <artifactId>glassfish-embedded-all</artifactId>
      <version>${glassfish.version}</version>
    </dependency>
```

```
    </dependencies>
  </plugin>
```

With this setup, you can run the following command to package the application as `war` and deploy it in GlassFish:

```
$ mvn package embedded-glassfish:run
```

To shut down the server, type *X* and *ENTER*.

Testing the application

Before starting to work on our application from the performance window, let's get a bit familiar with it. We will not browse and test all the endpoints but just check how to get a price using the JAX-RS layer and WebSocket layer. In other words, we will define two customer use cases of our application.

The goal here is to ensure that we know how to use the application to be able to write test scenarios later. To do so, we will execute some requests manually on both fronts (HTTP and WebSocket).

Get a quote price the JAX-RS way

The endpoint we saw previously has been deployed on `/<application_context>/api/quote/{quoteId}` with the context of the web application, `application_context`. If you used the previous setup, it is, most likely, the artifact ID of the Maven project. Let's consider from now on that it is `quote-manager`.

Here is what it returns for one of the quotes:

```
$ curl -v http://localhost:9090/quote-manager/api/quote/8
* Trying 127.0.0.1...
* TCP_NODELAY set
* Connected to localhost (127.0.0.1) port 9090 (#0)
> GET /quote-manager/api/quote/8 HTTP/1.1
> Host: localhost:9090
> User-Agent: curl/7.52.1
> Accept: */*
>
< HTTP/1.1 200 OK
< Server: Undefined Product Name - define product and version info in
config/branding 0.0.0
```

```
< X-Powered-By: Servlet/3.1 JSP/2.3 (Undefined Product Name - define
product and version info in config/branding 0.0.0 Java/Oracle
Corporation/1.8)
< Content-Type: application/json
< Content-Length: 54
<
* Curl_http_done: called premature == 0
* Connection #0 to host localhost left intact
{"id":8,"name":"JOBS","customer_count":0,"value":59.4}
```

This kind of application often needs a kind of index endpoint to be able to browse quotes (in a nice user interface or a command-line interface, for instance). In our case, it is our *find all* endpoint, which supports pagination through the query parameters. Here is how to use it and the kind of data it returns:

```
$ curl -v http://localhost:9090/quote-manager/api/quote?from=0&to=5
* Trying 127.0.0.1...
* TCP_NODELAY set
* Connected to localhost (127.0.0.1) port 9090 (#0)
> GET /quote-manager/api/quote?from=0 HTTP/1.1
> Host: localhost:9090
> User-Agent: curl/7.52.1
> Accept: */*
>
< HTTP/1.1 200 OK
< Server: Undefined Product Name - define product and version info in
config/branding 0.0.0
< X-Powered-By: Servlet/3.1 JSP/2.3 (Undefined Product Name - define
product and version info in config/branding 0.0.0 Java/Oracle
Corporation/1.8)
< Content-Type: application/json
< Content-Length: 575
<
{"total":10,"items":[{"id":1,"name":"FLWS","customer_count":0,"value":9.0},
{"id":2,"name":"VNET","customer_count":0,"value":5.19},{"id":3,"name":"XXII
","customer_count":0,"value":2.2},{"id":4,"name":"TWOU","customer_count":0,
"value":50.1},{"id":5,"name":"DDD","customer_count":0,"value":12.56},{"id":
6,"name":"MMM","customer_count":0,"value":204.32},{"id":7,"name":"WBAI","cu
stomer_count":0,"value":10.34},{"id":8,"name":"JOBS","customer_count":0,"va
lue":59.4},{"id":9,"name":"WUBA","customer_count":0,"value":62.63},{"id":10
,"name":"CAFD","customer_count":0,"value":14.42}]}
```

Get the price, the WebSocket way

The WebSocket endpoint is deployed on `/<application_context>/quote`, and some exchanges can look like the following:

```
connect> ws://localhost:9090/quote-manager/quote
send> {"name":"VNET"}
received< {"found":true,"value":5.19}
send> {"name":"DDD"}
received< {"found":true,"value":12.56}
disconnect>
Connection closed: Close status 1000 (Normal Closure)
```

What is interesting to see in this communication dump is the fact that the connection lasts for more than one request, and it is based on the symbol more than the identifier (compared to the previous JAX-RS samples).

Setting up MySQL

All the previous parts will work transparently in Glassfish, as it can provide you with a default database if none is set since Java EE 7. This default database is an Apache Derby one for Glassfish. Considering that we will work on the performance soon, we want a recent *production* database. To ensure this, we will set up MySQL.

Assuming that you installed MySQL for your operating system and that it runs on `localhost:3306` (the default), we need to create a new database. Let's call it `quote_manager`:

```
$ mysql -u root -p
Enter password: ******
...
mysql> create database quote_manager;
Query OK, 1 row affected (0.00 sec)
```

Now that we have a database, we can configure it in Glassfish and let JPA 2.2 create the tables for us based on our model. For this, we need to create `glassfish-resources.xml` in the `WEB-INF` folder of the `war` package (put it in `src/main/webapp/WEB-INF` in the Maven project):

```
<?xml version="1.0" encoding="UTF-8"?>
<!DOCTYPE resources PUBLIC "-//GlassFish.org//DTD GlassFish Application
Server 3.1 Resource Definitions//EN"
    "http://glassfish.org/dtds/glassfish-resources_1_5.dtd">
```

```
<resources>
  <jdbc-connection-pool allow-non-component-callers="false"
                        associate-with-thread="false"
                        connection-creation-retry-attempts="0"
                        connection-creation-retry-interval-in-seconds="10"
                        connection-leak-reclaim="false"
                        connection-leak-timeout-in-seconds="0"
                        connection-validation-method="auto-commit"
                        datasource-
classname="com.mysql.jdbc.jdbc2.optional.MysqlDataSource"
                        fail-all-connections="false"
                        idle-timeout-in-seconds="300"
                        is-connection-validation-required="false"
                        is-isolation-level-guaranteed="true"
                        lazy-connection-association="false"
                        lazy-connection-enlistment="false"
                        match-connections="false"
                        max-connection-usage-count="0"
                        max-pool-size="10"
                        max-wait-time-in-millis="120000"
                        name="MySQLConnectinoPool"
                        non-transactional-connections="false"
                        pool-resize-quantity="2"
                        res-type="javax.sql.DataSource"
                        statement-timeout-in-seconds="-1"
                        steady-pool-size="8"
                        validate-atmost-once-period-in-seconds="0"
                        validation-table-name="DUAL" wrap-jdbc-
objects="false">
    <property name="URL"
value="jdbc:mysql://localhost:3306/quote_manager"/>
    <property name="User" value="root"/>
    <property name="Password" value="password"/>
  </jdbc-connection-pool>
  <jdbc-resource jndi-name="java:app/jdbc/quote_manager" pool-
name="MySQLConnectinoPool" enabled="true"/>
</resources>
```

Alternatively, you can also do it through code using the `@DataSourceDefinition` annotation, which is more portable than the specific descriptor of GlassFish (this is the solution we will rely on from now on):

```
@DataSourceDefinition(
        name = "java:app/jdbc/quote_manager",
        className = "com.mysql.jdbc.Driver",
        url = "jdbc:mysql://localhost:3306/quote_manager",
        user = "root",
        password = "password"
)
public class DataSourceConfiguration {
}
```

If you recompile and restart the server, you will see that it has created the tables, thanks to our `persistence.xml` configuration:

```
mysql> show tables;
+------------------------+
| Tables_in_quote_manager |
+------------------------+
| CUSTOMER               |
| QUOTE                  |
| QUOTE_CUSTOMER         |
| SEQUENCE               |
+------------------------+
```

If you are waiting for the server to start and have kept the provisioning activated, you will also see some data in the QUOTE table:

```
mysql> select * from QUOTE limit 10;
+----+-------+-------+
| ID | NAME  | VALUE |
+----+-------+-------+
| 1  | FLWS  | 9     |
| 2  | VNET  | 5.19  |
| 3  | XXII  | 2.2   |
| 4  | TWOU  | 50.1  |
| 5  | DDD   | 12.56 |
| 6  | MMM   | 204.32|
| 7  | WBAI  | 10.34 |
| 8  | JOBS  | 59.4  |
| 9  | WUBA  | 62.63 |
| 10 | CAFD  | 14.42 |
+----+-------+-------+
```

Conclusion

Now we have our functional Quote Manager application, and we can deploy it in a Java EE 8 server (GlassFish here) and store our data in a *real* database (MySQL).

Till now, we have mainly worked on making the application functional. Thanks to the high-level APIs of Java EE, this was not so hard, but it is important to understand what we used and what the performance implications of each element of our stack are, to be able to validate/invalidate the performance figures once you have them in your hands.

Summary

In this chapter, we created an application responsible for managing quote prices and enabling clients to access them through HTTP and WebSockets. The application uses plain Java EE code (no external dependencies). We also saw how to link the application to a database. We used MySQL as the database, which is a free and very common choice.

In the next chapter, we will go deeper into the Java EE stack, and understand its role and what it implies for the application in terms of the application's performance.

2
Looking Under the Cover – What is This EE Thing?

Java EE can appear as a magic tool for deployment. However, it is actually just Java code. This chapter intends to look under the cover of the server and ensure that you understand what implications you should expect from the performance of your application. Since covering the entire Java EE space is quite impossible, this chapter will deal with the most common patterns and main specifications.

In this chapter, we will go through some commonly used specifications, and check out what their role is and what you should expect in terms of the impact on your runtime. In the end, you should be able to do the following:

- Know the services that you can expect from your container and the high-level associated overhead
- Evaluate whether a code pattern can impact the performance
- Judge whether your runtime (Java EE) overhead is normal

Context and Dependency Injection – what did you do to my beans?

Context and Dependency Injection (**CDI**) is the central specification of Java EE. Its role is to *manage* the beans you define. It is directly linked to the pattern called **Inversion of Control** (**IoC**), which provides a way to obtain loose coupling between your classes. The goal is to be flexible on the way so that the current instances are linked together. It also controls the life cycle and the instantiation of instances.

IoC – a pretty simple example

Before exploring the CDI, let's use a very simple example (I would say, a *handmade example*) to illustrate what a bean container is.

We will use an application that has `TimeService`, which simply provides a `now()` method returning the current `LocalDateTime`.

Here is what it can look like in terms of code:

```
public interface TimeService {
    LocalDateTime now();
}
```

A trivial implementation will rely on the native `now()` implementation:

```
public class TimeServiceImpl implements TimeService {
    @Override
    public LocalDateTime now() {
        return LocalDateTime.now();
    }
}
```

But you may also need to be able to switch to a mock (for tests or another customer, for instance):

```
public class MockTimeService implements TimeService {
    @Override
    public LocalDateTime now() {
        return LocalDateTime.of(2017, Month.SEPTEMBER, 4, 19, 0);
    }
}
```

In terms of code, you will likely implement the switch with a plain old factory:

```
public static class TimeServiceFactory {
    public TimeService create() {
        if (useDefault()) {
            return new TimeServiceImpl();
        }
        return new MockTimeService();
    }
}
```

Then, you need to use the factory everywhere in the callers, which is quite impacting, especially when you need to add a parameter to the `create()` method. To solve this issue, you can put all your application instances in a single place, which we will call `Container`:

```
public class Container {
    private final Map<Class<?>, Class<?>> instances = new HashMap<>();

    public <A, I extends A> Container register(final Class<A> api,
    final Class<I> implementation) {
        instances.put(api, implementation);
        return this;
    }

    public <T> T get(final Class<T> api) {
        try {
            return api.cast(
                    ofNullable(instances.get(api))
                        .orElseThrow(() -> new
                        IllegalArgumentException("No bean for api
                        <" + api.getName() + ">"))
                        .getConstructor()
                        .newInstance());
        } catch (final Exception e) {
            throw new IllegalArgumentException(e);
        }
    }
}
```

This is a very minimal and trivial implementation. But once it is done, you can just register all your application beans in your bootstrap class, and all the code will rely on `Container` to retrieve the instance. In other words, the lookup of the classes is centralized. This also means that the updates are simpler:

```
public class Main {
    public static void main(final String[] args) {
        final Container container = new Container()
                .register(TimeService.class, TimeServiceImpl.class)
                /*other registers if needed*/;

        final TimeService timeService =
        container.get(TimeService.class);
        System.out.println(timeService.now());
    }
}
```

As the last thing before starting to deal with the CDI itself, you can add services on top of the container, since the instances are created by `Container`. For instance, if you want to log any call to the method of a registered API, you can change the `get(Class<?>)` method in the following way:

```
public <T> T get(final Class<T> api) {
    try {
        final Object serviceInstance = ofNullable(instances.get(api))
                .orElseThrow(() -> new IllegalArgumentException("No
                bean registered for api <" + api.getName() + ">"))
                .getConstructor()
                .newInstance();

        return api.cast(Proxy.newProxyInstance(api.getClassLoader(),
        new Class<?>[]{api}, new LoggingHandler(serviceInstance,
        api)));
    } catch (final Exception e) {
        throw new IllegalArgumentException(e);
    }
}
```

The entire logic will be implemented in `LoggingHandler`, which will fully decorate the registered instance logic with logging invocations. In other words, each method invocation on the proxy instance will be forwarded to the handler:

```
public class LoggingHandler implements InvocationHandler {
    private final Object delegate;
    private final Logger logger;

    public LoggingHandler(final Object delegate, final Class<?> api) {
        this.delegate = delegate;
        this.logger = Logger.getLogger(api.getName());
    }

    @Override
    public Object invoke(final Object proxy, final Method method, final
    Object[] args) throws Throwable {
        logger.info(() -> "Calling " + method.getName());
        try {
            return method.invoke(delegate, args);
        } catch (final InvocationTargetException ite) {
            throw ite.getTargetException();
        } finally {
            logger.info(() -> "Called " + method.getName());
        }
    }
}
```

Now, if you call `TimeService.now()`, you will be able to observe the corresponding output. With the default logging setup, it looks something like this:

```
sept. 03, 2017 4:29:27 PM com.github.rmannibucau.container.LoggingHandler
invoke
INFOS: Calling now
sept. 03, 2017 4:29:27 PM com.github.rmannibucau.container.LoggingHandler
invoke
INFOS: Called now
```

By itself, it is not that useful, but if you add some metrics (timing), parameter logging, and so on, it can become really neat. Also, keep in mind that you can chain the handlers you add on top of the proxy.

What does this mean, regarding the performance? Well, it means that a simple call to a method we fully control (user method) can do really different things from the user code; it will be slow due to the `Container` class and not due to the user code. If you doubt it, take a case where the user method implementation is empty and the handler pauses for some minutes. Of course, the EE implementation doesn't do it, but it adds some complexity on top of the end user code.

The main features of CDI

CDI is quite a complete specification with a lot of features compared with our small container. However, the CDI works in a manner similar to the container, except that it scans the `classloader` application to find beans at startup instead of requiring a manual registration.

To understand how the CDI can impact the performance of your application, we will detail a few major features of the CDI, explaining the work the server has to do to provide them.

Injections

If you take a look at our quote manager application, you may have noticed that `QuoteService` was injected in `QuoteResource` or `DirectQuoteSocket`. We are exactly in the IoC area of the CDI container. Here, the algorithm globally looks as follows (in pseudo-code):

```
Object createInstance() {
    Object[] constructorArguments = createConstructorArguments(); <1>
    Object instance = createNewInstance(constructorArguments); <2>
    for each injected field of (instance) { <3>
```

```
          field.inject(instance);
    }
    return prepare(instance); <4>
}
```

To fulfill its role, the CDI will need to instantiate an instance and initialize it. To do so, it proceeds with the following steps which leads to provide you a ready to use instance:

1. The CDI allows injections from the constructor parameters, through field injections, or through setter injections. Therefore, before instantiating an instance, the CDI needs to resolve the required parameters and get one instance for each of them.
2. Now, the container can provide constructor parameters; it just creates a current instance from the bean constructor.
3. Now that the container has an instance, it populates its field/setter injections.
4. If needed, the instance is wrapped in a proxy, adding the required services/handlers (interceptors/decorators in CDI semantic).

In terms of the performance, this kind of logic has some consequences for us and the way we can rely on the CDI in high-performance environments and applications. A simple bean instantiation now requires operations which look simple but can be expensive to execute all the time due to the actual work they have to do, like allocating memory or using meta programming, or because of the complexity they hide:

*   Most of the steps imply some reflection (that is, Java reflection) and, therefore, the container must cache all it can to avoid wasting time in retrieving the reflection data again and again.
*   *Step 1* and *step 3* can imply calling back `createInstance()` for other instances, which means that if the complexity to create an instance without any injection is 1, the complexity to create an instance with N injections will be *1+N*. It will be *1+NxM* if the N injections have M injections.

Scopes

A very neat feature of the CDI is to handle the scope life cycle for you. Concretely, you decorate your beans with `@ApplicationScoped` and `@RequestScoped`, and the life of the bean is either bound to the application (it is a singleton) or the request duration (which means you can have as many different instances as you have concurrent requests).

The scope implementation is called *context*, and the context is mainly responsible for looking up in the right contextual instance or creating it. An application scoped instance will be looked up in a single map shared by the entire application. However, a request scoped instance will also be looked up in `ThreadLocal` associated with the request life cycle through `ServletRequestListener`.

The implications on the performance are quite immediate:

- The context setup can be pricey (depending on the scope) and can add some overhead that you may not require. In fact, if you have no `@RequestScoped` bean, you don't need the `ServletRequestListener` instance (even if not very expensive).
- Recreating your bean every time the context needs it will trigger the process we saw in the previous part and the life cycle hooks of the bean (`@PostConstruct` and `@PreDestroy`).

Interceptors/decorators

Interceptors are the CDI way of adding custom handlers on top of a bean. For instance, our logging handler will be this interceptor in CDI:

```
@Log
@Interceptor
@Priority(Interceptor.Priority.APPLICATION)
public class LoggingInterceptor implements Serializable {
    @AroundInvoke
    public Object invoke(final InvocationContext context) throws Exception
{
        final Logger logger =
Logger.getLogger(context.getTarget().getClass().getName());
        logger.info(() -> "Calling " + context.getMethod().getName());
        try {
            return context.proceed();
        } finally {
            logger.info(() -> "Called " + context.getMethod().getName());
        }
    }
}
```

Decorators do the same job but they are applied automatically based on the interface(s) they implement and get the current implementation injected. They don't require a binding (such as `@Log` to put on a method to activate `LoggingInterceptor`), but they are more specific to a set of types.

In terms of the performance, an interceptor/decorator will obviously add some logic and, therefore, some execution time. But it also adds a more vicious overhead: the context creation. This part depends on the implementation of the CDI your server uses (Weld, OpenWebBeans, CanDI, and so on). However, if you don't have any interceptor, the container doesn't need to create a context and, therefore, to populate it. Most of the context creation is cheap but the `getParameter()` method, which represents the parameters of the method, can be expensive, since it requires converting a stack call into an array.

CDI implementations have multiple choices here and we will not go through all of them. What is important to keep in mind here is the following equation:

```
business_code_execution_time + interceptors_code_execution_time <
method_execution_time
```

If you only have interceptors that don't do much, you can often assume that the container makes it as right as possible. If you compare this with a framework where you do it all manually, you will probably see this overhead.

By itself, the associated overhead is still acceptable, not big enough to not use interceptors in your code regarding the maintenance/complexity versus the performance trade-off. However, when you start adding a lot of interceptors, you need to ensure that they are well implemented too. What does this mean? To understand, we need to step back and see how interceptors are used.

To link an interceptor and an implementation, you need to use what we call an interceptor binding, which is the marker annotation of your interceptor (decorated with `@InterceptorBinding`). No big issues until here, but this binding often holds some configuration, making the interceptor behavior configurable.

If we use back our logging interceptor, the logger name is configurable:

```
@InterceptorBinding
@Retention(RUNTIME)
@Target({TYPE, METHOD})
public @interface Log {
    /**
     * @return the logger name to use to trace the method invocations.
     */
    @Nonbinding
    String value();
}
```

Now, `LoggingInterceptor` needs to get back the value, which will be passed to the logger factory to get the logger instance that our interceptor will use to decorate the actual bean invocation. This means that we can just modify our previous implementation, as shown in the following snippet, to respect the logger configuration:

```
@Log("")
@Interceptor
@Priority(Interceptor.Priority.APPLICATION)
public class LoggingInterceptor implements Serializable {
    @AroundInvoke
    public Object invoke(final InvocationContext context) throws Exception
{
        final String loggerName = getLoggerName();
        final Logger logger = Logger.getLogger(loggerName);
        logger.info(() -> "Calling " + context.getMethod().getName());
        try {
            return context.proceed();
        } finally {
            logger.info(() -> "Called " + context.getMethod().getName());
        }
    }
}
```

All the tricky part is in `getLoggerName()`. A bad and fragile - because it relies on plain reflection and not CDI metamodel - but common implementation is as follows:

```
private String getLoggerName(InvocationContext context) {
    return ofNullable(context.getMethod().getAnnotation(Log.class))
            .orElseGet(() ->
context.getTarget().getClass().getAnnotation(Log.class))
            .value();
}
```

Why is it fragile? Because there is no guarantee that the class handling works, as you can get a proxy instance and ignore the stereotype usage. It is bad because it utilizes reflection at every invocation and the JVM is not really optimized for such usage. The implementer should call `getAnnotation` only once.

Regarding the performances, a better implementation will be to ensure that we don't use reflection every time there is an invocation call, but only once, since the Java model (the `Class` metadata) doesn't change at runtime in general. To do it, we can use `ConcurrentMap` which will hold the already computed names in memory and avoid to do it again and again when the same method is called:

```
private final ConcurrentMap<Method, String> loggerNamePerMethod = new
ConcurrentHashMap<>();

private String getLoggerName(InvocationContext context) {
    return loggerNamePerMethod.computeIfAbsent(context.getMethod(), m ->
ofNullable(m.getAnnotation(Log.class))
            .orElseGet(() ->
context.getTarget().getClass().getAnnotation(Log.class))
            .value());
}
```

It simply caches the logger name per method and computes it once. This way, no reflection after the first call is involved; instead, we rely on the cache. `ConcurrentHashMap` is a good candidate for it and its overhead is negligible compared to a *synchronized* structure.

To be fast, do we just need to ensure that the interceptors are caching metadata? Actually, it is not enough. Remember that the interceptors are beans with an enforced scope: `@Dependent`. This scope means *create every time you need*. In the context of an interceptor, it means *create an instance of the interceptor every time you create an intercepted bean*.

If you think of a `@RequestScoped` bean, then its interceptors will be created for every request and the cache, which totally defeats the purpose.

To solve it, do not cache in the interceptor but in an `@ApplicationScoped` bean, which is injected into the interceptor:

```
@ApplicationScoped
class Cache {
    @Inject
    private BeanManager beanManager;

    private final ConcurrentMap<Method, String> loggerNamePerMethod = new
ConcurrentHashMap<>();

    String getLoggerName(final InvocationContext context) {
        return loggerNamePerMethod.computeIfAbsent(context.getMethod(), mtd
-> {
            // as before
        });
```

```
        }
    }

@Log("")
@Interceptor
@Priority(Interceptor.Priority.APPLICATION)
public class LoggingInterceptor implements Serializable {
    @Inject
    private Cache cache;

    @AroundInvoke
    public Object invoke(final InvocationContext context) throws Exception
{
        final String loggerName = cache.getLoggerName(context);
        final Logger logger = Logger.getLogger(loggerName);
        logger.info(() -> "Calling " + context.getMethod().getName());
        try {
            return context.proceed();
        } finally {
            logger.info(() -> "Called " + context.getMethod().getName());
        }
    }
}
```

This simple trick ensures that our cache is @ApplicationScoped itself and, therefore, computed only once per application. If you want to make sure you don't compute it at runtime at all, you can even enforce it to be initialized through a CDI extension in an observer of the AfterDeploymentValidation event (but this is less impacting on the performance).

To conclude this part, note that the specifications now rely on interceptors to provide their features and integrate together (Security API, JTA, JSF, JAX-RS, and so on). The EJB specification was providing the JTA integration until Java EE 7 (replaced by @Transactional) and the security API until Java EE 8 (replaced by Security API). It was an ad-hoc implementation of these integrations (such as our Container at the beginning of this chapter), but it is strictly equivalent to the interceptor functional use. And in terms of the performance, both implementations (EJB and CDI based) are often very close.

Events

CDI events globally provide an event BUS inside the application. They can be synchronous or asynchronous. To let you have an idea, here is what the code can look like:

```
@ApplicationScoped
public class LifecycleManager {
    @Inject
    private Event<Starting> startingEvent;

    public void starting() {
        final Starting event = new Starting();

        startingEvent.fire(event);
        startingEvent.fireAsync(event);
    }
}
```

As both types of invocations are exclusive, what we can note here is that these snippets call `fire()` and `fireAsync()`. To be able to target all the observers, you need to invoke both. This means that the associated logic will be twice.

Without entering into the details that do not impact our performance, both cases share the same resolution mechanism:

1. Resolve the observers based on the event type.
2. Remove the observers not matching the fire type (asynchronous or synchronous).
3. Sort the observers by priority.
4. Handle the invocations.

The difference between synchronous and asynchronous cases is *point 4*. In the synchronous case, it just means, *invoke the observers*, whereas in the asynchronous case, it means, *call asynchronously and return* `CompletionStage` *representing all the invocation results*.

The parts impacting the performance are the resolution of the observers and the invocation, which can require some bean resolution.

We already saw bean resolution, so let's dig into the observer resolution here. Indeed, the implementation is specific to the vendor you are using. But, as it is impossible to use static analysis to implement this part, the resolution is done at runtime with a cache per event type. Note that the caching depends a lot on the implementation. Most will only cache raw type events.

This concretely means that the invocation without generics, as shown in the following code, will be way faster than the invocation that implements generics and enforces the CDI container to do some more resolution:

```
event.fire(new MyEvent());
```

In terms of the code, and to let you compare it with the previous example, the code with generics would be exactly the same except the event would be parameterized:

```
event.fire(new MyEvent<String>());
```

Then, once you have the potential set of observers, you need to reduce the set based on the qualifiers that the caller configures for the event. This also implies some reflection, more or less cached, depending on the implementation.

Finally, some runtime checks are enforced by the set of tests that the vendors have to pass so that we can claim to be compliant with the specifications.

All these steps are more or less optimized by vendors depending on the cases they may have received complaints about. But in all of them, you can end up on code paths where everything is done at runtime for the firing of each event, which can be a pain in terms of the performance.

Dynamic lookups

Another great feature of the CDI is to be able to control a lazy instantiation or resolution of a bean. This is done with the `Provider<?>` and `Instance<?>` APIs. *Instance* is a *Provider* allowing you to resolve a bean at runtime. *Provider* is an instance wrapper allowing you to decide when to instantiate the underlying instance.

Take a look at the following code snippet:

```
@ApplicationScoped
public class DynamicInstance {
    @Inject
    private Provider<MyService> myServiceProvider;

    @Inject
    private Instance<MyService> myServices;

    public MyService currentService() {
        return myServiceProvider.get(); <1>
    }
```

```
    public MyService newService(final Annotation qualifier) {
        return myServices.select(qualifier).get(); <2>
    }
}
```

Let's look at the underlying mechanism of the preceding code snippet:

- Calling `Provider.get()` will trigger the creation of an underlying instance (`MyService` here). It delays the instantiation of the injection or makes the instantiation conditional. Note that it depends on the scope of the bean and that a normal scoped bean won't benefit much from this use.
- Calling `Instance.select(...)` will make the bean definition more specific based on the injection point. In this case, we start from a bean type (`MyService`) with the implicit `@Default` qualifier and replace the implicit qualifier with the one passed as the parameter. Then, we resolve the bean and get its instance. This is useful for switching the implementation dynamically and conditionally.

Since an *Instance* is a *Provider*, the implementations share the same code for both. This means their performances will be the same.

Now the question is, what is the cost of using a programmatic lookup versus a plain injection? Is it more expensive or not? In terms of implementation, the code is quite comparable, it has to resolve the bean to instantiate and then instantiate it so that we are very close to an injection. We will ignore the small differences that do not impact the performance much. One issue here is its use: if you get a *Provider* injected and resolve it for each use, you will then increase a lot of the time spent on *resolving and instantiating* versus *just using an already resolved and created instance*.

JAX-RS – the servlet router

Even if JAX-RS is not fully bound to HTTP and is usable over JMS, WebSockets, and so on, we will just consider the HTTP case here and, more particularly, the case it runs on top of the servlet specification (which is the most common one).

The goal of JAX-RS is to provide a command pattern based on the API to implement the HTTP communications. In other words, it abstracts the I/O with Java modeling. You can see it as a HTTP Java object binding solution. This is what `QuoteResource` uses.

The role of JAX-RS is to provide all the necessary tooling to make servlet abstraction directly usable for most cases. For this purpose, it provides the following:

- A routing layer letting developers directly map the request based on its path
- A serialization layer allowing the conversion of Java objects into HTTP models and streams
- An exception handling layer enabling the mapping of an exception to an HTTP response

The router

JAX-RS is command-oriented. It means that a request must be bound to a Java method. To do so, the matching takes multiple parameters of the request into account:

- The patch
- The Accept header
- The Content-Type header

Here is the simplified algorithm for routing:

1. Find the class matching the request based on the path (this is a regex-like logic).
2. From the class found in *step 1*, find the method matching the request based on the path. (This is close to *step 1* but applied to methods with subresource handling.)
3. From the methods found in *step 2*, find the one that will handle the request based on mime types (Accept/Content-Type headers). This level parses the media types to handle the quality of service options (q, qs, and so on) of the header.

This is not a complicated algorithm, but it is quite dynamic and depends on the incoming requests. So most of the time, it is done at runtime by the providers and can add a small overhead, which you can notice during benchmarks.

Marshalling

(Un)Marshalling is what will (read/)write a Java object to a communication format. It is commonly the part converting an object to a XML or JSON payload but can really be any format, including binary formats.

This conversion is normally synchronous in the implementation and can be costly depending on the model you use and the serializer that is activated. Compared with the servlet API, where you yourself serialize the payload you want to read/return, here, the task is done by the framework and is, therefore, a bit hidden.

A crucial point at this stage is to make sure that the manipulated object has almost no logic and is fast to initialize/read. If you don't respect this point, you may end up holding the HTTP stream for too long which would badly impact your scalability and on a more general practice, you would risk to have some lazy loading of data with JPA which can fail or imply an unexpected connection usage depending the JPA provider and configuration. Another bad case would be to start writing and, then, compute some costly value before continuing to write and therefore force the marshalling process to pause and delay the write after having started it. This not only has a direct impact on the request thread pool but also on the HTTP I/O.

In the same spirit as the algorithm used to match a method to invoke (see the previous part), the JAX-RS runtime must resolve the provider to use (`MessageBodyReader` or `MessageBodyWriter` depending on whether you read or write) in order to make the link with the Java model. Here again, this resolution depends on the incoming request (or the response being built) and media type headers and is not as flat as expected even if it is cacheable and generally fast.

Filter and interceptors

JAX-RS 2.0 added `ContainerRequestFilter` and `ContainerResponseFilter` to modify the request context. It is executed around the method invocation but has already passed the method resolution. On a high level, it can be seen as a CDI interceptor but only at the HTTP layer. These filters do not impact significantly the performance until they do a lot of logic, and there are a few cases where it is a good place to put some logic. One very common example is to validate a security token or log in a user based on the HTTP headers. Don't be surprised to see this kind of component while investigating what your application is doing.

In the same spirit, `ReaderInterceptor` and `WriterInterceptor` intercept `MessageBodyReader` or `MessageBodyWriter`. They are intended to wrap the input/output streams to add some support such as GZIP compression. However, since we are close to the current I/O, we need to take care to not add too much logic here if the payloads are huge or if the algorithm is complex. In fact, since the stream operations are called very often, a badly implemented wrapper can affect the performance.

@Suspended or asynchronous operation

JAX-RS 2.1 got a brand new reactive API to integrate with Java 8 CompletionStage but the server also has a nice integration to be reactive: `@Suspended`. For instance, the `findAll` method of `QuoteResource` could look like the following:

```
@Path("quote")
@RequestScoped
public class QuoteResource {
    @Inject
    private QuoteService quoteService;

    @Resource
    private ManagedExecutorService managedExecutorService;

    @GET
    public void findAll(@Suspended final AsyncResponse response, <1>
                        @QueryParam("from") @DefaultValue("0") final int
from,
                        @QueryParam("to") @DefaultValue("10") final int to)
{
        managedExecutorService.execute(() -> { <2>
            try {
                final long total = quoteService.countAll();
                final List<JsonQuote> items = quoteService.findAll(from, to)
                        .map(quote -> {
                            final JsonQuote json = new JsonQuote();
                            json.setId(quote.getId());
                            json.setName(quote.getName());
                            json.setValue(quote.getValue());
json.setCustomerCount(ofNullable(quote.getCustomers())
                                .map(Collection::size).orElse(0));
                            return json;
                        })
                        .collect(toList());

                final JsonQuotePage page = new JsonQuotePage();
                page.setItems(items);
                page.setTotal(total);
                response.resume(page); <3>
            } catch (final RuntimeException re) {
                response.resume(re); <3>
            }
        });
```

```
        }

    // ...
  }
```

In the synchronous flavor of a JAX-RS method, the returned instance is the response payload. However, when going asynchronous, the returned instance is no more used as the payload in JAX-RS 2.0; the only option is to use the `AsyncResponse` JAX-RS API to let the container be notified of the state of processing of the request. Since JAX-RS 2.1 (Java EE 8), you can also return a Java 8 CompletionStage instance, which gives you the same hooks, and the server can integrate with it to be notified of the success or failure of the invocation. In any case, both kinds of APIs imply the same kind of logic:

1. The `@Suspended` annotation marks a parameter of the `AsyncResponse` type to be injected. This is the callback holder you use to notify JAX-RS that you have finished the execution and have made JAX-RS resume the HTTP request. If you use the `CompletionStage` API flavor, you don't need this parameter and can directly use your `CompletionStage` instance almost the same way.

2. This asynchronous API makes sense when the computation of the response is asynchronous. So, we need to submit the task in a thread pool. In EE 8 the best way to do it correctly is to rely on the EE concurrency utility API and, therefore, `ManagedExecutorService`.

3. Once the computation is finished, `resume()` is used to send back the response (normal payload or `throwable`), which will use `ExceptionMappers` to be translated in payload.

With this pattern, you need to take into account the fact that there is another thread pool apart from the HTTP one. It will impact at different levels, which we will deal with later, but an important point is that increasing the number of threads doesn't mean improving the performance in all cases, and for fast execution, you can even decrease your performance.

JPA – the database link

The **Java Persistence API (JPA)** is the link to the database (MySQL for our quote application we created in chapter 1). Its goal is to enable an application to map the database model to Java objects. The gain is that we can use the database as any object.

For instance, consider the following table, which matches our quote representation in the database:

The preceding table can be converted into the following object in Java, thanks to JPA annotations:

```
@Entity
public class Quote {
    @Id
    @GeneratedValue
    private long id;

    @NotNull
    @Column(unique = true)
    private String name;

    private double value;|
```

While the tables are *flat*, mapping them in JPA is pretty straightforward, but the more the model complexity will increase, the more you will realize the two opposed worlds: building a great Java model can lead to an awful database model or the opposite. Why? Because both don't share exactly the same philosophy and can lead to some anti-patterns.

For instance, in our model, we linked our *Quote* to *Customer* mapping. Since a customer can have multiple quotes (and the opposite as well), we used a @ManyToMany relationship. If you check the database generated by JPA, you will be surprised to see one table that is not modelized:

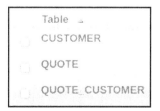

The **QUOTE_CUSTOMER** table model is pretty simple if you open it:

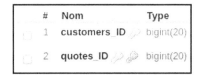

#	Nom	Type
1	customers_ID	bigint(20)
2	quotes_ID	bigint(20)

As you can see, it just makes a link between the **QUOTE** and **CUSTOMER** tables. This is what we would manually do on the database side, except that we would modelize this table (it wouldn't be implicit) and potentially add some attributes owned by the relationship (something we can't do with our current Java model).

Of course, you can always modelize this join table and link it to *Quote* and *Customer* with @ManyToOne relationships if you need more flexibility or want to be closer to the database model.

This example is interesting at two levels:

- What will the JPA provider do to fetch the quotes of a customer, since there is this join table in the middle?
- The model is symmetric: a customer can get the quotes he can access, and we can access the allowed customers from a quote. In Java, it will just be translated by quote.getCustomers() and customer.getQuotes(). Are both doing the same thing? Are they similar in terms of performance? In Java, they really look the same, right?

To dig into the role of the provider, we must start by checking how by using some object-related code and query language the provider can actually make it work on the database-side, which uses a different paradigm. To do so, we will first investigate how our Java code is converted to native SQL and, then, check how the modeling can impact the performance.

From JPA to the database

JPA let's you represent your database in plain Java. Said otherwise it let's you represent the relational model as an object model. It is very common for the development and maintenance but at some point, and in particular when you will validate your performances, you will need to check what the mapper (JPA implementation) is doing and how it does translate your object code/model to the relational one (SQL).

When you check the JPA caller code, you often have something like the following:

```
final Quote quote = entityManager.find(Quote.class, id);
....
entityManager.persist(quote);
```

For more complex queries, it is like the following:

```
final Number count = entityManager.createQuery("select count(q) from Quote
q", Number.class);
```

I will not deal with named queries versus this kind of query in this part, but what is important here is that the model is object/Java-based. Even the JPQL query is related to an object and not plain SQL.

This leads to the main role of the JPA provider: translating all the code from the object/Java model to the relational/SQL model.

To understand this, we will configure the JPA provider of our server to log what it does. Since we are using GlassFish, we need to configure EclipseLink, which is the JPA provider. To do so, we just add the following properties in the persistence unit:

```
<property name="eclipselink.logging.level" value="FINEST"/>
<property name="eclipselink.logging.logger" value="JavaLogger"/>
```

This configuration will activate Eclipselink to log at `FINEST` level of the logger a lot of information. To see these information, we need to ensure the `FINEST` log level is written somewhere and not skipped as it is done by default. To do that, you need to configure the EclipseLink logger level to `FINEST` as well. This way Eclipselink would log with a level the logger would output. You can do it in GlassFish add this line to your `logging.properties`:

```
org.eclipse.persistence.level = FINEST
```

Note that if we use the maven plugin that we set up in Chapter 1, *Money – The Quote Manager Application* to run GlassFish, it will fallback on JVM `logging.properties` and you will need to either modify it from `$JAVA_HOME/jre/lib/logging.properties` or set another one when launching the server. Here is the potential content to activate logging in the console:

```
# output configuration - console here
java.util.logging.ConsoleHandler.level = FINEST
java.util.logging.ConsoleHandler.formatter =
java.util.logging.SimpleFormatter
```

```
# global configuration (default)
.level = INFO
.handlers = java.util.logging.ConsoleHandler

# eclipselink specific logging level
org.eclipse.persistence.level = FINEST
```

Finally, to use this file when launching the server, simply set the system property, `java.util.logging.config.file` (assuming you put the file in `src/main/glassfish/conf/logging.properties`), as follows:

```
MAVEN_OPTS="-
Djava.util.logging.config.file=src/main/glassfish/conf/logging.properties"
mvn package embedded-glassfish:run
```

The logger name uses this pattern:

```
org.eclipse.persistence.session./file:<path to the webapp>/WEB-
INF/classes/_<entity simple name in lowercase>.[sql|query]
```

Now, if you start the server, you have a few more lines:

```
...
Sep 09, 2017 5:21:51 PM
org.eclipse.persistence.session./file:/home/rmannibucau/dev/quote-
manager/target/quote-manager-1.0-SNAPSHOT/WEB-INF/classes/_quote.sql
FINE: SELECT ID, NAME, VALUE FROM QUOTE WHERE (NAME = ?)
  bind => [1 parameter bound]
...
Sep 09, 2017 5:41:53 PM
org.eclipse.persistence.session./file:/home/rmannibucau/dev/quote-
manager/target/quote-manager-1.0-SNAPSHOT/WEB-INF/classes/_quote.sql
FINE: INSERT INTO QUOTE (ID, NAME, VALUE) VALUES (?, ?, ?)
  bind => [3 parameters bound]
....
Sep 09, 2017 5:44:26 PM
org.eclipse.persistence.session./file:/home/rmannibucau/dev/quote-
manager/target/quote-manager-1.0-SNAPSHOT/WEB-INF/classes/_quote.sql
FINE: SELECT t1.ID, t1.NAME FROM QUOTE_CUSTOMER t0, CUSTOMER t1 WHERE
((t0.quotes_ID = ?) AND (t1.ID = t0.customers_ID))
  bind => [1 parameter bound]
```

These lines are generated by our JPA provider (EclipseLink here) every time a query is issued to the database. The queries use bound parameters. This is interesting at two levels. The first one is about the security and intends to prevent SQL injections - note that for security reasons as well, the values are not logged by default `eclipselink.logging.parameters` can be set to true in your persistence unit properties if you want to see them instead of the number of bound parameters only. The second interesting consequence is directly linked to the performance and the fact that the provider can use prepared statements instead of creating a statement every time it creates a query. Combined with a datasource pool which can most of the time cache these prepared statements, it makes pretty cheap to execute statement compared to an implementation which would create them each time it is needed.

Depending on your JPA provider, you need to change the properties to activate the query logging. Hibernate and OpenJPA use other properties and logger names, for instance. Alternatively, some containers or JDBC drivers will let you configure it at another level. For instance, in Apache TomEE you can set `LogSQL=true` in your `DataSource` resource directly.

What is interesting to see is the effect of what we write in Java on the SQL side.

The `INSERT` case is straightforward and directly converts the JPA model to the corresponding SQL statement to insert all the values into the corresponding database:

```
INSERT INTO QUOTE (ID, NAME, VALUE) VALUES (?, ?, ?)
```

`SELECT` is a direct binding too, which selects all the columns with a clause on the idenfitier of the entity:

```
SELECT ID, NAME, VALUE FROM QUOTE WHERE (ID = ?)
```

Here, the role of the JPA provider is quite obvious; it makes the link to SQL, which means the following:

- Convert the JPA API and JPQL to the current SQL. Note that in all the JPA providers, there is a notion of database SQL language so that they can handle the database specifics (such as the column types or the pagination). EclipseLink calls it *platform*, Hibernate, *dialect* and OpenJPA, *dictionary*.
- Handle Java to database mapping: database column names are converted to field names, table names to class names, and so on.

However, if you look closer to the logs when you query a quote through the JAX-RS endpoint, you may be surprised:

```
SELECT t1.ID, t1.NAME FROM QUOTE_CUSTOMER t0, CUSTOMER t1 WHERE
((t0.quotes_ID = ?) AND (t1.ID = t0.customers_ID))
```

Where does it come from? If you investigate a bit, you will quickly identify this line in the JAX-RS layer:

```
json.setCustomerCount(ofNullable(quote.getCustomers()).map(Collection::size
).orElse(0));
```

What does it do? It just sets the number of customers linked to *Quote*. Which part triggers this additional query? A simple call on the relationship collection triggers it. In our case, it is `size()`:

```
quote.getCustomers().size();
```

Since the relationship between *Quote* and *Customer* is lazy, this simple line will trigger an additional query with EclipseLink. What is interesting is that if you check the JAX-RS resource, it is not `@Transactional` and this query may fail depending on the JPA provider, as lazy handling must be done in a transaction.

 The provider is clever enough to not trigger any query and just call `getCustomers()`. But it will do when calling any method of the returned collection such as `size()` here. Depending on the provider, null may or may not be possible, which is why the original code assumes it can be null.

We will discuss about modelling in another chapter but the obvious solution to make the relationship eager is not a real solution, since you will slowly load all your object graphs everywhere, doing which can lead to performance issues and even memory issues. So try to resist this temptation.

While you are playing with the JPA and SQL, I recommend that you disable EclipseLink's default shared cache, which easily hides queries (later on, we will discuss why to disable it even in production). This can be done with the following property added to your persistence unit:

```
<property name="eclipselink.cache.shared.default" value="false"/>
```

Model and implications

This section does not intend to go through all the cases; other books centered on JPA do it very well. In order to avoid doing things that can have a negative impact on the performances, this part will show you that the abstraction JPA does need some attention.

To illustrate this statement, we will reuse the **Customer**/**Quote** relationship. As it is *@ManyToMany*, it relies on a join table. Here is a representation of the model:

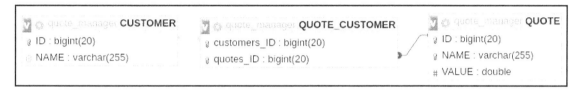

The use case is when you want to access the other side of the relationship: *Quotes* from a *Customer* (getQuotes()) or the opposite (getCustomers().size()).

Here, the provider will find all the entities that have the current entity identifier in the join table.

This sounds perfectly fine but how can it affect the performance? If you check the structure of the join table in MySQL, you will immediately see a minor difference:

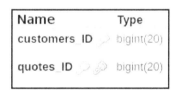

The quotes_ID column has an index, whereas the customers_ID column does not. Do not be fooled by the picture and the fact that both the columns have a yellow key. The primary key is the composed key of both the columns, so the index is not useless and allows us to select fast rows from quotes_ID. Why does quotes_ID have an index and customers_ID hasn't? Because the *Quote* entity is the owner of the relationship. However, it will always be faster to select columns by the *Quote* identifier rather than by the *Customer* identifier.

Now the interesting part is to compare both the calls:

```
quote.getCustomers()
customer.getQuotes()
```

The first call will load the customers from an already loaded quote whereas the second call will load the quotes related to an already loaded customer.

Now let's see what the corresponding generated SQL will be. The first invocation will be converted to the following statement:

```
SELECT t1.ID, t1.NAME FROM QUOTE_CUSTOMER t0, CUSTOMER t1 WHERE
((t0.quotes_ID = ?) AND (t1.ID = t0.customers_ID))
```

The second invocation (`customer.getQuotes()`) will be converted to the following:

```
SELECT t1.ID, t1.NAME, t1.VALUE FROM QUOTE_CUSTOMER t0, QUOTE t1 WHERE
((t0.customers_ID = ?) AND (t1.ID = t0.quotes_ID))
```

A join is done with the known sides of the relationship, which means the entity containing the relationship (set of entities). Yet, we saw that only one of the two columns of the join table has an index. This means that one side will be slower than the other side. If you use bi-directional relationships, you should ensure that you make the owner of the relationship either of the following:

- The one that is way more used than the other one (if there is a huge difference)
- The one that will bring back a smaller set of entities than the other one

This is just an example of how a very fast model can impact the performance. This is a general statement that is valid for any modeling. Anyway, since JPA makes modeling very easy and not as much database-related, it is easier to make it wrong.

The Java Transaction API

The **Java Transaction API (JTA)** is the element responsible for providing the API responsible for ensuring the consistency of your data in the widest sense. In our quote manager, it is only applied to the database data but it can be applied to JMS messages, potentially files if you use connectors, and so on.

Without going through the details and protocol, the idea is to ensure, across multiple systems, that either all commits or all rollbacks but not something in between are done ensuring the consistency of the system (which is one common issue mixing NoSQL systems).

To do that, JTA uses what we call a *two phases commit protocol*:

- Ask all systems to prepare the commit which means the system must verify and ensure it will be able to commit in next phase
- Ask all systems to actually do the commit

A lot of transaction manager or servers are optimized for the case of a single resource to limit all the associated overhead.

In our quote manager application we only have a database, so we should benefit from these optimizations in most servers. Nonetheless, we still use JTA backbone and don't fallback on JPA transaction management (*RESOURCE_LOCAL*) which is faster.

What is important to know with JTA is that a transaction is bound to a thread. Each resource has its representation and identifier, a complete lifecycle (see *XAResource*). There is a transaction bound registry to store the data (a bit like a *@TransactionScoped* bean) and the listeners to integrate with the transaction lifecycle.

All of that is not true in terms of memory and CPU cycles but can be justified if you need it, either because you have multiple systems or because you use your server JTA monitoring (you rarely have monitoring with *RESOURCE_LOCAL* in administration UI).

Server resources

At several layers, the server provides your application with some resources. In our quote manager we have our datasource injected into the persistence unit through its JNDI name:

```
<jta-data-source>java:app/jdbc/quote_manager</jta-data-source>
```

This datasource can also be injected anywhere else in the code:

```
@Resource(lookup = "java:app/jdbc/quote_manager")
private DataSource datasource;
```

But the server manages way more resources. Resources are important because they are provided and handled by the server but used from the application. In other words it is a way to control how the application behaves from the outside of it. It enables you to develop without having to care about the configuration and to tune it later or to adapt it depending on the environment you deploy your application to. The next table lists a subset of the most useful JavaEE resource types which can impact your performances and you can need to watch out if your application uses some of them.

Resource Type	Description	Example
ManagedExecutorService	An EE *ExecutorService* which is used to ensure you inherit the EE context in custom asynchronous tasks. Very useful to link to JAX-RS *@Suspended* or third party libraries for instance.	`@Resource private ManagedExecutorService mes;`
ManagedScheduledExecutorService	Close to the `ManagedExecutorService`, it reuses the `ScheduledExecutorService` API adding the EE integration.	`@Resource private ManagedScheduledExecutorService mses;`
DataSource	As seen before it allows to connect to a database providing a `DataSource` instance.	`@Resource private DataSource ds;`
XADataSource	Same as `DataSource` but supporting two phases commit.	`@Resource private XADataSource ds;`
Queue	JMS *Queue*, it defines a destination of type queue. In term of configuration, its name can be interesting to distinguish the logical name (application) and real name (deployment).	`@Resource private Queue queue;`
Topic	Same as `Queue` but for a destination of type `topic`.	`@Resource private Topic topic;`
ConnectionFactory	Defines the way to integrate with JMS and get *Connections* (or *JMSContext* since Java EE 7).	`@Resource private ConnectionFactory cf;`

There are other types of resources, but those are the main ones linked to the outside of the application and with performance related configuration, like pooling configuration.

DataSource configuration

To illustrate the configuration let's use the one we rely on in the quote manager: the datasource. As shown in Chapter 1, *Money – The Quote Manager Application* you can define the datasource this way:

```xml
<?xml version="1.0" encoding="UTF-8"?>
<!DOCTYPE resources PUBLIC "-//GlassFish.org//DTD GlassFish Application
Server 3.1 Resource Definitions//EN"
    "http://glassfish.org/dtds/glassfish-resources_1_5.dtd">
<resources>

  <1>
  <jdbc-connection-pool allow-non-component-callers="false"
                        associate-with-thread="false"
                        connection-creation-retry-attempts="0"
                        connection-creation-retry-interval-in-seconds="10"
                        connection-leak-reclaim="false"
                        connection-leak-timeout-in-seconds="0"
                        connection-validation-method="auto-commit"
                        datasource-
classname="com.mysql.jdbc.jdbc2.optional.MysqlDataSource"
                        fail-all-connections="false"
                        idle-timeout-in-seconds="300"
                        is-connection-validation-required="false"
                        is-isolation-level-guaranteed="true"
                        lazy-connection-association="false"
                        lazy-connection-enlistment="false"
                        match-connections="false"
                        max-connection-usage-count="0"
                        max-pool-size="10"
                        max-wait-time-in-millis="120000"
                        name="MySQLConnectinoPool"
                        non-transactional-connections="false"
                        pool-resize-quantity="2"
                        res-type="javax.sql.DataSource"
                        statement-timeout-in-seconds="-1"
                        steady-pool-size="8"
                        validate-atmost-once-period-in-seconds="0"
                        validation-table-name="DUAL" wrap-jdbc-
objects="false">
    <property name="URL"
value="jdbc:mysql://localhost:3306/quote_manager"/>
    <property name="User" value="root"/>
    <property name="Password" value="password"/>
  </jdbc-connection-pool>
```

```
<2>
<jdbc-resource jndi-name="java:app/jdbc/quote_manager" pool-
name="MySQLConnectinoPool" enabled="true"/>
</resources>
```

This XML configuration defines the datasource our JPA provider will use thanks to two declarations allowing the container to create the datasource instance and allowing the JPA provider to find this datasource:

- The pool definition which defines how the database connections will be created, cached and validated
- The link between the pool and the application through its JNDI name to let the application use it - this is how JPA will look up the instance

The properties are the datasource instance (based on the configured class) configuration but the `jdbc-connection-pool` attributes are mostly the pool configuration.

It is very important to note that the configuration depends on the server. As an example, in Wildly, you would use this kind of declaration:

```
<datasources>
  <xa-datasource jndi-name="java:jboss/quote_manager" pool-
name="QuoteManagerPool">
    <driver>mysql</driver>
    <xa-datasource-property name="ServerName">localhost</xa-datasource-
property>
    <xa-datasource-property name="DatabaseName">quote_manager</xa-
datasource-property>
    <pool>
      <min-pool-size>10</min-pool-size>
      <max-pool-size>50</max-pool-size>
    </pool>
    <security>
      <user-name>root</user-name>
      <password>secret</password>
    </security>
    <validation>
      <valid-connection-checker class-
      name="org.jboss.jca.adapters.jdbc.extensions.mysql
      .MySQLValidConnectionChecker"></valid-connection-checker>
      <exception-sorter class-
name="org.jboss.jca.adapters.jdbc.extensions.mysql.MySQLExceptionSorter"></
exception-sorter>
    </validation>
  </xa-datasource>
  <drivers>
```

```
    <driver name="mysql" module="com.mysql">
      <xa-datasource-
  class>com.mysql.jdbc.jdbc2.optional.MysqlXADataSource</xa-datasource-class>
    </driver>
  </drivers>
</datasources>
```

Here again we find a property part and a pool part. Still, it is no more in attributes but with plain tags.

In Apache TomEE the same resource declaration looks like:

```
<Resource id="quote_manager" type="DataSource">
  JdbcDriver = com.mysql.jdbc.Driver
  JdbcUrl = jdbc:mysql://localhost:3306/quote_manager?tcpKeepAlive=true
  UserName = root
  Password = secret
  ValidationQuery = SELECT 1
  ValidationInterval = 30000
  NumTestsPerEvictionRun = 5
  TimeBetweenEvictionRuns = 30 seconds
  TestWhileIdle = true
  MaxActive = 50
</Resource>
```

Here the configuration is not fully XML but it is mixed with properties (as `java.util.Properties`) that contains the pool configuration and connection information which will be passed either to tomcat-jdbc or commons-dbcp2 pooling library.

What is interesting to note is the overall idea. Most of the servers share the same kind of configuration and here are the crucial configuration entries you need to care about:

Configuration type	Description
Max pool size	How many connections can be created by the pool. This is a key configuration which must be set consistently with the scalability you need across your deployments and the database max connection configuration.
Max wait	The time a caller can wait before getting a timeout from the pool. For performances it is not bad to deactivate it (0) to ensure you identify a too small pool. If you set 10 seconds for instance, the benchmark can be slow because all callers are waiting for a connection.
Idle timeout	How many times a connection is kept if idle.

Validation	How connections are validated, this is very important to ensure connections are valid when kept in the pool and not corrupted. For instance MySQL will close each connection after 8h by default and therefore if your pool doesn't renew the connection you will get errors. The validation type is important because it can generally be done by a background thread from time to time or actively when borrowing or releasing a connection. All have impacts on consistency and/or performances so it is a trade off choice and if you can rely on your database it is generally better to have a background evictor than an active one.
Min (or steady) pool size	The size the pool should enforce as a minimum. The goal is to ensure that when the application is idle and get a new request it doesn't have to create a connection at that moment and can just reuse an existing one because creating a connection is an expensive operation.
Initial (or steady) pool size	The number of connections to create when creating the resource (at startup generally). In GlassFish this is merged with the minimum pool size (*steady-pool-size*).

Last note about resources is that most servers allow multiple ways to configure them:

1. Plain configuration files (often XML based).
2. A command line interface.
3. A REST API.
4. A UI. For instance, here is a screenshot of Glassfish JDBC pool configuration where you will find all the parameters we talked about:

Java EE and performances

As a reminder, this book is not about Java EE role, so we can't go through all the specifications and detail them all but it is important to understand what Java EE is and what its role is to be able to start working on Java EE performances serenely.

Very often, a small annotation or line of code can hide a lot of logic. The entity manager is a good example: most of the methods are hiding some SQL generation and execution which is not a trivial operation.

With the standardization of CDI in applications, a simple call to a method with a simple complexity can imply to:

- Validate the call (BeanValidation) which can be impacting if the object graph is huge
- Validate the logged in user and its permissions (Security API) which can sometimes contact external systems depending on the configuration and implementations
- An integration of multiple external systems (JTA), and so on

All these features can be done with CDI interceptors and are additional logic virtually added to a method.

Ensure you know the server

When you will start to investigate your application performances, before or during profiling, it is therefore important to understand what the server does to know what you should expect in terms of performances. At runtime, the server is part of your application. This means that if the server has a bug (it is still a software like anyone, so it can have bugs or issues even if widely tested), or a performance bottleneck, you will directly be impacted.

Some servers can be embedded with your application, and some can't. Yet, in any case, you will need to ensure you validate your application as well (as your server) to fully understand your runtime and be able to have an impact on it if needed.

Here the choice of your server will be very impacting. You may need to ask yourself what to do in case the server has a bug or a performance bottleneck. In the following, you will find some criteria you can investigate before the benchmark or when starting the development:

Criteria	Comment
Is the server Open Source?	If the server is Open Source, you will be able to check issues you identify against the source code and validate them. You will also be able to recompile it with patches and potentially don't wait for the server team to fix the issue but fix it yourself, which can be very interesting during benchmarks if it has some associated cost (like locating servers or dedicated locals).
Is the server supported?	Having a company you pay for fixing performance issues (or bugs) can be important too. However, mind that some servers will answer quite slowly if you don't pay enough, and this doesn't help a lot during benchmarks. If you go with this solution, make sure to have appropriated SLA or go rather for the Open Source solution.
Is the application portable?	If the application is portable, you would be able to compare servers and use the fastest one. This is not a trivial work to do even if since Java EE 6 it is easier and you will need to ensure it is the case during development. But this can be worthy if one version of a server has a performance issue.

Until recently, Java EE philosophy was to host applications. This is where was coming the *application server* name. The intent, which is still valid today, was to ensure the server is managed by another team than the application (typically, operation team and development team).

Yet, with Docker and embeddable containers (Apache TomEE, Wildfly Swarm, Payara micro, and so on), the operation responsability started being reconsidered and developers have more and more control over the server. This means that you will then ask yourself the same question (how can I easily patch my server?), but also that you will need an expert developer either from your development team or from a computer support company.

Ensure you know your application

In case it was not explicit enough before, it is crucial to know what the server does for your application. It is already key in development, but when you start working on performances, it is a must. This means that you need to know the application good enough to know which part of the server it will use and which implication it will have on your performances.

In other words, you will need to fully understand the use case of your application but also what technology was used to implement it. A simple example is if your application used *RESOURCE_LOCAL* mode for JPA but you see a lot of JTA use, then you will need to identify why. If you don't have this kind of insight, you will just think the application uses JTA and that it is ok. Yet, this kind of fact can mean *something is not well configured*, which can not only impact the application's behavior, but also its raw performances and even its scalability.

It is also very important to know what part of the specifications is used. To illustrate it we'll use JPA again here. JPA is integrated with Bean Validation. This means that each time you will persist/merge an entity, the entity will be validated to ensure it passes the model constraints. This is a great feature but if you validate your model on the outbounds of your application (JAX-RS for instance) then you rarely (never in theory, if the application is done correctly) need to revalidate it internally (JPA). This means that the Bean Validation layer is useless here and can be disabled. This particular example is done by updating the `persistence.xml` and adding the `validation-mode` tag in the right persistence unit:

```
<validation-mode>NONE</validation-mode>
```

Ensure you know your resources

It is crucial to properly tune the resources (databases, thread pools, and so on). Since Java EE 6, some resources can be defined in the application. For instance, a `DataSource` can be defined with:

```
@DataSourceDefinition(
        name = "java:app/jdbc/quote_manager",
        className = "com.mysql.jdbc.Driver",
        url = "jdbc:mysql://localhost:3306/quote_manager",
        user = "root",
        password = "password"
)
public class DataSourceConfiguration {
}
```

This is often a bad idea since you can't externally configure it (it is hardcoded). Thus, you often end up configuring the resources in server specific files or UI.

This is a good practise to avoid in the application. But outside the application, Java EE doesn't define any way or standard to configure the server. Everything is vendor specific. However, you will need to tune it! For that reason, it is crucial to ensure you know:

- What kind of resources your application needs
- How to create them and configure them in your server

This is a great start for the application side but resources are generally linked to an *external* side like a database. Here again, it will be very important to know the resource itself, how it is configured and potentially how to tune it if needed. A very simple example is the number of connections you can use on a database. If you can only use 20 connections, no need to configure 100 in the application, this would generate a lot of errors and slow down the application, or just make it fail depending on how the pool is configured.

Summary

In this chapter, you understood that the Java EE server's role is to make the development of the application easier and faster, providing out-of-the-box services and implementations. We browsed through some common examples, detailed their implications in terms of the code, and, therefore, the performance. We saw that the JPA handles statement creation automatically, securely, and correctly and that your code can imply some unoptimized queries if not designed close enough of the data. This is a good example showing that Java EE is here to enable you to build the best application as easily as possible even though you need to take care of some points (often related to design) in order to ensure you meet your performance requirements.

At this point, we have an application (Chapter 1, *Money – The Quote Manager Application*), we know what it does, and how the Java EE server helps it (this chapter). So, before working on the performance, we need to be able to measure it. This is what our next chapter will be about.

3
Monitor Your Application

When it comes to an application's performance, you will quickly need to know what your application does and get the metrics of performance. In this chapter, we will identify a few ways to get insights on applications.

Thus, in this chapter, we will learn how to monitor our application's behavior in order to be able to compare it with the response times and execution times we observe. This will therefore show you the following:

- How to add monitoring or profiling to an existing application
- How to read important figures corresponding to the monitoring of an application
- How to ensure that the application performance is monitored and that any unexpected changes are visible

Java tools to know what my application is doing

Two critical factors are directly linked to performance when you take an application as a black box:

- **Memory usage**: If too much memory is consumed, it can slow down the application or even make it dysfunctional
- **CPU time**: If an operation is too slow, it will consume a lot of CPU cycles and impact the overall performance

Without too much external tooling (except the **Java Development Kit** (**JDK**) and/or operating system tools), you can easily extract a lot of information and start working on the performance.

The jcmd command – the small command line utility that does a lot

Since Java 8, the JDK has been coming with the `jcmd` command, which allows you to execute commands on a local Java instance using the same user/group as the instance you want to check.

The usage of `jcmd`, although command-based, is quite simple. To understand it, we will first start our quote manager application with the command we saw in `Chapter 1`, *Money – The Quote Manager Application*:

```
mvn clean package embedded-glassfish:run
```

Now in another console, just execute `jcmd`. On my system, it will dump what follows:

```
$ jcmd
4981 com.intellij.idea.Main
7704 sun.tools.jcmd.JCmd
7577 org.codehaus.plexus.classworlds.launcher.Launcher clean package
embedded-glassfish:run
5180 org.jetbrains.idea.maven.server.RemoteMavenServer
```

The first column is the **process ID** (**PID**) of the program and what follows is the launching command (main and parameters). Since we launched our server with maven, we can identify it with the maven main (`org.codehaus.plexus.classworlds.launcher.Launcher`) or with the parameters that exactly match the command we launched (`clean package embedded-glassfish:run`).

If you launch a standalone GlassFish, you will probably have a line like the following:

```
7877 com.sun.enterprise.glassfish.bootstrap.ASMain -upgrade false -
domaindir /home/dev/glassfish5/glassfish/domains/domain1 -read-stdin true -
asadmin-args --host,,,localhost,,,--port,,,4848,,,--secure=false,,,--
terse=false,,,--echo=false,,,--interactive=true,,,start-domain,,,--
verbose=false,,,--watchdog=false,,,--debug=false,,,--
domaindir,,,/home/dev/glassfish5/glassfish/domains,,,domain1 -domainname
domain1 -instancename server -type DAS -verbose false -asadmin-classpath
/home/dev/glassfish5/glassfish/lib/client/appserver-cli.jar -debug false -
```

```
asadmin-classname com.sun.enterprise.admin.cli.AdminMain
```

This one is pretty verbose but you can identify that the main (first string) references `glassfish` and you can find the domains directory to distinguish between multiple instances.

To just give you another idea, if you use Apache Tomcat or TomEE, you will identify it with this line:

```
8112 org.apache.catalina.startup.Bootstrap start
```

Now, we have the PID of our Java process; we can pass it to `jcmd`:

```
jcmd <PID> help
```

For example, for our previous maven GlassFish instance, it will look like the following:

```
jcmd 7577 help
```

The output should look like the following:

```
7577:
The following commands are available:
JFR.stop
JFR.start
JFR.dump
JFR.check
VM.native_memory
VM.check_commercial_features
VM.unlock_commercial_features
ManagementAgent.stop
ManagementAgent.start_local
ManagementAgent.start
GC.rotate_log
Thread.print
GC.class_stats
GC.class_histogram
GC.heap_dump
GC.run_finalization
GC.run
VM.uptime
VM.flags
VM.system_properties
VM.command_line
VM.version
help
```

As you can see, the output is basically a list of commands that you can invoke using `jcmd`. A lot of these commands are informative, such as `VM.version` (which will just log which JVM you are using), but some commands are actual actions, such as `GC.run` (which will call `System.gc()`). Concerning the performance, we are interested in `Thread.print`, which is a replacement of `jstack`. GC data commands, such as `GC.class_histogram`, are related to the garbage collection data, while the `JFR` commands are related to **Java Flight Recorder**.

Let's start with the most basic but also probably the most important command: `Thread.print`. This will allow us to see what our application is doing by digging into the *current* thread stack of our application.

Thread.print

If you execute the `Thread.print` command, the output will look like the following:

```
$ jcmd 7577 Thread.print
7577:
2017-09-10 16:39:12
Full thread dump Java HotSpot(TM) 64-Bit Server VM (25.144-b01 mixed mode):

"....." #xxx [daemon] prio=xxx os_prio=xxx tix=0x.... nid=0x....
[condition]
  java.lang.Thread.State: XXXXX
  at ......
  at ......
  ...


"....." #xxx [daemon] prio=xxx os_prio=xxx tix=0x.... nid=0x....
[condition]
  java.lang.Thread.State: XXXXX
  at ......
  at ......
  ...


"....." #xxx [daemon] prio=xxx os_prio=xxx tix=0x.... nid=0x....
[condition]
  java.lang.Thread.State: XXXXX
  at ......
  at ......
  ...
```

Since reproducing the full output of this command will take the entire chapter, it has been replaced by a skeleton of sorts of the thread stacks. What is important here is to identify that each block starting with a line that has quotes is a thread.

Therefore, the dump repeats this pattern:

```
"thread_name" #thread_id_as_int [daemon if the thread is daemon]
prio=java_priority os_prio=native_priority tid=thread_id_pointer_format
nid=native_id [state]
    thread_stack_trace
```

When the server is idle—that is, when it is not serving any request or executing any scheduled tasks—we can identify that most of the threads are just waiting for a task (in thread pools):

```
"dol-jar-scanner" #50 daemon prio=5 os_prio=0 tid=0x00007f3b7dd0a000
nid=0x1ddf waiting on condition [0x00007f3ae6bae000]
    java.lang.Thread.State: WAITING (parking)
  at sun.misc.Unsafe.park(Native Method)
  - parking to wait for <0x00000000877529a8> (a
java.util.concurrent.locks.AbstractQueuedSynchronizer$ConditionObject)
  at java.util.concurrent.locks.LockSupport.park(LockSupport.java:175)
  at
java.util.concurrent.locks.AbstractQueuedSynchronizer$ConditionObject.await
(AbstractQueuedSynchronizer.java:2039)
  at
java.util.concurrent.LinkedBlockingQueue.take(LinkedBlockingQueue.java:442)
  at
java.util.concurrent.ThreadPoolExecutor.getTask(ThreadPoolExecutor.java:107
4)
  at
java.util.concurrent.ThreadPoolExecutor.runWorker(ThreadPoolExecutor.java:1
134)
  at
java.util.concurrent.ThreadPoolExecutor$Worker.run(ThreadPoolExecutor.java:
624)
  at java.lang.Thread.run(Thread.java:748)
```

To understand this dump, you will need to know how `ExecutorService` works. It basically creates threads with tasks called *Workers*, and each work can take some tasks from a queue (to simplify things). Here we can see the following:

- `ThreadPoolExecutor$Work`, which means that we are in a thread pool task handler
- `LinkedBlockingQueue.take`, which means that the thread is waiting for a new task

We can also identify in this dump some incoming requests in the I/O layer, such as waiting for a socket to connect to an NIO `Selector`:

```
"http-listener-kernel(1) SelectorRunner" #27 daemon prio=5 os_prio=0
tid=0x00007f3b7cfe7000 nid=0x1dc8 runnable [0x00007f3b1eb7d000]
   java.lang.Thread.State: RUNNABLE
  at sun.nio.ch.EPollArrayWrapper.epollWait(Native Method)
  at sun.nio.ch.EPollArrayWrapper.poll(EPollArrayWrapper.java:269)
  at sun.nio.ch.EPollSelectorImpl.doSelect(EPollSelectorImpl.java:93)
  at sun.nio.ch.SelectorImpl.lockAndDoSelect(SelectorImpl.java:86)
  - locked <0x000000008675cc20> (a sun.nio.ch.Util$3)
  - locked <0x000000008675cc10> (a java.util.Collections$UnmodifiableSet)
  - locked <0x000000008675c1f8> (a sun.nio.ch.EPollSelectorImpl)
  at sun.nio.ch.SelectorImpl.select(SelectorImpl.java:97)
  at
org.glassfish.grizzly.nio.DefaultSelectorHandler.select(DefaultSelectorHand
ler.java:115)
  at
org.glassfish.grizzly.nio.SelectorRunner.doSelect(SelectorRunner.java:339)
  at org.glassfish.grizzly.nio.SelectorRunner.run(SelectorRunner.java:279)
  at
org.glassfish.grizzly.threadpool.AbstractThreadPool$Worker.doWork(AbstractT
hreadPool.java:593)
  at
org.glassfish.grizzly.threadpool.AbstractThreadPool$Worker.run(AbstractThre
adPool.java:573)
  at java.lang.Thread.run(Thread.java:748)
```

An important line here is either `epollWait` (if you are familiar with OS natives) or `Selector*.select` (if you are more familiar with the Java side of the code, which means it is waiting for a connection).

Now, if we inject some requests into our application (let's just use Apache Bench or **AB** to undertake some `GET` requests on our `findById` endpoint), we can see some threads that are actually working. (Note that because of its length and to avoid having several pages of thread stacktrace, the `[...]` have been shortened):

```
"http-listener(3)" #23 daemon prio=5 os_prio=0 tid=0x00007f3b7d063800
nid=0x1dc4 runnable [0x00007f3b1ef7d000]
   java.lang.Thread.State: RUNNABLE
  [...]
  at
com.sun.enterprise.connectors.ConnectionManagerImpl.internalGetConnection(C
onnectionManagerImpl.java:254)
  [...]
  at
```

```
com.sun.gjc.spi.base.AbstractDataSource.getConnection(AbstractDataSource.ja
va:115)
   at
org.eclipse.persistence.sessions.JNDIConnector.connect(JNDIConnector.java:1
35)
   [...]
   at
org.eclipse.persistence.queries.ObjectLevelReadQuery.executeDatabaseQuery(O
bjectLevelReadQuery.java:1221)
   at
org.eclipse.persistence.queries.DatabaseQuery.execute(DatabaseQuery.java:91
1)
   at
org.eclipse.persistence.queries.ObjectLevelReadQuery.execute(ObjectLevelRea
dQuery.java:1180)
   at
org.eclipse.persistence.queries.ReadAllQuery.execute(ReadAllQuery.java:464)
   [...]
   at
org.eclipse.persistence.indirection.IndirectSet.size(IndirectSet.java:624)
   [...]
   at java.util.Optional.map(Optional.java:215)
   at
com.github.rmannibucau.quote.manager.front.QuoteResource.findById(QuoteReso
urce.java:48)
   [...]
   at
org.glassfish.jersey.servlet.WebComponent.service(WebComponent.java:370)
   at
org.glassfish.jersey.servlet.ServletContainer.service(ServletContainer.java
:389)
   [...]
   at
org.apache.catalina.core.ApplicationFilterChain.doFilter(ApplicationFilterC
hain.java:208)
   at
org.apache.catalina.core.StandardWrapperValve.invoke(StandardWrapperValve.j
ava:256)
   at
org.apache.catalina.core.StandardContextValve.invoke(StandardContextValve.j
ava:160)
   [...]
   at
org.glassfish.grizzly.http.server.HttpHandler.runService(HttpHandler.java:2
06)
   at
org.glassfish.grizzly.http.server.HttpHandler.doHandle(HttpHandler.java:180
)
```

```
   [...]
   at
org.glassfish.grizzly.threadpool.AbstractThreadPool$Worker.doWork(AbstractT
hreadPool.java:593)
   at
org.glassfish.grizzly.threadpool.AbstractThreadPool$Worker.run(AbstractThre
adPool.java:573)
   at java.lang.Thread.run(Thread.java:748)
```

There are other kinds of thread stacks but this one is particularly interesting, as we can identify most of our endpoint stacks. Keep in mind that we are calling a JAX-RS endpoint that calls JPA to find a quote that will rely on `DataSource` to connect to the current database. We can identify the JAX-RS layer with `org.glassfish.jersey` lines, the JPA layer with the `org.eclipse.persistence` lines, our application with our own package (`com.github.rmannibucau`, in this example), and the datasource connection retrieval with the `ConnectionManager` lines. We can also identify that Jersey (JAX-RS implementation of GlassFish) is deployed over Tomcat, thanks to the `org.apache.catalina` packages (but only for the application pipeline management) and Grizzly for I/O handling (`org.glassfish.grizzly` packages).

This analysis is interesting as it shows something you need to take care of in Java EE: Java EE defines APIs but the runtime actually runs implementations. You rarely see `javax.*` entries in thread dumps, so you may need to check which implementations your server uses to make your analysis easier and faster.

Now the question is, can we conclude anything about this stack? Yes, of course! We can conclude that our application goes through the stack we expected. However, in terms of the performance, it doesn't mean anything. What will be impacting is how often you see the same stack being called. Concretely, if you see 30 threads over 100 waiting in a particular call, it may mean that this is a good place to optimize. If the stack even adds BLOCKED next to the line, it means that you need to ensure it is normal for the application to lock here and, maybe, change something (either the code or the configuration).

Before going on to the next section, keep in mind that you can get the same kind of output in multiple ways. The `jstack` tool is another Java tool that you can use for doing more or less the same thing, but an interesting tip is to use Linux (or Windows) native tools to get exactly the same information. If you have JRE (Java without the development tools) instead of JDK, here is how to do it on Linux:

```
kill -3 $JAVA_SERVER_PID
```

Memory

The GC.class_histogram command allows you to get a heap histogram. We will deal with this in the coming sections. But just to sum up very quickly, the heap is where most of your Java objects will go. Therefore, it is important to see how it is used.

If we execute the GC.class_histogram command in our process, the output will look as follows:

```
$ jcmd 7577 GC.class_histogram
7577:

 num #instances #bytes class name
----------------------------------------------
   1: 192795 16202648 [C
   2: 10490 4667040 [B
   3: 191582 4597968 java.lang.String
   4: 38779 3412552 java.lang.reflect.Method
   5: 20107 2243296 java.lang.Class
   6: 70045 2241440 java.util.HashMap$Node
   7: 24429 2078312 [Ljava.util.HashMap$Node;
   8: 47188 1887520 java.util.LinkedHashMap$Entry
   9: 28134 1745104 [Ljava.lang.Object;
  38: 2175 121800 com.sun.tools.javac.file.ZipFileIndex$DirectoryEntry
  39: 1890 120960
com.mysql.jdbc.ConnectionPropertiesImpl$BooleanConnectionProperty
1739: 6 192 java.util.regex.Pattern$3
2357: 1 96 com.sun.crypto.provider.SunJCE
2478: 4 96 org.glassfish.jersey.server.AsyncContext$State
2548: 1 88 org.glassfish.ejb.startup.EjbDeployer
2558: 2 80 [Lcom.mysql.jdbc.StringUtils$SearchMode;
2649: 2 80 org.glassfish.kernel.embedded.EmbeddedDomainPersistence
2650: 2 80 org.glassfish.persistence.jpa.PersistenceUnitInfoImpl
2652: 1 80 org.hibernate.validator.internal.engine.ConfigurationImpl
2655: 5 80 org.jboss.weld.manager.BeanManagerImpl
2678: 1 72 [Lorg.glassfish.jersey.uri.UriComponent$Type;
2679: 2 72 [Lsun.security.jca.ProviderConfig;
2680: 1 72 com.github.rmannibucau.quote.manager.model.Quote
2689: 3 72
com.sun.enterprise.container.common.impl.ComponentEnvManagerImpl$FactoryFor
EntityManagerWrapper
2770: 3 72 org.eclipse.persistence.jpa.jpql.parser.TableExpressionFactory
6925: 1 16 sun.reflect.ReflectionFactory
Total 1241387 61027800
```

Here again, it is a partial output (truncated in multiple places) since it is too verbose for this book. If we find most of the environments we know, it is important to notice the following things:

- `com.mysql` for the JDBC driver our application uses
- `com.github.rmannibucau` for our application (the quote entity in particular)
- `com.sun.enterprise` for the GlassFish server
- `org.jboss.weld` for the CDI container of GlassFish
- `org.hibernate.validator` for the GlassFish bean validation implementation
- `sun`, `com.sun`, `java`, and so on for the JVM

Now, an important thing is to be able to interpret these figures. The first column is not very important but the next two are. As written in the table header, they represent the number of instances and their size in bytes.

If you run several concurrent requests on your server and filter the output for your quote entity, you can see the following:

```
 138:            591           42552
 com.github.rmannibucau.quote.manager.model.Quote
```

This line means that the heap currently has 591 instances of `Quote` and it takes 42,552 bytes.

This means that it is a statistic you can check in real time while the server is running. But as it is written in the command help, it impacts the server (slows it down), so you need to use it for tuning purposes only.

The last interesting figure of the `GC.class_histogram` command is the total size of the heap, which is the last number printed. In our previous output, it was 61,027,800 bytes (about 61 MB).

JVisualVM – the UI for JVM monitoring

The `jcmd` command is a great command-line tool but is a bit raw. However, the JVM provides additional tooling to yield metrics linked to performance and, in particular, the CPU and memory. `JVisualVM` and `JConsole` are two such tools packaged with the JDK (not the JRE). Since both are pretty similar, we will only deal with `JVisualVM` in this section, but most of the information and tools can be used with `JConsole` as well.

To launch `JVisualVM`, you just have to execute a command of the same name:

```
$ $JAVA_HOME/bin/jvisualvm
```

Once launched, you will see the welcome screen of `jvisualvm`:

To start using `jvisualvm`, you will need to select a JVM. This is done through the tree on the left-hand side of the screen. The two options are **Local** and **Remote**. In this case, we'll run the server on our local machine, so it is automatically detected by `jvisualvm` (just ensure to start it from the same JDK as the one the server is using). In the previous screenshot, you can see three processes:

- `VisualVM`: This is a Java process and detects itself.
- `GlassFish`: This is a standalone GlassFish server.
- `org.codehaus.plexus.classworlds.launcher.Launcher`: This is a maven process. If you start GlassFish with maven, as we saw in `Chapter 1`, *Money – The Quote Manager Application*, this is the process to choose.

Once you have identified your process in the list, you need to double-click on it and you will get the following screen showing high-level information about the process:

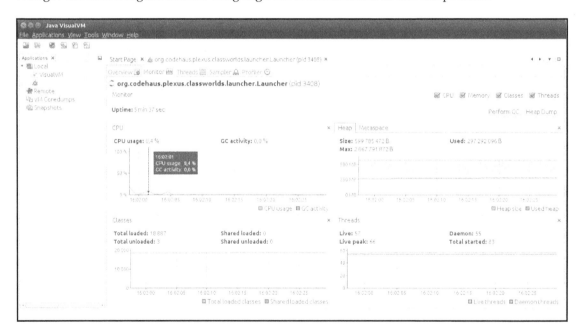

Once you have selected a JVM on the left, the right pane will show information about the JVM. It is organized in tabs:

- **Overview**: This gives high-level information about the JVM (process ID, main class, arguments, Java version, system properties, and so on).
- **Monitor**: This gives an overview of the CPU usage, the memory usage (in particular, the heap), the number of classes loaded, and the number of threads.
- **Threads**: This gives a live view of the existing threads managed by the JVM and shows the thread state over time (whether it is idled or active). Here is a screenshot:

The legend is in the bottom-right corner and uses colors to help this view to be readable: green for running, purple for sleeping, yellow for wait, red for fork, and orange for monitor.

What is interesting are the green blocks. This is when a thread does something. If you take the **http-listener(x)** threads for instance, you can see that they are orange and green. The orange part is when the threads are waiting for requests and the green part is when they are serving something. This view must be coupled with the thread dumps (or thread stack view) to ensure that the waiting threads are actually waiting for something relevant (such as waiting for some I/O), which the application does not control.

- **Sampler**: This tab is very interesting and allows you to capture what the server is doing in terms of CPU and memory. We find some information that we had with jcmd, but this is easier to use. All you need to do is to click on the **CPU** or **Memory** button and jvisualvm will start capturing the related information. Here is the memory view that you will get once some samples have been captured:

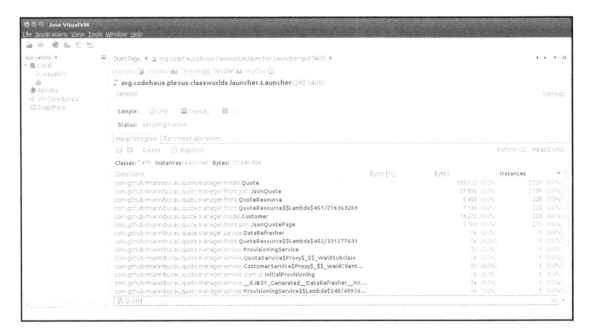

This view is really close to the GC histogram command of `jcmd`; you'll find the class name, the corresponding size in bytes, and the number of instances. You can filter the visible classes at the bottom using any pattern related to your application; in this screenshot, we filtered by **Quote**.

If you capture some CPU samples, the view is centered on the methods and their execution time:

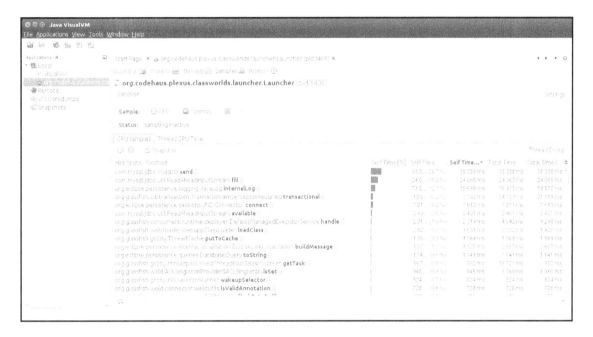

The first column is the method identifier and the other columns show the corresponding time for the respective methods. **Self Time** is the time of the method itself. **Self Time (CPU)** is the same but ignores waiting time (locks and so on). Same goes for the **Total Time** columns. What is the main difference between the **Self Time** and the **Total Time** columns? The **Total Time** columns include further method calls, which the **Self Time** columns don't.

While on the CPU view, you can click on **Thread Dump** to get a thread dump, the same as for `jcmd` but it is directly accessible in `jvisualvm`.

- **Profiler**: This is the last tab of the JVM view and provides more or less the same view as the **Sampler** tab. The main difference is the way it captures the data. Don't worry if the time between your click and the first data you can see is quite long in **Profiler**. While the **Sampler** tab just takes a *screenshot* of the JVM (memory or thread stacks) from time to time and generates approximate statistics from them, the **Profiler** tab modifies the classes (actual bytecode) to capture accurate data. This implies that the sampling overhead is not very huge but the profiling overhead can be if it affects all the codebase, including the fast methods (which are instrumented by default). If you want precise metrics, you will need to use the profiler, but it is recommended that you hit the **Settings** checkbox to precisely tune which classes you want to get the metrics for and not let the defaults, which are too wide to not affect the system.

How to connect remotely

Connecting locally is easy since `jvisualvm` will just locally look up the running JVM. But for connecting remotely, you will need some more setup.

All the communication relies on JMX and, therefore, you need to set up a remote JMX connection. This relies on what is called a connector (can be seen as a small embedded JMX server). There are multiple protocols available but out of the box; they rely on RMI communications and system properties to be configured.

To add these system properties, the fastest and easiest way is as follows:

```
-Dcom.sun.management.jmxremote.port=1234
-Dcom.sun.management.jmxremote.ssl=false
-Dcom.sun.management.jmxremote.authenticate=false
```

It will enable JMX on port 1234 and disable SSL and security. For performances, we don't need more, but if you want to keep it in production, you may need to configure the security and SSL. For more details on how to do so, you can refer to the Oracle website at `https://docs.oracle.com/javase/8/docs/technotes/guides/management/agent.html`.

Once this is configured, you just have to right-click on the **Local** item in the tree on the left side, select **Add JMX Connection**, and fill in the related information (host/port and the potential credentials if you've configured the security).

Java Mission Control

Since Java 7u40, the JDK has included the Java Flight Recorder tool. If you remember the available commands in `jcmd`, you had some `JFR.*` options, which are directly related to this tool. It allows you to capture a set of JVM events. It is coupled with **Java Mission Control** (**JMC**), which enables you to analyze and exploit the JVM events.

Launching it is easy:

```
$ $JAVA_HOME/bin/jmc
```

Once it is launched, you'll get a welcome screen; the view looks similar to the `jvisualvm` view, with a list of the available processes on the left-hand side:

You can use the same kind of hints as for `jvisualvm` to identify the process. If you are not quite sure, don't hesitate to use the `jps -v` command, which will show you the command line and its PID for each running JVM (which will allow you to identify the number in parentheses in JMC).

Once you've identified your process, you can right-click on it and select the **Start JMX** console to have a view similar to `jvisualvm` and specific to the selected JVM:

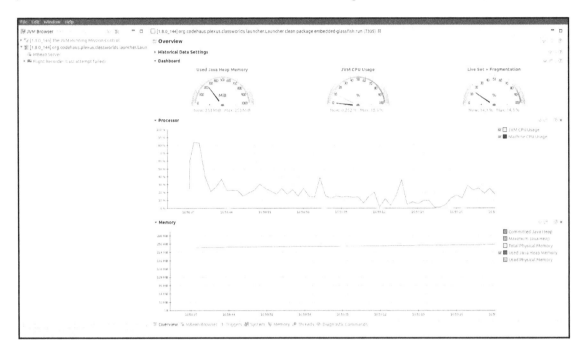

You find the CPU (processor here), the memory, and thread information, and also the MBean view, which is how the JVM can export the internal data in a standard manner.

One interesting thing is when you go to the **Diagnostic Commands** tab you will recognize the jcmd commands listed:

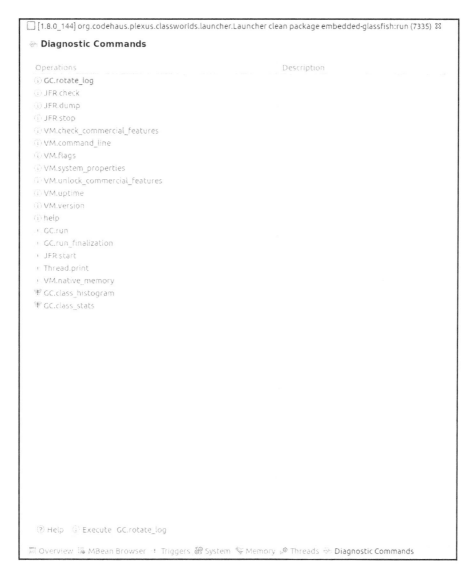

This pane allows you to execute the jcmd commands directly from the UI. Here, we are interested in the **Java Flight Recorder** (**JFR**) commands, as we want more information about our JVM.

In the previous screenshot, you may have noted that there is a **Flight Recorder** item on the left tree. It provides a UI for these commands. However, if you hit **Start Recording**, you will get the following error:

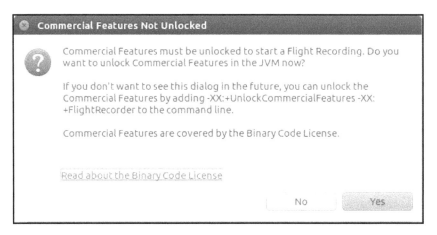

To use Java Flight Recorder, you need to add the following options to your JVM:

```
-XX:+UnlockCommercialFeatures -XX:+FlightRecorder
```

These two options will activate the Java Flight Recorder features. To add them to GlassFish, you can edit the $GLASSFISH_HOME/glassfish/domains/domain1/config/domain.xml file and add it to the java-config block after jvm-options. Alternatively, you can use the create-jvm-options command line's glassfish command. In any case, you will need to restart (or start) your server after this modification.

If you want to test it using our maven GlassFish, you can just add them to MAVEN_OPTS:

```
$ MAVEN_OPTS="-XX:+UnlockCommercialFeatures -XX:+FlightRecorder" mvn
embedded-glassfish:run
```

Now the options are activated on the JVM; you can go back to Java Mission Control and hit **Start Recording** on the **Start Flight Recorder** item. It will ask you a file location to store the recording and either a duration or a limit (size/age) for the recording. Finally, you can select whether you want to profile your server or just to monitor it. Here again, the difference is in the associated overhead. Let's select profiling for now. You can then hit **Next** and select what you want to monitor. An important parameter is the heap one, but if you continue through the wizard, you will see that you can precisely customize what you monitor, including the I/O. Once everything is well configured, simply hit **Finish**. It will proceed with the recording and open it once done.

> For the first time, select **1 min** as the recording duration; it will prevent you from waiting for too long.

After the recording is done, you should get a view similar to the following one, showing the captured data:

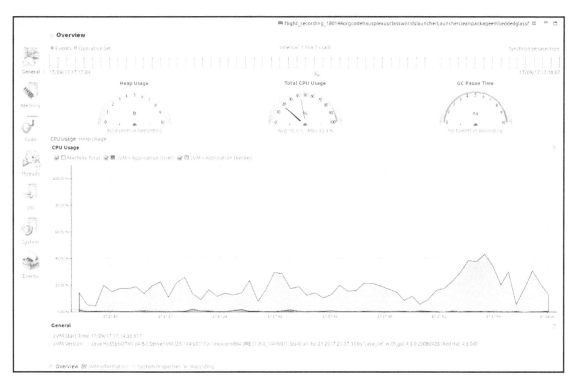

Looking at the top, we can see the event timeline. You can click on it to refine the time-slot selection. The counters show the summary of the capture in terms of memory and CPU. Finally, at the bottom, you have the CPU and memory graph.

What makes this tool more advanced than the previous one is the fact that you can visualize the code hotspot in the **Code** tab (the tabs are on the left in this tool) and the I/O in a single tool. The in-built JDK also makes it quite easy to use, whereas the overhead is not as important (if you select continuous monitoring, a counterpart is that the statistics won't be very accurate but close enough so as to give you an idea). A major strength of this tool is the **Call Tree** view of the **Code** tab. It allows you to associate, through a stack, the method execution time cost with the method calls. For instance, while the server was running, this capture shows that the cost of our `findAll` method is mainly related to the way we are mapping each quote that requires using the JPA layer (eclipselink) and the database:

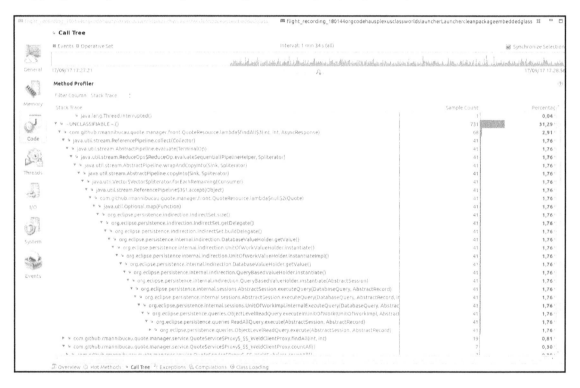

This view is a really great way to investigate the hotspots of the application. It kind of merges the thread dumps and the profiling views (sometimes called *Path Tracking*) and enables you to get directly to the costly operations.

GlassFish ad hoc monitoring

Many servers have inbuilt monitoring capabilities. This depends highly on the server, but it can give some interesting insights without having to use another tool. This is precious when you don't control the machine or don't have the permissions to access/configure the server.

To illustrate this kind of monitoring, let's use our Java EE reference implementation: GlassFish.

Once started with the normal `./bin/asadmin start-domain` command, you can activate monitoring with this additional command:

```
$ ./bin/asadmin enable-monitoring
Command enable-monitoring executed successfully.
```

Indeed, there is a symmetric command if you want to deactivate monitoring:

```
$./bin/asadmin disable-monitoring
```

You can list the monitors available with the `get` command:

```
$ ./bin/asadmin get server.monitoring-service.*
server.monitoring-service.module-monitoring-levels.cloud=OFF
server.monitoring-service.module-monitoring-levels.cloud-elasticity=OFF
server.monitoring-service.module-monitoring-levels.cloud-orchestrator=OFF
server.monitoring-service.module-monitoring-levels.cloud-tenant-manager=OFF
server.monitoring-service.module-monitoring-levels.cloud-virt-assembly-
service=OFF
server.monitoring-service.module-monitoring-levels.connector-connection-
pool=OFF
server.monitoring-service.module-monitoring-levels.connector-service=OFF
server.monitoring-service.module-monitoring-levels.deployment=OFF
server.monitoring-service.module-monitoring-levels.ejb-container=OFF
server.monitoring-service.module-monitoring-levels.http-service=OFF
server.monitoring-service.module-monitoring-levels.jdbc-connection-pool=OFF
server.monitoring-service.module-monitoring-levels.jersey=HIGH
server.monitoring-service.module-monitoring-levels.jms-service=OFF
server.monitoring-service.module-monitoring-levels.jpa=OFF
server.monitoring-service.module-monitoring-levels.jvm=OFF
server.monitoring-service.module-monitoring-levels.orb=OFF
server.monitoring-service.module-monitoring-levels.security=OFF
server.monitoring-service.module-monitoring-levels.thread-pool=OFF
server.monitoring-service.module-monitoring-levels.transaction-service=OFF
server.monitoring-service.module-monitoring-levels.web-container=OFF
server.monitoring-service.module-monitoring-levels.web-services-
container=OFF
server.monitoring-service.dtrace-enabled=false
```

```
server.monitoring-service.mbean-enabled=true
server.monitoring-service.monitoring-enabled=true
Command get executed successfully.
```

This output shows that the Jersey monitoring level is `HIGH` but other ones are disabled (`OFF`).

An alternative is to use the administration UI (by default on `http://localhost:4848`, for a standalone installation). Going to your configuration part on the left tree, you will have a **Monitoring** item where you can access the exact same entries:

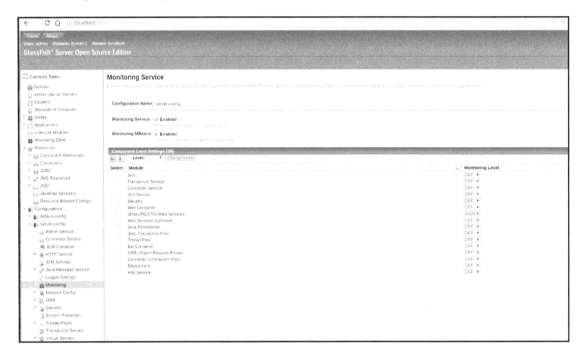

Selecting the level you want on the left of the table for the corresponding module will activate the associated monitoring. Once the monitoring is activated, you'll generally need to restart the server to let GlassFish take it into account.

Once it is done, you can access the associated information through the **Monitoring Data** item of the left tree:

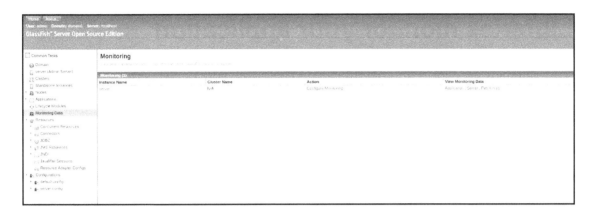

Here, you can see the monitored instances. (If you use a standalone GlassFish, you will probably have a single entry.) The **View Monitoring Data** column will let you select the data you want to see. If you click on **Application**, for instance, you will obtain the corresponding screen with the information filled in, depending on the monitoring level you activated before. Here is a sample screenshot:

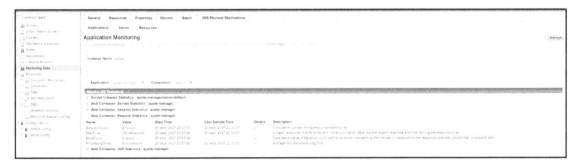

Depending on the application, this is more or less useful. However, for us (a JAX-RS service), the **Request Statistics** block is interesting even if it gives high-level information. We can use it to monitor the maximum response time and error count. By itself, it will not be enough to improve the performance, but it will enable us to compare it with the client-side information; we can then easily obtain and validate our performance testing.

It is important to keep in mind that servers often give aggregated performance figures for recent production monitoring, not performance tuning. This doesn't mean that it is useless but that you will only rely on ad hoc monitoring to validate your performance measurement pipeline (your client or your request injector, to put it simply).

Libraries monitor your application

We saw what the JVM provides us with tools and what the server gives us performance hints, but there are a lot of libraries intended to help you work on the performance.

Counters, gauges, timers, and more

The most famous library is probably *Metrics* from Dropwizard (`http://metrics.dropwizard.io`) but all libraries share more or less the same sort of API. The metrics are centered around a few important concepts:

- **Gauges**: These provide the measure of a value at a certain time. They are intended to build a time series. Most famous examples are the CPU or memory usages.
- **Counters**: These are long values, often associated with a gauges in order to build time series.
- **Histogram**: This structure allows you to compute the statistics around a value, for instance, the mean or the percentiles of request lengths.
- **Timers**: These are a bit like histograms; they compute other metrics based on one metric. Here, the goal is to have information about the rate of a value.
- **Health checks**: These are less related to the performance; they allows you to validate that a resource (such as a database) is working or not. Health checks throw a warning/error if the resource isn't working.

All these libraries provide different ways to export/expose the collected data. Common configurations are related to JMX (through MBeans), Graphite, Elasticsearch, and so on, or just the console/logger as the output.

How can these concepts be linked to the performance? The most important features for us will be the gauges and the counters. The gauges will enable us to make sure the server is doing well (for example, the CPU is not always at 100%, the memory is well released, and so on). The counters will enable us to measure the execution time. They will also enable us to export the data in an aggregated storage if you test against multiple instances, allowing you to detect some potential side effects of one instance on another one (if you have any clustering for example).

Concretely, we want to measure some important segments of our code. In the extreme case, if you don't know anything about the application, you will likely want to measure all parts of the code then refine it when you have more knowledge about your application.

To be very concrete and illustrate what we are trying to achieve, we want to replace application methods by this kind of pattern:

```
@GET
@Path("{id}")
public JsonQuote findById(@PathParam("id") final long id) {
    final Timer.Context metricsTimer =
getMonitoringTimer("findById").time();
    try {
        return defaultImpl();
    } finally {
        metricsTimer.stop();
    }
}
```

In other words, we want to surround our business code with a timer to collect statistics about our execution time. One common and *poor man* solution you can be tempted to start with is to use loggers to do it. It often looks as follows:

```
@GET
@Path("{id}")
public JsonQuote findById(@PathParam("id") final long id) {
    final long start = System.nanoTime();
    try {
        return defaultImpl();
    } finally {
        final long end = System.nanoTime();
        MONITORING_LOGGER.info("perf(findById) = " +
        TimeUnit.NANOSECONDS.toMillis(end - start) + "ms");
    }
}
```

The preceding code manually measures the execution time of the method and, then, dumps the result with a description text in a specific logger to identify the code portion it is related to.

In doing so, the issue you will encounter is that you will not get any statistics about what you measure and will need to preprocess all the data you collect, delaying the use of the metrics to identify the hotspots of your application and work on them. This may not seem like a big issue, but as you are likely to do it many times during a benchmark phase, you will not want to do it manually.

Then, the other issues are related to the fact that you need to add this sort of code in all the methods you want to measure. Thus, you will pollute your code with monitoring code, which is rarely worth it. It impacts even more if you add it temporarily to get metrics and remove it later. This means that you will try to avoid this kind of work as much as possible.

The final issue is that you can miss the server or library (dependency) data, as you don't own this code. That means that you may spend hours and hours working on a code block that is, in fact, not the slowest one.

Instrumenting the code

The immediate question is *how do you instrument the code you want to measure without having to modify it?* The first goal is to avoid being too intrusive in the code and, also, to avoid affecting the entire application just for the duration of a benchmark. The second goal is to be able to *toggle* the instrumentation and to be able to deactivate it in order to measure the application without monitoring (particularly, if you put it everywhere) and ignore the associated overhead on the metrics you take.

Nowadays, in Java and Java EE state, you have several options to instrument the code. We will browse through most of them, but here is an overview of the choices you have:

- **Choice 1 – manual**: In this solution, you wrap the instance you use with a *Factory* of the monitoring framework you rely on, and the returned instance is wrapped in a monitored proxy (new instance delegating to the original one). Concretely, it can look like the following:

```
@ApplicationScoped
public class QuoteResource {
    @Inject
    private QuoteService service;

    @PostConstruct
    private void monitorOn() {
        service = MonitoringFactory.monitor(service);
    }
}
```

  From what we talked about earlier, this has a drawback of impacting the code and limiting the instrumentation to the code you own (or can modify). However, the big advantage is that it is simple to integrate and works with any kind of code (managed by the EE container or not). Concretely, most of the monitoring libraries will have such a utility and often just use it internally in other kinds of integrations.

- **Choice 2 – through CDI (or the interceptor API)**: The Java EE standard way to *inject* logic into a service is to use an interceptor. We will detail how it works in a dedicated part but the overall idea is to flag a method as being monitored. Here again, the limitation will be to have access to the code you want to monitor through the CDI container. However, it is less impacting than the previous solution in terms of coding.

> If your application relies on Spring, the Spring framework has the same kind of tooling (referenced as *AOP* in their documentation). So, the same concept applies even if it is activated a bit differently.

- **Choice 3 – through a javaagent**: The javaagent is the most powerful way to instrument the code. The drawback is that you need to configure it directly on the JVM, while the good point is that you can monitor almost every class (except for a few of the JVM itself).

> Some containers (such as Tomcat/TomEE for instance) allow you to configure `java.lang.instrument.ClassFileTransformer`. This will basically enable you to perform bytecode instrumentation at load time (dynamically). This allows you to benefit from almost the same power as that of a javaagent, except that you will not be able to instrument the container—and potentially, a part of the JVM—but only the classes of the application. However, it is still more powerful than CDI instrumentation as it sees all the classes of the application, not only the ones that the CDI processes.

CDI instrumentation

If we focus back on the Metrics library, we will find several CDI integrations. The global idea is to decorate the code with some annotation and automatically get the metrics associated with the executed code. Clearly, it will impact your code this way (using `https:/ /github.com/astefanutti/metrics-cdi` for instance):

```
@Transactional
@ApplicationScoped
public class QuoteService {
    @PersistenceContext
    private EntityManager entityManager;

    @Timed(name = "create")
```

```
    public Quote create(final Quote newQuote) {
        entityManager.persist(newQuote);
        entityManager.flush();
        return newQuote;
    }
}
```

The `@Timed` annotation will automatically wrap the method execution in a Metrics timer and will therefore provide the statistics about the execution time of the method. The relevant code of the interceptor associated with the `@Timed` annotation is very close to this logic:

```
private Object onInvocation(InvocationContext context) throws Exception {
    Timer.Context time = findTimer(context).time();
    try {
        return context.proceed();
    } finally {
        time.stop();
    }
}
```

This is exactly what we want to achieve but it has one trap we didn't think about yet: the exception handling. To understand this point, we can compare the code used in the retired project (called Apache Sirona), which had the following differently implemented feature:

```
protected Object doInvoke(final InvocationContext context) throws Throwable
{
    final Context ctx = before(context);
    Throwable error = null;
    try {
        return proceed(context);
    } catch (final Throwable t) {
        error = t;
        throw t;
    } finally {
        if (error == null) {
            ctx.stop();
        } else {
            ctx.stopWithException(error);
        }
    }
}
```

What is important to see here is that the code path changes in the case of an exception. In terms of statistics, this implies that failures will have a different marker from successful calls in the metrics report. This is important to notice because the execution time of a failure is rarely comparable to a success, even for simple methods. Let's take a simple finder example from our quote manager application and observe this. Here is the line we will investigate:

```
entityManager.find(Quote.class, id)
```

A normal call with a valid ID will be around 6 to 7 ms (on my reference machine, with my personal configuration). The `EntityManager#find` method can take any type for the identifier, so if we pass a wrong type (such as `String` instead of `long`) then the call should compile and execute. Eclipselink will complain with an exception but the performance impact is something interesting: 0 ms! Indeed, this example is very extreme and is a bug, but if you have some rate limiting on an endpoint or some sanity checks at the beginning of the methods, the same impact can be observed.

This means that if the framework you are using is putting all the invocations (with errors or not) in the same bucket, you can have a very good performance but a very slow application, since the average of the success/failure makes the figures look good.

Implementing your own configurable monitoring interceptor

Implementing a CDI interceptor is not that complicated. Thus, you may want to have your own if you do not find a library matching your expectations. It can have two kinds of direct impact on the way you use monitoring:

- Be able to control the counters you use depending on the case you are in. This includes success/failure handling, but it can also be tenant-related (if your application is handling multiple tenants). This can be very important if you do not use the exact same system as the tenant (one can have a slower database than the other, for instance).
- Be able to configure the monitored beans. Yes, with CDI you can also avoid having to decorate the beans you want to monitor and just do it automatically from a configuration.

The first step to create a CDI interceptor is to have what CDI calls *interceptor binding*. It is the annotation you will use on your beans that will mark the method as being monitored. Here is a simple one:

```
@InterceptorBinding
@Target({ElementType.TYPE, ElementType.METHOD})
@Retention(RetentionPolicy.RUNTIME)
public @interface Monitored {
}
```

It is a normal annotation that you can put in a method (or a class to mark all the methods as being monitored). The only particular thing is its @InterceptorBinding marker.

Then, to link this interceptor bind to the actual interceptor implementation, you create an interceptor with the same annotation:

```
@Interceptor
@Monitored
@Priority(Interceptor.Priority.PLATFORM_BEFORE)
public class MonitoredInterceptor implements Serializable {
    @AroundInvoke
    @AroundTimeout
    public Object monitor(final InvocationContext invocationContext) throws
Exception {
        final Context ctx = newContext(invocationContext);
        Exception error = null;
        try {
            return invocationContext.proceed();
        } catch (final Exception t) {
            error = t;
            throw t;
        } finally {
            if (error == null) {
                ctx.stop();
            } else {
                ctx.stopWithException(error);
            }
        }
    }
}
```

The method being decorated with @AroundInvoke will handle the method invocation, and being decorated with @AroundTimeout, it will also support EJB timer callbacks (@Timeout).

Note that if you also want to monitor the constructors, you can do so, but you will need to implement an `@AroundConstruct` method (with the same sort of implementation as our `monitor` method). The fact that our interceptor is decorated with `@Priority` automatically enables it, and you do not need to activate it in `beans.xml`.

With this code, you can decorate any method with `@Monitored` and, assuming that your `Context` stores the metrics, you will get your figures in the reporting solution you used.

However, one goal of writing a custom implementation was also to be able to configure it. With CDI, it can be done with `Extension`. The global idea will be to observe the application types/methods, and if one is configured to be monitored, we will add `@Monitored` automatically. This way, we'll have no code impact in the application and we can easily activate/deactivate monitoring by simply changing our configuration. For the configuration, we can just start with a `performance.properties` resource as follows (note that it will be easy to change to a particular file outside the application):

```
public class PerformanceExtension implements Extension {
    private final Annotation monitored = new
    AnnotationLiteral<Monitored>() {};
    private final Properties configuration = new Properties();
    private boolean enabled;

    void loadConfiguration(final @Observes BeforeBeanDiscovery
    beforeBeanDiscovery) {
        try (final InputStream configStream =
        Thread.currentThread().getContextClassLoader()
        .getResourceAsStream("performances.properties")) {
            if (configStream != null) {
                configuration.load(configStream);
            }
        }   catch (final IOException ioe) {
            throw new IllegalArgumentException(ioe);
        }
        enabled =
        Boolean.parseBoolean(configuration.getProperty("enabled",
        "true"));
    }

    <A> void processAnnotatedType(final @Observes
    ProcessAnnotatedType<A> pat) {
        if (!enabled) {
            return;
        }
```

```
        final String beanClassName =
        pat.getAnnotatedType().getJavaClass().getName();
        if(Boolean.parseBoolean(configuration.getProperty(beanClassName
        + ".monitor", "false"))) {
            pat.setAnnotatedType(new WrappedAnnotatedType<>
            (pat.getAnnotatedType(), monitored));
        }
    }
}
```

This code uses the `BeforeBeanDiscovery` event (beginning of the CDI lifecycle) to load our configuration. Here, you can read from whatever place you want. A small optimization is to have a special key to check whether the extension is activated or not. If it is set to something other than true, then we will just skip all other events. In case it is enabled, we'll observe all the discovered types through the `ProcessAnnotatedType` event. If the bean should be monitored (our test is very simple here, we just check whether the class name suffixed with *monitor* is true in our configuration), then we override `AnnotatedType`, keeping all its information but adding `@Monitored` into the set of the class's annotations.

You can do exactly the same at the method level, wrapping `AnnotatedMethod` returned by `AnnotatedType#getMethods`. The logic is the same; you just need to have one more configuration level (for methods).

The `WrappedAnnotatedType` implementation is a simple delegation implementation, except for the annotation accessors, where a new set is used instead of the original one:

```
public class WrappedAnnotatedType<A> implements AnnotatedType<A> {
    private final AnnotatedType<A> delegate;
    private final Set<Annotation> annotations;

    public WrappedAnnotatedType(final AnnotatedType<A> at, final
    Annotation additionalAnnotation) {
        this.delegate = at;

        this.annotations = new HashSet<Annotation
        >(at.getAnnotations().size() + 1);
        this.annotations.addAll(at.getAnnotations());
        this.annotations.add(additionalAnnotation);
    }

    @Override
    public Set<Annotation> getAnnotations() {
        return annotations;
    }
```

```
    @Override
    public <T extends Annotation> T getAnnotation(final Class<T>
    annotationType) {
        for (final Annotation ann : annotations) {
            if (ann.annotationType() == annotationType) {
                return annotationType.cast(ann);
            }
        }
        return null;
    }

    @Override
    public boolean isAnnotationPresent(final Class<? extends
    Annotation> annotationType) {
        return getAnnotation(annotationType) != null;
    }

    // other methods fully delegate the invocations to the delegate
    instance
}
```

As you can see, the only logic is in `getAnnotation` and in the constructor where a new set of annotations is created to replace the original one.

Finally, to enable `Extension` and let the CDI find it, we just put its qualified name in `META-INF/services/javax.enterprise.inject.spi.Extension` in our project resources.

Once this extension is added to your application (you can develop it as a library and just add the `jar` file inside your `war` package if you want), you can configure it through `performances.properties`.

In our case, monitoring our quote service looks like this:

```
# activate the monitoring
enabled = true

# monitor the QuoteService class
com.github.rmannibucau.quote.manager.service.QuoteService.monitor = true
```

What's more, you can add a line by the class you want to monitor. Don't forget to restart between updates in this file, since the configuration and the CDI model's wrapping is done only at startup.

Javaagent – a complex but powerful instrumentation

If you go back again to metrics, you can find existing javaagents even if they are less numerous, since writing an agent is a bit more complicated.

A javaagent is a particular kind of the main method provided by the JVM that enables you to register `ClassFileTransformer`, which is a way to modify the classes' bytecode before they get loaded. In other words, you will write some code and compile it, but the JVM will never execute it. Instead, it will execute a rewritten version of the code.

We will not detail how to do it here. In fact, it is more complicated than writing an interceptor (you need to take care of the classloaders, write low-level bytecode with the ASM library or an equivalent, and so on). However, it is important to see that the scope of a javaagent is the JVM—not an application, not a container, but the full JVM. For technical reasons, as you may guess, you can not instrument all the JVM classes, but all the classes that are loaded after the javaagent are started (which is already far enough).

Instrumenting `java.net.HttpURLConnection` is a good example of instrumentation using a javaagent.

This class is often used to implement a Java HTTP client, but it is often hidden by libraries (such as a JAX-RS client implementation). Therefore, it is not easy to have the current request and framework time if you cannot measure this specific class.

That is how a javaagent will be way more powerful than a CDI or a Spring instrumentation.

To give you an idea of what you can do with a javaagent, we will configure the Sirona project in our quote manager application.

Sirona javaagent

To keep it simple and easy to understand, we will use maven, but you can follow the same steps on any application server, since javaagent is set up on the JVM and not on a particular server.

The first step is to download the javaagent `jar` file. To do so with maven, you can just add the dependency maven plugin in your `pom.xml`:

```
<plugin>
  <groupId>org.apache.maven.plugins</groupId>
  <artifactId>maven-dependency-plugin</artifactId>
  <version>3.0.2</version>
  <executions>
    <execution>
      <id>sirona</id>
      <goals>
        <goal>copy</goal>
      </goals>
      <configuration>
        <artifactItems>
          <artifactItem>
            <groupId>com.github.rmannibucau.sirona</groupId>
            <artifactId>sirona-javaagent</artifactId>
            <version>0.6</version>
            <type>jar</type>
            <classifier>shaded</classifier>
            <overWrite>true</overWrite>
            <outputDirectory>${project.basedir}</outputDirectory>
            <destFileName>sirona-javaagent.jar</destFileName>
          </artifactItem>
        </artifactItems>
      </configuration>
    </execution>
  </executions>
</plugin>
```

It is configured to download sirona-javaagent shaded JAR (all in one bundle). Now, if you execute this maven command, you should obtain the javaagent JAR in your maven project:

```
$ mvn dependency:copy@sirona
```

Once this command is executed, you should find a `sirona-javaagent.jar` file next to your pom.

Now that we have the javaagent, we need to configure it. To make it simple, sirona supports a `sirona.properties` configuration file in the current directory, so we will use it. Here's what it will contain to activate monitoring in our application:

```
com.github.rmannibucau.sirona.javaagent.listener.CounterListener.includes=p
refix:com.github.rmannibucau.quote.manager
com.github.rmannibucau.sirona.javaagent.listener.CounterListener.excludes=c
ontainer:jvm
```

```
com.github.rmannibucau.sirona.store.counter.CounterDataStore=com.github.rma
nnibucau.sirona.store.counter.CsvLoggingCounterDataStore

com.github.rmannibucau.sirona.csvlogging.counter.period=5000
com.github.rmannibucau.sirona.csvlogging.counter.clearAfterCollect=true

com.github.rmannibucau.sirona.javaagent.path.tracking.activate=false
```

The `CounterListener`-related configuration is about the scope of the monitoring: what is instrumented and what is not. Here, we just instrument our application package and make Sirona ignoring the JVM classes (*container* is an alias for a set of built-in exclusions). Then, we configure `CounterDataStore` where the metrics are stored. In this example, we use a logging flavor (the metrics will then be outputted in a logger) and a CSV formatting. This is the simplest way, but you can also configure it to output the data in Elasticsearch, Graphite or any external system. Then, we configure our storage to log every 5 seconds (5000 ms)—this is mainly for demonstration, but in real life, you will probably want to wait for a minute or so. Next, we request the storage to be cleared after collection. This last point means that every time the data is logged, the data is reset. It avoids keeping the startup data from having side-effects on the runtime data. Finally, the last line deactivates the path tracking feature of Sirona, which is built in with the javaagent, but we do not need it here.

Now that everything is configured, we just need to ensure that our application is ready to run (you can re-execute `mvn clean package` if you have a doubt) and then launch it with the javaagent on the JVM (maven if you launch GlassFish with maven or directly GlassFish if you use a standalone instance):

```
MAVEN_OPTS="-javaagent:sirona-javaagent.jar" mvn embedded-glassfish:run
```

As you can see, adding a javaagent is as simple as adding the `-javaagent` option on the JVM, followed by the path of the JAR.

 If the agent is natively developed and not done in Java, the command would be quite similar (but using `-agentlib`). This is how you can distinguish between Java and native agents, but the principle remains the same.

Once you have started the server, if you wait for a few seconds (~5 seconds as for our configuration), you will start getting some output related to the metrics Sirona took:

```
sept. 23, 2017 12:16:32 PM
com.github.rmannibucau.sirona.store.counter.LoggingCounterDataStore
pushCountersByBatch
INFOS:
"com.github.rmannibucau.quote.manager.service.ProvisioningService$Data.getQ
```

```
uoteSummary()";"performances";70;1;3045.0;157.0;842.514285714286;58976.0;62
2.1554571298391
sept. 23, 2017 12:16:32 PM
com.github.rmannibucau.sirona.store.counter.LoggingCounterDataStore
pushCountersByBatch
INFOS:
"com.github.rmannibucau.quote.manager.service.QuoteService$Proxy$_$$_WeldSu
bclass.weld$$$46()";"performances";1;1;6054.0;6054.0;6054.0;6054.0;0.
```

The output format depends on the logger configuration. Out of the box, it is not that fancy, but if you configure your logger, you will get a plain CSV output. By default in Sirona, the logger name will be `com.github.rmannibucau.sirona.counters`. If you want to configure this particular logger in a specific file without a specific formatter pattern, you will have to use the logger name and not the class name.

To keep it simple for us, we will just change the `SimpleFormatter` format in the JVM (it will affect all loggers using this formatter):

```
MAVEN_OPTS="-Djava.util.logging.SimpleFormatter.format=%5\$s%6\$s%n -
javaagent:sirona-javaagent.jar"
```

Note that depending on your operating system, you may (or may not) need to escape the dollars, as in the previous example (it was for Linux).

Once the server starts with this new configuration, the output is more readable:

```
"com.github.rmannibucau.quote.manager.service.QuoteService$Proxy$_$$_WeldSu
bclass.weld$$$94()";"performances";1;1;4347.0;4347.0;4347.0;4347.0;0.0
"com.github.rmannibucau.quote.manager.service.QuoteService$Proxy$_$$_WeldSu
bclass.weld$$$98()";"performances";1;1;3842.0;3842.0;3842.0;3842.0;0.0
"com.github.rmannibucau.quote.manager.service.QuoteService$Proxy$_$$_WeldSu
bclass.weld$$$102()";"performances";1;1;4186.0;4186.0;4186.0;4186.0;0.0
"com.github.rmannibucau.quote.manager.model.Quote._persistence_new(org.ecli
pse.persistence.internal.descriptors.PersistenceObject)";"performances";11;
1;15760.0;4272.0;8134.545454545455;89480.0;3191.1807959949983
"com.github.rmannibucau.quote.manager.service.QuoteService.mutate(java.lang
.String,java.util.function.Function)";"performances";10;1;1.3095653E7;55178
05.0;9319597.6;9.3195976E7;2502831.398655584
"com.github.rmannibucau.quote.manager.service.ProvisioningService$Data.getQ
uoteSummary()";"performances";70;1;7909.0;519.0;1455.4142857142854;101879.0
;1239.6496056226922
```

What is interesting here is that you can directly import this in a CSV editor, including Microsoft Excel or LibreOffice Calc, and work on the data (sort it, compare it, and so on).

To efficiently work on the data, you need to know what the columns are. For this particular datastore, here is the header list:

- Timer/counter name
- Timer/counter role (*performance* means the execution time is measured, *failure* means an exception has occurred)
- Hits (indicates how often the method has been called in the measuring window)
- Max concurrency (indicates what the maximum of a concurrent call for a method in the measuring window is)
- Max (gives the maximum execution time)
- Min (gives the minimum execution time)
- Mean (gives the the average execution time)
- Sum (gives the sum of all the execution times)
- Standard deviation of all the execution times of the window

In your investigations into finding the bottleneck of a method to dig into (in order to optimize the performance), you will have to take multiple datasets into account. The first data will be the *sum*. If you sort by *sum* (decreasing order), the first method will be the one consuming a lot of time for your application. However, you need to validate it against the number of hits. For instance, if you have a single hit, then you know that caching this method's data will not be helpful. The standard deviation (or comparing the min/max range) will also give you an idea of the method's behavior. If the range is high, then you need to investigate what this method does, and why it is fast sometimes and slow some other times.

Once you've found a good method to investigate, you can reuse the tools we talked about earlier to dig into the method. Having this level of information to start working is generally easier to deal with and more centered on the application overview than the detailed view, which can be hard (or long) to organize. It is always easier to drill down the performance data than starting from the detailed view.

Now, to show you how powerful a javaagent can be, we will temporarily change our sirona configuration a bit. We will exclude the Oracle package (just to override the default exclusion, which is the whole JVM), and we will include `HttpURLConnection`.

The goal for our application can be to compare the time we spend in the provisioning versus the current network cost, which we can not optimize as it is linked to our environment, which we assume to be constant during the benchmark phase.

Here is what the configuration looks like now:

```
com.github.rmannibucau.sirona.javaagent.listener.CounterListener.includes=p
refix:com.github.rmannibucau.quote.manager,\
    prefix:sun.net.www.protocol.http.HttpURLConnection
com.github.rmannibucau.sirona.javaagent.listener.CounterListener.excludes=p
refix:oracle

com.github.rmannibucau.sirona.store.counter.CounterDataStore=com.github.rma
nnibucau.sirona.store.counter.CsvLoggingCounterDataStore

com.github.rmannibucau.sirona.csvlogging.counter.period=5000
com.github.rmannibucau.sirona.csvlogging.counter.clearAfterCollect=true

com.github.rmannibucau.sirona.javaagent.path.tracking.activate=false
```

Only the two first lines change, and you can see that the JVM is no more excluded to be able to instrument the sum package and that `HttpUrlConnection` is now included in the white list of instrumented classes.

We relaunch our server, and after the provisioning, we get these new outputs:

```
"sun.net.www.protocol.http.HttpURLConnection.plainConnect()";"performances"
;1;1;1.288844214E9;1.288844214E9;1.288844214E9;1.288844214E9;0.0
"sun.net.www.protocol.http.HttpURLConnection.getNewHttpClient(java.net.URL,
java.net.Proxy,int)";"performances";1;1;1.288132398E9;1.288132398E9;1.28813
2398E9;1.288132398E9;0.0
....
```

The configuration change includes the JVM HTTP client monitoring, and we can now have a part of the time spent in the actual network as well as the time spent in the client code itself, with retries and all the logic it embeds. This is the kind of information you cannot get without a javaagent.

Modern architectures tend to encourage microservices. This means that you will mainly split your overall system into subsystems with a clear responsibility separation. It implies a lot of issues, such as the requirement to handle transactions across different systems (what XA was doing in its time), the addition of multiple remote communications, which slows down the overall process, and so on, but it comes with the advantage of allowing you to develop systems more rapidly and to go into production more easily in general. There is always a trade-off.

In any case, if you work on the performance, you may have to deal with such a system now and, therefore, need to know which tools can help you.

There are mainly two kinds of solutions that will help a lot:

- **Data aggregation**: All the data of all the applications will be aggregated in a single system. For instance, the previously captured execution times of N instances will be stored in a single *database* (such as InfluxDB or Elasticsearch).
- **Tracing**: The entire system will propagate a single *transaction ID* (also called *request ID*), which will enable you to identify the request (user action) across all the systems and the stage you are at (third system of the pipeline, for instance).

SQL Monitoring

In a lot of applications, most of the time will be taken by the SQL queries' execution. Therefore, it is important to monitor them. You can use one of the previous techniques but there are also some specific ways to monitor them.

Generally, the idea is to replace the native driver you use (the Oracle, MySQL ones, for instance) with a monitoring driver, which will wrap the default driver and delegate all the logic to the original one, adding some metrics on top of it.

For instance, using sirona JDBC driver (`http://repo.maven.apache.org/maven2/com/github/rmannibucau/sirona/sirona-jdbc/0.6/`) for our datasource, we will define the application DataSource this way:

```
@DataSourceDefinition(
        name = "java:app/jdbc/quote_manager",
        className = "com.github.rmannibucau.sirona.jdbc.SironaDriver",
        url =
"jdbc:sirona:mysql://localhost:3306/quote_manager?delegateDriver=com.mysql.
jdbc.Driver",
        user = "root",
        password = "password"
)
public class DataSourceConfiguration {
}
```

The driver's class name is now the monitoring one, and the URL changed a bit to configure the monitoring driver. Here, with Sirona, you append `sirona` before the native driver URL and after the `jdbc:` prefix, and you add the `delegateDriver` query parameter to the URL with the classname of the native driver as the value.

Once done, Sirona will automatically create counters for each statement and add it to its report.

> This kind of solution works very well with prepared statements, as you will reuse the same *key* (the SQL value). This is generally what any JPA provider does.

This visualization, between Java and the database, can help determine the slow queries. There are a lot of implementations of such a type. Just pick the one you prefer, between Sirona, Jamon, JavaSimon, Log4jJDBC, P6Spy, and others.

Data aggregation

Microservices—or more generally services with small scopes—are fast-moving applications in general, and it is easy to add/remove them in a global system. In this condition, the performance will need to be comparable and validatable against any change of the sibling services (which can impact the central service by overusing or misusing it).

Being able to have a centralized vision of all the systems is a key to understanding how optimizing another application can make your application go faster. The corollary of this statement is that when you depend on another application, which is too slow for your SLA, you need to be aware of it as soon as possible. Once identified, you can add caching or alternative ways to make your application less dependent on others and behave faster.

It is not always possible—for instance, in our quote manager application, we can't get data about Yahoo—but in a microservice structure, you will often get a company policy or at least contacts to be able to discuss it and implement it.

In practice, it is mainly about agreeing on a way of identifying the application (which is just about defining a convention in the overall system, shared by all the subsystems) and the data format put inside the aggregator. For instance, you can say that you will use the `Company-ID` HTTP header as a request identifier and the log format will be `${Company-Id} | ${Tenant-Id} | ${Machine-Id} | ${Execution-Time} | ${action/method} | ${message}`.

This is just a simple example, but the idea is to be able to browse the log across applications pretty quickly.

Once you know what you will log, you need to select a system to store your data. Here, you have a lot of choices but do not forget to check whether you can exploit the data once it is stored. It means that you need to ensure you have a good user interface that will fulfill your expectations on top of the storage.

The most known are these:

- Elastic stack: It is based on Elasticsearch to store the data and Kibana to visualize it. It is available for free.
- Splunk: It is a custom stack dedicated to the aggregation of data.
- Grafana: It is mainly a UI tool, but it is pluggable on most of the monitoring databases, including Elasticsearch, Graphite or InfluxDB.

Tracing

There are multiple options for tracing (Zipkin, Dapper, and others) but a few of them seem to have become mainstream. One of them is the OpenTracing initiative (`http://opentracing.io/`). All share more or less the same design based on spans.

The global idea is to let each transaction's actors mark their presence with a span. A span contains an identifier, some metadata about the invocation, and the execution time. The identifier is generally composed of multiple values representing the overall trace identifier (the request marker), the span identifier, and, often, the parent identifier.

When correctly installed, the tracing happens on the client and server sides, so you have a full vision of the system handling, and it is associated with the processing time of each part of the system. It is really about ensuring that every part of your system is properly instrumented—each time you exit or enter a system, you must be set up to handle the associated tracing. This includes HTTP clients/servers, and also the JDBC or NoSQL drivers.

As for the monitoring libraries, this relies on storage, but there are also local implementations (a bit like our CSV logger when we talked about the Sirona javaagent) you can use to test your configuration or use as fallbacks if you can't have a real monitoring database. However, using local outputs with such systems will make your work harder and longer, since it is really about aggregating multiple data to have a consolidated vision. What you need to understand is that you shouldn't hesitate to invest in setting a server dedicated to the data collection. It will not only help you for performance, but also for tracing your system. So, it is a worthy investment!

APM

You can find tools called **Application Performance Management** (**APM**) on the market. These are really the Rolls Royce of monitoring tools and allow you to trace completely all the steps of the application, to go back in time to understand what happened, and to deduce the cause of a support issue very quickly. The paid offers generally include the infrastructure as well, which is not a negligible point, since it leads to a lot of data manipulation.

Technically, they reuse several of the previous techniques but are really an all-in-one solution, which makes them very valuable. However, they are generally expensive and rarely open source.

Nonetheless, you can find a few open source implementations, such as PinPoint(`https://github.com/naver/pinpoint`), InspectIT(`https://github.com/inspectIT/inspectIT`), and Glowroot(`https://glowroot.org/`). In terms of a leading proprietary, solution you can find New Relic (`https://newrelic.com/java`), DripStat (`https://dripstat.com`), or DynaTrace (`https://www.dynatrace.com/`).

Summary

In this part, we saw a lot of ways to gather information about the JVM and your application. We also saw that the JVM itself provides a set of tools to give you information about the memory, CPU, and garbage collection. Most of them are available through the command line (which can be very handy when benchmarking a machine without any UI), but they also come with several user interfaces, enabling you to get the information easily once you can connect to the JVM. One of these tools is the JMC: it gives you a lot of information and even allows you to drill down into the method invocations to have a detailed view of your application.

However, it is not enough and you may need to get access to the server information about the pool usage, and in this case, the server can give you some more information about configuration issues (such as a pool configured too small). Then, a set of libraries allows you to get the monitoring information in a more efficient and performance-oriented way, which enables you to investigate the application without a deep knowledge or any assumption about it. Note that these tools (such as Metrics or Sirona) also aggregate more data and often have plugins for the servers, which can prevent you from using the server-specific monitoring to get a more global vision.

Finally, we saw that in multisystem applications, you will need to ensure you can monitor your applications and also the ones linked to them so that you can identify the impacts on your own applications and try to decrease them if too impacting.

All of these tools, in some way, have some kind of overlap, but they all fulfill different needs and answer to a different trade-off between ease, information completeness, and investment. Depending on the knowledge you have about the application you are working on, and the investment you can afford for the code and infrastructure of the application of the benchmarking platform, you will pick a solution.

In the next chapter, we will investigate the impact of resources on applications and their performance. We will go through the Java memory management and the server resource handling, such as `DataSource` and `ConnectionFactory`.

4

Application Optimization – Memory Management and Server Configuration

We now know how to get information about the performance of our application. From high-level execution time to deep container internals, we can determine which part of the code is slowing us down.

However, this is mainly about our code or stack (the Java EE container). There are other criteria that can influence the performance of the same machine (considering that the CPU and the memory are fixed).

In this chapter, we will investigate the following:

- How JVM manages the memory and automatically releases unused objects
- Compare different options to release the memory that JVM offers
- See how the server configuration can also impact the performance

Java and the memory

Java is a high-level language, which means that it is doing a lot of work for you. Nowadays, most languages do that (such as Scala, Go, and even recent C++ updates), but to understand the memory challenge, we need to go back to the early programming days and compare two simple code segments.

The first one is a simplified version of our provisioning service, directly taken from our quote manager application:

```
public void refresh() {
    final Client client = ClientBuilder.newClient();
    try {
        final String[] symbols = getSymbols(client);
        for (String symbol : symbols) {
            final Data data = client.target(financialData)
                        .resolveTemplate("symbol", symbol)
                        .request(APPLICATION_JSON_TYPE)
                        .get(Data.class);
            quoteService.createOrUpdate(new UpdateRequest(data));
        }
    } finally {
        client.close();
    }
}
```

The variable usage is interesting to observe. With respect to the Java variable scope, `client` is available to the complete `refresh` method, the `symbols` array is available in the `try` block. Therefore, the `for` loop and `data` are only for one iteration of the loop. However, we never really allocate any object memory explicitly; we can call `new` to reference a constructor but we do not have the memory vision, the pointer, or the size.

If we compare the same code block to a version where you need to manage the memory, it will look as follows:

```
public void refresh() {
    final Client client = ClientBuilder.newClient();
    try {
        final String[] symbols = getSymbols(client);
        try {
            for (String symbol : symbols) {
                final Data data = client.target(financialData)
                        .resolveTemplate("symbol", symbol)
                        .request(APPLICATION_JSON_TYPE)
                        .get(Data.class);
                try {
                    final UpdateRequest updateRequest = new
                    UpdateRequest(data);
                    try {
                        quoteService.createOrUpdate(updateRequest);
                    } finally {
                        releaseMemory(updateRequest);
                    }
                }
```

```
                } finally {
                    releaseMemory(data);
                }
            }
        } finally {
            releaseMemory(symbols);
        }
    } finally {
        client.close();
    }
}
```

The code gets way more complex even if this example assumes that `client.close()` handles the releasing, which cannot be true. In fact, each allocated object needs to call the `releaseMemory()` function to release the allocated structure. It also implies that we should not miss any call. Otherwise, we would be leaking memory. The previous code example uses a lot of nested `try`/`finally` to guarantee this.

What should we learn from this simple example? We should learn that Java allows the developer not to care about memory management in most cases. If you use some native integration through JNI, for instance, you may still need to handle it. To ensure that the application behaves well and does not leak—which is important for a server that is not supposed to be restarted—the JVM provides several solutions for memory management. This is transparently done but directly impacts the performance, since memory allocation is sensitive for a process and memory deallocation has some challenges.

Garbage collector

Garbage collector is the name of the part of the JVM that handles the memory. To make it very simple, it is the part releasing the memory held by some unused objects and reallocating this memory space to new objects.

This part is dependent on the JVM you are using, but all the algorithms use the same sort of logic. So, it is important to understand how it works in the high level, and then you can investigate the specifics of your particular JVM.

In the context of this book, we will limit ourselves to the HotSpot JVM (the Oracle one).

The heap memory is divided into two main spaces: the young generation and the old one. The young generation is itself divided into multiple spaces: the Eden and the survivors (there are two survivors). Both the generations also have a *virtual* space that is mainly there to support either garbage collection operations or generation resizing.

Since Java 8, the permanent space (used until Java 7) has been dropped and replaced by metaspace. Its role is to hold the metadata of the application in memory, such as the classes (name, annotations, fields, and so on). If you remember the previous chapter on how to monitor your applications, you will probably be thinking about the `jcmd GC.class_stats` command that gives you information about this space of memory. In terms of the performance, it is important to ensure that this space is constant once the JVM is *hot*. Concretely, it means that once we have executed all the possible code paths of our application, we should not see many changes on the memory allocated to that space. If you still see it moving significantly after that time, you may have a leak or a classloader issue that you'll need to investigate before you continue working on the performance.

From now on, we will just deal with the heap. It is the part of the memory that you need to start with when you start tuning an application for production deployment or benchmark. To summarize what we have just talked about, you can visualize the way the memory is split with the following diagram:

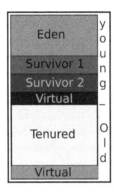

The global idea is to start filling the *first* zone (the **Eden** zone of the young generation) with *dynamic* objects—you can visualize it as request-related objects with a mental model—and once it is full, the garbage collector will move objects still used to the next zone (**Survivor 1**, **Survivor 2**, and, finally, the **Tenured** zone). This is a very high-level understanding of the generations. The point behind splitting the memory this way is that the garbage collector works on zones smaller than the full memory when it needs to run, and it can apply different algorithms to each zone and be more efficient. Keep in mind that the more you go to the old generation, the more objects survive the garbage collection cycles and stay in the memory in terms of the application runtime.

The main difference between the young and old generations is the way the garbage collector impacts the application. While working on the young generation and running, it will execute what is called a *minor collection*. This browses through the corresponding zone, is generally fast, and has low impact in terms of the application's performance.

However, when a collection is executed in the old generation, it is called a *major collection* and generally blocks the application. This means that your application may not be responding during the collection time, which highly affects the performance.

Now there are several more detailed ways to delve into the ways the JVM garbage collection works, and each of them has an impact on the performance.

Garbage collector algorithms

Over the years, the garbage collector algorithms have been enhanced and there are multiple algorithms available now. They match several sorts of applications and are more or less adapted, depending on the product:

- **Serial collector**: This is a mono-threaded implementation and the default algorithm for client-side machines (32 bit or single processor).
- **Parallel collector**: The serial collector algorithm adapts to server resources (fast CPU and big memory sizes). The parallel collector is the default one for server machines (>= 2 processors).
- **Parallel compacting collector**: This allows to paralellize the tenured generation processing.
- **Concurrent Mark Sweep (CMS) collector**: With this collector, the tenured generation is processed in parallel with the application.
- **Garbage first collector (G1)**: This collection is concurrently performed with the application that targets the server application we are dealing with in the context of this book. This will be the default collector with Java 9 but is already available with Java 8.

The serial collector

To force using the serial collector, you will need to add the following option to your JVM:

```
-XX:+UseSerialGC
```

Once this option is added to the JVM, you will have a garbage collector using a single thread and potentially lock the application for collection.

The first collection will move the still used objects from eden to the first empty survivor space. If the used objects are too big, they are directly moved to the tenured space. Younger objects of the *survivor 1* (also known as *survivor from*) space are then moved to the *survivor 2* (also known as *survivor to*) space if there is space; otherwise, they are moved directly to the tenured space. Older objects are moved to the tenured space.

Once all these moves are done, the eden and survivor spaces (which were full) can be freed. Note that the survivor space is then reversed in terms of its role, which means that the survivor space is always empty.

Here is a way to represent the algorithm:

We start from a state where the eden becomes full and the first survivor has some objects:

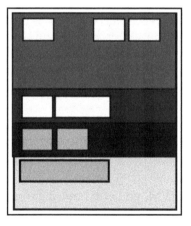

In the first phase, the used objects are moved from eden to the second survivor if they fit (the two small green blocks) or directly to the tenured space if too big (the large block in the end):

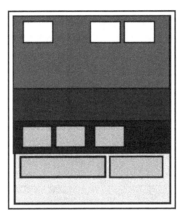

Now, the same logic is applied to the first survivor space, so we have the small used objects moving to the other survivor and the big ones to the tenured space. At this stage, you can still have unused objects in the first survivor:

Finally, the last step is to free the unused memory: the eden and first survivor in our example. In the next cycle, exactly the same logic will be followed, but the two survivor spaces will be reversed.

This algorithm mainly concerns how the young generation is managed, but it is not sufficient in itself, since it will fill the old one pretty quickly. For this reason, a complete cycle requires a second algorithm called the Mark-Sweep-Compact, which is applied on the tenured space.

As you can guess from its name, the algorithm has three phases:

1. **Mark**: In this phase, the collector identifies the still used instances and marks the associated memory space
2. **Sweep**: The unmarked memory in the previous step is freed
3. **Compact**: The previous step may have created holes in the memory space, so the collector compacts it, ensuring that all the objects are placed side by side for faster access

You can visualize it—for a single memory zone—with the following diagram:

Let's assume that our initial state is the previous diagram. We have five objects filling the space. The first step is then to *Mark* the still used objects to be able to remove the remaining ones (no more used). It can be illustrated with the following diagram:

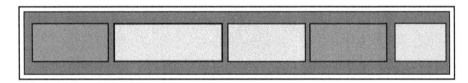

The darker blocks are the no-more-used ones in this illustration, and the lighter ones are the still-used ones. Now that we have proceeded from the *Mark* phase, we will execute the *Sweep* phase and remove the unused blocks:

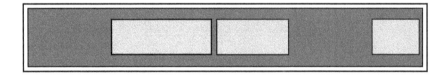

At this point, we are fine in terms of the memory volume. This means that we've freed all the memory we can and we could almost stop the collection here. However, as you can see in this diagram, there are some holes in the free space.

One issue is that if we need to allocate a big object, then it can be split into multiple memory zones and the memory access may become slower. To optimize this, we have the last step, that is, *Compact*:

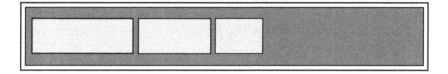

After this last step, the memory is optimized (compacted); all the objects are side by side and we have the biggest possible available memory zone vacant at the end.

For a server (don't forget that we're talking about Java EE in this book), this is rarely the fastest garbage collector mode, but the concepts are quite important to understand and if you write a Java EE client (using the JAX-RS client API, for instance) it can still apply to your final delivery, which will not require a lot of memory allocation.

Parallel and parallel compacting collectors

The parallel collector is close to the serial collector (which is why it is important to understand the serial algorithm). The main difference will be how it sets up the collection. We saw that, in a serial collection, a single thread is responsible for the collection, but with the parallel collector, multiple threads adopt the role. This means that you can hope to reduce the *stop the world* duration (when the garbage collector enforces the application to stop responding and do its job) by the number of threads (theoretically).

This can be activated/enforced (this is supposed to be the default for a server machine) by adding this option on the JVM: `-XX:+UseParallelGC`.

The parallel collector can be tuned with several JVM options, but here are some you may want to customize:

- `-XX:MaxGCPauseMillis=N`: You configure the value (`N`) to the maximum duration you desire for the pauses of the garbage collector. Note that this is just a hint and there is no guarantee that you will obtain the desired result, but it can be interesting as a first attempt. Also keep in mind that it will optimize the garbage collector pause duration (and, maybe, not the throughput of the application, which can be an issue for the server). In the end, you may manually tune the heap size and ratio, but starting to test this JVM option can give you some hints about the way to go.

- `-XX:GCTimeRatio=N`: This is also a hint, allowing you to request that no more than *1/(1+N)* of the application time is spent in garbage collection. This is intended to optimize the throughput of the application—which is generally the case for a server. This is not the easiest configuration to understand, so let's use a small example. If you set *N* to 19, then 1/20 of the application time (5%) will be allocated to garbage collection. The default is 99 so only 1% of the application time is allocated to garbage collection.
- `-XX:ParallelGCThreads=N`: This allows you to configure the number of threads allocated to parallel garbage collection.

There are no magic values for these flags, but once you have identified the memory needs of your application, it is very interesting to tune them a bit to be aligned with the application requirements.

What is interesting to know is that the garbage collector can adjust the generation sizes, depending on the configured ratio to try to respect it. This is done by increasing the generation sizes to decrease the collection times. By default, a generation size is increased by 20% and decreased by 8%. Here again, you can customize this adjustment with some JVM flags.

There are lots of flags, and their name and supported values can depend on the JVM you use. Since they are not portable flags, you may need to check them against your JVM documentation. With the Hotspot, you can do it with the following command:

```
java -XX:+PrintFlagsFinal -version
```

This command prints the Java version (just to avoid any error) and also prints the JVM flags, allowing you to list them all, which is the part we care about. Once you have the output, you just need to filter the flags you want. In our case, we want to customize the way the generation sizes are increased/decreased, so we can filter the flags with the `grep` command (on Unix) using the `Generation` keyword:

```
$ java -XX:+PrintFlagsFinal -version 2>&amp;amp;1 | grep Generation
    uintx TenuredGenerationSizeIncrement = 20 {product}
    uintx TenuredGenerationSizeSupplement = 80 {product}
    uintx TenuredGenerationSizeSupplementDecay = 2 {product}
     bool UseAdaptiveGenerationSizePolicyAtMajorCollection = true {product}
     bool UseAdaptiveGenerationSizePolicyAtMinorCollection = true {product}
    uintx YoungGenerationSizeIncrement = 20 {product}
    uintx YoungGenerationSizeSupplement = 80 {product}
    uintx YoungGenerationSizeSupplementDecay = 8 {product}
```

+PrintFlagsFinal allows you to list the options, their value (after the equal sign), their type (first string), and the flag type (in braces).

 If you add other options to the JVM (such as -client or -server), it will adjust the values to reflect these flags.

As you can see in the previous capture, you can use -XX:YoungGenerationSizeIncrement to customize the increase percentage of the young generation when needed to respect the configured ratio. YoungGenerationSizeSupplement is a supplement for the young generation size increment used at startup, and the decay flag is the decay factor to the supplement value. Indeed, the tenured generation has the same sort of configuration.

These configurations are very advanced and you must ensure that you can explain why you tune them before doing it; otherwise, you can just mess up your JVM configuration and make your application behave badly.

Finally, parallel GC still uses a single thread for the tenured generation collection.

Now, there is also a compacting parallel collector. It is the same as the parallel collector in the young generation, but in the tenured one, the algorithm differs a bit. It is close to the *Mark/Sweep/Compact* algorithm, except it divides the space in more zones to let the collector work in parallel on them. Then, the sweep phase is replaced by a *summary* phase, where the density is verified to request a compaction. Finally, the compaction is done in parallel. To use this option, you need to activate another JVM flag: -XX:+UseParallelOldGC. This option is supposed to be good for applications with large heaps, which is the case with applications handling a lot of concurrent requests and using some caching mechanism.

Concurrent Mark Sweep (CMS)

The goal of the CMS is to reduce GC pauses, enabling you to execute the GC while the application is running. For this, it uses multiple threads. The main idea is to be able to free some memory before the tenured generation is full, and the GC needs to pause the application threads. If it happens too frequently, you will need to adjust the application tuning (CMS configuration) to avoid it as much as possible and to keep it behaving correctly. You can identify this type of issue checking verbose:gc output and Concurrent Mode Failure messages.

Compared to the standard *Mark* phase, the one of the *CMS* algorithm will pause the application twice: first pause to mark objects directly reachable from the root of the memory graph and the second pause to identify the objects missed in the concurrent tracing phase. This concurrent tracing phase will take resources that the application will not be able to use anymore, and the throughput will potentially decrease a bit.

A collection mainly has two triggers:

- A kind of timeout based on the historical statistics of the memory, with a safety bound added to avoid a concurrent mode failure, which is very costly. This safety bound can be controlled based on a percentage, customizable with the – XX:CMSIncrementalSafetyFactory=N flag.
- Based on the remaining size on the tenured space. This trigger can be controlled with -XX:CMSInitiatingOccupancyFaction=N, *N* being the percentage of the tenured space that should trigger a collection if it is full. By default, it is 92% (N=92).

When investigating long GC pauses, you may need to tune the safety factor and, potentially, the occupancy fraction options to see if triggering the GC earlier (or later) can help.

One last thing to note about this algorithm is that there is no compaction, so the memory access can become slower with time.

Garbage First (G1)

The Garbage First collector is the most recent implementation. It is a server-side implementation that tends to decrease the pauses and concurrently works with the application. It introduces a new way of visualizing the heap.

The heap is divided into constant-sized regions. The G1 starts to mark the regions concurrently. After this phase, it knows which regions are almost empty and then starts collecting the memory from these regions, allowing the G1 to get a lot of memory pretty quickly and without much effort. This is where the name of this algorithm comes from. Then, in the compact phase, G1 can copy objects from multiple regions to a single region to ensure that it stays efficient.

An important thing to know about the G1 implementation is that it is based on statistics and can have a few glitches in the execution, even if the model is quite accurate in practice.

The fact that G1 splits the heap in regions also means that it is intended for applications using a lot of memory (Oracle claims more than 6 GB) and requiring small pause times (less than 0.5 seconds). This implies that switching from the CMS to the G1 is not always worth it; you should ensure that you meet one of these criteria before switching to the G1:

- ~50% of the heap is used by live data
- The statistics are not that accurate with the CMS algorithm (if the allocation rate varies a lot)
- You have identified long GC pauses

The G1 also has several JVM flags that you can use to customize the behavior the garbage collector should take. For instance, `-XX:MaxGCPauseMillis` sets the pause duration that you accept in milliseconds (statistically once again) and `-XX:ConcGCThreads=N` defines the concurrent number of threads used to mark the regions (recommended setting is about 25% of the parallel GC thread count). Default settings are intended for the most common use cases but you may need to refine the configuration to adapt it to your application and the way it uses (or reuses) memory.

Here again, activating the G1 collector needs its own JVM flag: `-XX:UseG1GC`.

Common memory settings

We saw how the memory was collected and that there are a lot of tuning options (once again, don't forget to check your particular JVM options). However, there are some very common memory settings that you will want to customize before finely tuning the collector. Here is a small table with these memory settings:

Option	Description
`-Xmx<size>`	The maximum memory size allocated to the heap, for example, `-Xmx1g` to allow the heap to grow until 1GB
`-Xms<size>`	The starting memory size allocated to the heap, for example, `-Xms512m` to allocate 512 MB to the heap
`-Xss<size>`	The stack size (can avoid `StackOverflowError`)
`-XX:SurvivorRatio=N`	Ration between eden and survivor spaces
`-XX:MinHeapFreeRatio=N` and `-XX:MaxHeapFreeRatio=N`	The ratio to trigger a heap resize, the min flag will trigger a heap increase, and the max flag will trigger a heap size decreasing

With all that we saw previously, it means that tuning the JVM memory can lead to a big set of options/flags, but don't be afraid, it is just a matter of taking control over its application. Here is a complete flag set example:

```
-Xms24G -Xmx24G -XX:+UseG1GC -XX:MaxGCPauseMillis=150 -
XX:ParallelGCThreads=16 -XX:ConcGCThreads=4 -
XX:InitiatingHeapOccupancyPercent=70 ....
```

This command is a common server memory configuration for a server with a lot of available memory for the application(s) you deploy:

- Allocate 24 Gigabytes for the heap (fixed since the min and max memory size are set to the same size).
- Enforce the JVM to use the G1 collector (accurate, as we use more than 6 GB of heap) and customizes G1 configuration. It defines a targeted max GC pause of 150 ms and requests G1 to use 16 parallel threads for the memory collection and four threads to mark regions once collected.
- Finally, the collection cycles will start if the heap is occupied at 70%.

This is not a bad setting to start with for a server (you can increase the number of threads a bit, but not too much, as they can be used at the same time your application is running); increase the max GC pause if you can accept it.

The parameter you will probably tune the most is the heap size (24 GB in the previous example), depending on the requirements of your application.

Debugging GC behavior

Now that we know how to tune the memory quite finely, we need to know what our application does, to be able to adjust the configuration. To do so, the JVM provides several ad hoc tools.

The most common and, probably, the most useful tool for the memory is the `-verbose:gc` option that you can pass launching your JVM. It will output memory information. If we activate it on our quote application, you will quickly see these sorts of lines:

```
[GC (Allocation Failure) 41320K->14967K(153600K), 0.0115487 secs]
[GC (Metadata GC Threshold) 44213K->20306K(153600K), 0.0195955 secs]
[Full GC (Metadata GC Threshold) 20306K->13993K(139264K), 0.0596210 secs]
[GC (Allocation Failure) 77481K->23444K(171008K), 0.0081158 secs]
[GC (Metadata GC Threshold) 69337K->23658K(207360K), 0.0094964 secs]
[Full GC (Metadata GC Threshold) 23658K->20885K(248320K), 0.0792653 secs]
[GC (Allocation Failure) 144789K->27923K(252416K), 0.0078509 secs]
[GC (Allocation Failure) 155923K->36753K(252416K), 0.0174981 secs]
[GC (Metadata GC Threshold) 68430K->37173K(275968K), 0.0146621 secs]
[Full GC (Metadata GC Threshold) 37173K->31086K(321536K), 0.1868723 secs]
```

We can distinguish two kinds of lines corresponding to different generation zone collection:

- **GC**: This is a young generation collection
- **Full GC**: This is a tenured generation collection

Each collection is associated with a reason:

- **Allocation failure**: The GC is asked to run because no more memory is available
- **Metadata GC threshold**: The metaspace threshold is reached

Then, you can see the resizing of the memory; for instance, `41320K->14967K(153600K)` means that the used memory is resized from ~41M to ~15M. The number in the parentheses is the available space (~150 MB here).

Don't be afraid to see the GC running often and even the full GC lines. While their executions are fast and you see that the memory size is acceptable, it is not an issue at all. However, if the execution is long and the memory stays high even after the collection, then you will need to tune the GC or update the application to ensure it comes back to something fast and reliable.

You can activate this output at runtime through JMX if you go on the `java.lang:type=Memory` MBean and set the `Verbose` attribute to `true`.

If you want even more details about the GC, you can add the `-XX:+PrintGCDetails` option and the lines will be more verbose:

```
[GC (Allocation Failure) [PSYoungGen: 145920K->16360K(162304K)]
177095K->54877K(323072K), 0.0152172 secs] [Times: user=0.03 sys=0.01,
real=0.02 secs]
```

We can recognize the previous information but there is new data as well:

- `PSYoungGen`: This is the collector type; this value means minor GC
- The resizing after (`X->Y(Z)`) shows the young generation size
- The last resizing is the full heap one
- Finally, the duration is expressed in terms of user time, system time, and real time

If you want to save all this information (log lines) in a file, you can add a flag with a file path and the JVM will dump this output in the file instead of the console:

```
-Xloggc:/path/to/output.log   -XX:+PrintGCDetails
```

This will allow you to analyze the GC behavior *offline*. There are some tools able to parse this output and let you visualize it directly. One of them is *GCViewer*, which you can find at `https://github.com/chewiebug/GCViewer/wiki/Changelog`. Once the JAR is downloaded, you can run it with Java directly:

```
java -jar gcviewer-1.35.jar
```

Then, just open the `output.log` file in the interface and you should visualize your GC as follows:

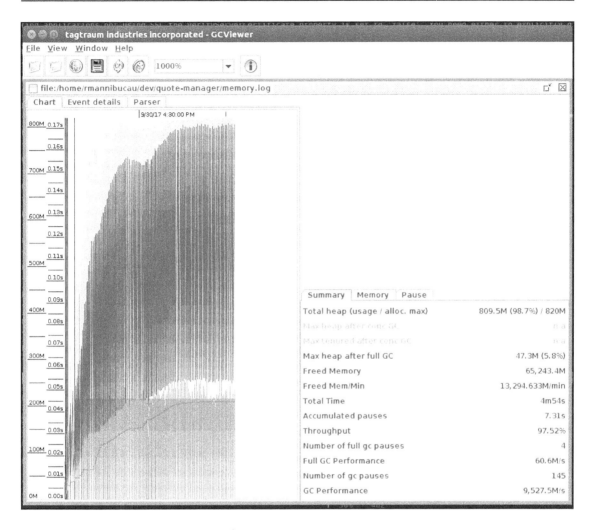

This tool has two main interesting features:

- The temporal graph deduced from the log output
- The statistics tabs (on the right) showing the statistic summary of the GC, and the number and duration of the pauses

This last information can let you validate the behavior of your application once you add some caching or some background task parallelly executed with the main application.

It will let you ensure the impact of one part of the application on the other in terms of memory and potentially find a performance issue if the memory is too impacted by this new feature.

Here is the legend associated with the colors of the graph:

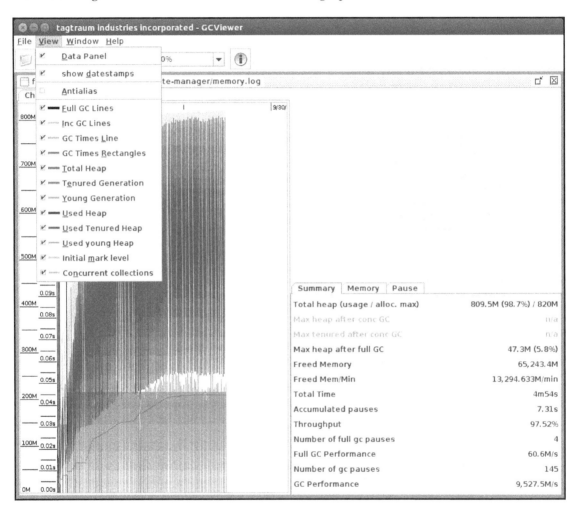

We find most of the information we talked about in the previous part and, particularly, the collections, generations, and so on. Note that the *Y* axis can be read with two units (time and memory size) depending on which graph you are looking at. You will likely filter the printed graphs to see it clearly, but you will find all the information you need to see when your GC is running.

Heap dump

Sometimes, you will need to get a heap dump to investigate what is in memory and why the GC runs so often or for so long. To do so, the JDK provides a tool called `jmap` that allows you to take a dump from the Java PID:

```
jmap –dump:format=b,file=/path/to/dump.hprof <PID>
```

This command will stop the application (a bit like a *stop the world* pause) and write all the instances into the configured file. Opening the output with `jvisualvm` will enable you to investigate the instances, and, in particular, the number of instances and the corresponding allocating size.

Here is what it can look like:

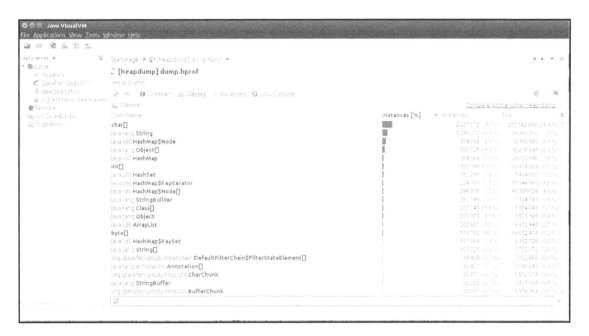

Normally, you should mainly see JVM classes such as `char[]`, `String`, `Map`, and so on.

If you double-click on a type, you will see the instances. For example, on `String` for our quote manager dump, we will have a view like this one:

Here, we visualize the `String` instances related to the request (the request URL or a subpart of it, such as the protocol, the host, or the port). So we can deduce that the instances are related to the request and its parsing. This is perfectly normal, but if you start seeing a lot of your own classes in the classes, view, and/or a few classes but with a huge allocation size, you can double-click on these types and get the instance details to identify why it happened.

If we double-click on `JsonQuotePage`, we will see something like this:

The reference of the instance on the left side (in the list of instances) doesn't help us much, but the detailed view (on the right side) of a single instance shows the actual data structure with its values.

As a reminder, our POJO page model is the following one:

```
@JsonbPropertyOrder({"total", "items"})
public class JsonQuotePage {
    private long total;
    private List<JsonQuote> items;

    // getters/setters
}
```

Our structure (class) has two fields: `total` and `items`, and we can find these two entries in the detailed view of the instance we obtained from the dump. As shown in the screenshot, we can even browse the `items` values. This will let you identify whether there is something particular with the values and whether you will need to customize the query you use to retrieve the data.

Java EE and the resources

With Java EE, you will likely have a lot of volatile objects (with a short lifespan) that are bound to a request. If we take `QuoteResource`, we will first allocate our JSON model, then our entity model, and so on. All these instances will be needed for the request only and nothing more. Thus, the garbage collector will quickly collect them. The garbage collector is quite good for such dynamic applications. However, it doesn't mean that we do not have long living instances. Even without an application cache, the server caches a lot of metadata to ensure that it works and runs fast. One example is the CDI container, which will keep the metadata of all the beans in the memory to make sure that it can create them when requested by the application. This takes memory and will never be released until the application is not deployed. This means that by tuning the memory of your application, you will also need to ensure that you tune the memory of the server. As already explained earlier, in performance tuning, the application is not only composed of your code but also the server code; otherwise, you will miss most of the logic and you can't be accurate tuning your application.

In general, the server adds some long live instances to ensure that the server layer does not slow your application down. However, there is a particular kind of logic that the server implements for you that directly impacts the performance of your application, and that you will need to watch out for: the resources.

What we call resources in an application server is generally what is managed by the server. It is often something you want to be able to configure outside the application even if Java EE 6 introduced some `@XXXDefinition` annotations to be able to do it from the application itself. The goal is to inject a preconfigured—and adapted to the current environment—instance. It is also often connected to something external or directly related to the machine resources. Since the next chapter will be about threading, here, we will focus on the external resources.

On top of the list of the most used resources, we find `DataSource`. This represents a connection to a database such as MySQL in our quote application. To cite a few other well-known resources before digging into the `DataSource` case, you can encounter the following:

- Concurrent resources (`ManagedExecutorService`) to handle concurrency. We will deal with them in the next chapter.
- `DataSource`, which connects to the databases.
- The JMS resources, such as `ConnectionFactory`, which connects to a broker, and `Queue` and `Topic`, which represent a destination.

- The Java mail `Session`, which allows you to interact with a mail box (often used to send mails from the application).
- The resource adapters, which provide a way of handling inputs/outputs in an EE fashion (integrated with security and transactions).

All these resources are configurable in the server—most of them from the application—and allow the operation team (or the person responsible for the deployment) to tune the resource the application is using. It also keeps the developer from having to care about the configuration and ensure that the deployment will be customizable enough.

DataSource

To illustrate it, we will refer to our `DataSource` example. In the first chapter, we configured a pool and a data source. The data source was just a name in the JNDI that the application was using to find the data source and later uses it in its JPA layer. This is pretty much what a data source is: a connection factory. What is crucial here is the way the connections are managed.

Most of the time, the production data sources are remote processes or, at least, require a network connection. If you remember our MySQL connection URL, we used the following:

```
jdbc:mysql://localhost:3306/quote_manager
```

This is a very common *development* configuration and it connects to `localhost`. Thus, the network cost is the machine local loop cost, which is generally optimized to be very fast. In real deployment, you will more likely connect to the following:

```
jdbc:mysql://application.mysql.company.com:3306/quote_manager
```

This URL will mark a remote host, and obtaining a connection will imply some real latency. Indeed, it will not be as slow as an internet connection, where the network has a lot of switches, routers, and hops. However, going over the network always implies some milliseconds of latency.

What is interesting with data sources (it is also the case for JMS resources in general) is that the protocol associated with the connection is a connected protocol. Understand that once the connection is obtained, sending a command is faster, as you don't have to create another connection.

If you ran the quote manager application, you would probably get some warning like this one:

```
Sat Sep 30 17:06:25 CEST 2017 WARN: Establishing SSL connection without
server's identity verification is not recommended. According to MySQL
5.5.45+, 5.6.26+ and 5.7.6+ requirements SSL connection must be established
by default if explicit option isn't set. For compliance with existing
applications not using SSL the verifyServerCertificate property is set to
'false'. You need either to explicitly disable SSL by setting useSSL=false,
or set useSSL=true and provide truststore for server certificate
verification.
```

This warning is issued by the MySQL driver and encourages you to use SSL for the network communication. This is mainly for security reasons, but the SSL connection is even slower. You can check out the HTTP2 protocol (introduced in Servlet 4.0 release, included in Java EE 8) that introduces the push protocol to avoid doing too many connections from the browser over SSL, because it was starting to be really slow with modern applications having a lot of web resources.

This means that reusing the same connection over and over is always a good idea because it will cut down the actual connection step and will just let the application issue commands and do its business.

To solve this *connection* issue, the server configures the data source as a connection pool. A pool is a set of reusable connections. Each server has its own pool and its own configuration, which are more or less advanced but all share the same logic:

- **Some size configuration**: The number of connections to keep in the memory while the server is idled (min), the number of connections that can be created (max), how long a connection can be awaited, and so on
- **Some eviction configuration**: The way to determine a connection should be dropped from the pool

The eviction is very important as the pool is related to long running connections. You, therefore, need to be able to remove transparently the corrupted connections. For instance, the MySQL server drops a connection after 8 hours by default. So, if you run your application for 8 hours and 1 minute, all the requests will start failing if you don't have any eviction. For a data source, this is generally done with `ValidationQuery`, which is a SQL query executed from time to time. If this fails, it is considered as invalidating the connection and removing it from the pool. The *time to time* can generally be configured too, and can mainly mean three moments: *before the connection is shared and given to the application*, *when the connection is given back to the pool* (the application is done with it), or *in a background thread when the connection is idled*.

The choice is a trade-off between *do you accept a few requests failing because the connection was not yet evicted by the background thread* and *do you accept it to be a bit slower because the connection is validated every time*. You can even mix all these validation types. A very important point here is to make sure that the validation query is very fast to execute. Never use `SELECT * from CUSTOMER`, which can return back thousands (or more) lines. Always use a constant result set query. For MySQL, it is recommended that you use `SELECT 1`, which will just return `1`. Each database has this kind of query, so check it out and ensure that it is well configured in your pool.

You will indeed find other configurations depending on the pool you rely on, but they are less impacting on the performance, so we will not detail them here.

One crucial thing about the connection pools—data source ones or not—is to make sure you are not waiting for them. As suggested earlier, if you are waiting for connections, then you are slower than you should be, as the pool should avoid this case. This means that when it comes to the performance, you don't have to hesitate and should just ask your pool to never wait for a connection. This parameter is often called *Max Wait Time*. Setting it to 0 or something very small can cause your application to start failing with exceptions saying that the application was not able to retrieve a connection in the configured time. This is exactly what we want! This means that the pool is too small for the application's needs and, thus, you need to increase the pool size. Alternatively, you can also decrease the load sent to the server. It doesn't mean you shouldn't configure any wait time in production. This is a parameter that can ensure you respond to your clients, but it will potentially increase your response time. If it is acceptable, don't hesitate to increase the value once you've tuned the application, but don't do it before ensuring that you are not using a wrongly configured pool.

If your pool size is too small, you will likely see it in the stack traces or in the monitoring you set up with the invocation, such as `allocateConnection` or `getConnection`, depending on your server.

In terms of size tuning, it is tempting to simply set as many connections as possible, but you need to keep in mind a few important points:

- The database connection count can be limited. Never allocate all of them to your application cluster, and ensure that you can keep at least a few for maintenance purposes. For instance, if your MySQL allows 152 connections (default `max_connections` of MySQL is 151 and `mysqld` allows `max_connections+1` actual connections), then your application—as a cluster—can use 140 connections.

- The pool handling requires you to deal with concurrency. Your application will request connections from all its threads and then the container pool will need to give different connections to all the threads to ensure that there is no data corruption of cross-thread connection usage. On the other hand, eviction will also happen at the same time the application is running and will potentially lock the pool (it is close to the GC algorithm problem). The smaller the work needed to be done on the pool, the better it will behave and the less it will impact the application.

This means that not over adjusting the pool is also important. It is generally a heuristic you should do based on your application and the targeted SLA. If you have no idea about the size you must use, you can start setting the maximum size of the pool to 25% of your maximum concurrent threads (HTTP pool size, for instance) and then increase it until you don't get an error anymore, with a maximum wait time of 0.

Java EE and pools

Java EE has a lot of pool types involved in its stack. Here is a summary of the ones you may want to have a look at while tuning your application. Each time, the tuning logic will be based on the same logic: no wait time and start with a medium size in order not to over allocate resources and impact the application too much.

Pool Type	Description
The `DataSource` pool	This handles and recycles database connections.
The `ConnectionFactory` pool	This handles JMX connections to the broker.
The `@Stateless` pool	This handles the recycling of stateless instances. Today, it is relevant when stateless instances are used as a poor man throttling implementation (max instance = max concurrency) or when the instances access some thread of unsafe resources, which is very expensive to instantiate. It can be seen as the Java EE pool API for application needs.
The HTTP thread pool	These threads are used to server the requests. They often have some sibling threads to accept the connection (selector threads).

The managed thread pool	This is usable by the application; these thread pools are used to execute custom tasks. They are often used in reactive programming to inherit from EE features in a reactive stack, such as RxJava.
The Resource Adapter / JCA Connector pool	The JCA specification defines multiple pools: the instance pools that are configured in a dependent way but share the same principle as the other pools, and the thread pool using `WorkManager`, which is the pre EE concurrency utility way to have a user thread pool injected by the server into the application (connector here). Applications rarely use JCA connectors today, but if you have inherited one, ensure that it is well tuned and integrated with your server.

Java EE and HTTP pools

Even if Java EE containers are more and more commonly used for daemons and standalone applications, most of the developed applications are still web applications and, therefore, use HTTP either as clients of another server or as the server themselves.

In the last sentence, *Java EE containers* include the wide embedded varieties of containers such as TomEE Embedded, Apache Meecrowave, WildFly Swarm, and so on, and is not limited to standalone containers or full profile servers.

This means that the Java EE configuration will have to deal with HTTP configuration. It needs to be handled at multiple levels (networks, HTTP caching, and so on) but also in multiple layers (server/HTTP connector, client connection pooling, SSL tuning, and so on).

We will delve into more details about this in Chapter 5, *Scale Up: Threading and Implications* for the pooling - related configuration and in Chapter 6, *Be Lazy, Cache Your Data* for the caching configuration.

Java EE implicit features

The Java EE philosophy has always been *to work out of the box*. However, it may have some impact on the performance as, sometimes, features are activated without your application requiring them at all. If you know that you don't need a feature, don't hesitate to disable it.

For instance, in `persistence.xml`, we disabled bean validation integration adding this line:

```
<validation-mode>NONE</validation-mode>
```

This avoids the JPA provider adding the bean validation listeners it uses to validate the entities and, thus, saves some CPU cycles without impacting the application. If you check the chain of our application, we use JAX-RS (has a bean validation integration) and then JPA (has another bean validation integration).

The rule for validation can be to always validate the data when it is entering the system (JAX-RS for us) and not validate them internally. In fact, it is redundant in terms of application logic. This is why it is fine to disable it at the JPA layer, for instance.

Summary

In this chapter, we saw how memory is managed with Java, and how to influence it to optimize and adapt it to your application requirements. We also saw how the Java EE server-provided resources help you save time, as they not only enable you to skip reconnection time between usages but also imply a dedicated tuning to not abuse the server memory and CPU.

The idea behind this chapter is to ensure that you have the keys and knowledge to be able to investigate any issue with memory and to be able to tune the memory and resources without being lost or using some random numbers.

Also, this part is probably the most unportable one and will be related to the JVM (for the memory) and server (for the resources) you'll use in your deployment. All the concepts will still apply but the way you tune them can differ, since this is not something standardized yet—even if the JVM tuning does not change as much as server configurations. However, don't hesitate to check out your JVM or server documentation and make sure to have read it before entering into a benchmark phase in order not to lose time in testing options you don't know upfront.

In the next chapter, we will see how to make the most of Java EE concurrent programming and how it is linked to the Java EE threading model to ensure that your application can scale. The memory and the CPU are the two most central resources a server uses on a machine: we just saw the memory resource, and we will now deal with the CPU through the threading study.

5
Scale Up – Threading and Implications

Scalability has always been a concern for Java and, thus, a thread-related API was introduced in Java version 1.0. The idea is to be able to benefit from the most modern hardware updates in order to parallelize the processing of applications.

Being able to handle multiple requests in parallel is crucial for a Java EE server to scale, but in our modern Java world, you also need to be able to control your own threads. Also, Java EE introduced the required API to do it in good conditions.

In this chapter, we will go through the following topics:

- Java EE threading model
- Data consistency across threads
- Java EE hidden thread usages
- How to integrate reactive programming with the Java EE programming model

Java EE threading model

The Java EE philosophy has, for a long time, been able to give its users a well-defined and safe programming model. This is why most of the Java EE defaults are about being thread-safe, and that several specifications such as **Enterprise Java Beans** (**EJB**) defaults were preventing custom thread usage. It does not mean Java EE was ignoring threads at all, but explicitly using thread pools from an application was not very natural. Also, most of the time, the adopted coding style was either against Java EE's (strict) rules or were very verbose.

Before detailing the new API added by Java EE to help you develop concurrent applications, let's see the basic Java EE model and how it can already help you to scale.

If we take back the specifications included in Java EE 8 (full profile), we'll get a long list. Now, if we check which specifications use threads, the list will be shorter and we can find some common points among them. Here is a table trying to represent whether the specifications manage dedicated threads or not and whether they explicitly interact with threads (handling cross-thread calls by using the provided threads) or simply use the caller (contextual) thread:

Specification	Manage dedicated threads	Interacts with threads	Comment
EJB 3.2	Yes	Yes	`@Asynchronous` allows you to execute tasks in a dedicated thread pool. `@Lock` used with `@Singleton` allows you to control the thread safety of the bean.
Servlet 4.0	Yes	Yes	Every request is executed in a single thread provided by the container by default. When using `AsyncContext`, you can execute the task in a custom thread and resume the request from another thread later.
JSP 2.3/JSP Debugging 1.0	No	No	Inherits from the servlet model.
EL 3.0	No	No	Uses the caller context.
JMS 2.0	Yes	No	By itself, JMS can be seen as a specific sort of connector (as in *Connector 1.7*) but put a few specific words on this case. JMS has two sorts of usages: on the server side and on the client side. The server side is generally a network server expecting connection. This is where dedicated threads will be used (such as any socket server). Then, the processing will be fully delegated to the connector. On the client side, it generally inherits from the caller context but also uses custom threads, as it is asynchronous by design. So, it needs its own thread pools to handle this part of the JMS specification.

JTA 1.2	No	Yes	JTA doesn't manage threads but *binds* its context to threads. Concretely, when a transaction starts, it is only valid for the initial thread.
JavaMail 1.6	Yes	No	JavaMail being the link between your Java code and the way mails are sent/received, the implementation is, here again, linked to a socket, and thus, it often relies on dedicated threads.
Connector 1.7	Yes	Yes	Connector specification is the standard way to interact with external systems (bi-directional ways even if connector implementations often handle only one way). However, it generally uses dedicated threads in two layers, the first one being related to the network interactions and the second one being related to the container interaction that generally goes through `WorkManager`, which is the ancestor of the *Concurrency Utilities for Java EE* specification. Like JTA, it also uses context-related information that is often bound to the thread. Finally, since it interacts with the JTA, a part of the interactions is, by design, bound to threads.
Web Services 1.4 / JAX-RPC 1.1	No	No	Web services generally just inherit from the servlet contextual threading model.
JAX-RS 2.1	Yes	Yes	JAX-RS inherits from the servlet contextual model, but since JAX-RS 2.0, the server can asynchronously handle the requests, thanks to Servlet 3.0 `AsyncContext`. In this case, the developer must notify the container when a request is completed and interacts with threads, as it is generally done from a different thread from the servlet one. On the client side, JAX-RS 2.1 now has a reactive API, able to use custom threads to do the execution.

WebSocket 1.1	Yes/No	Yes/No	Normally, the WebSocket specification was designed to be implemented on top of the servlet specification, which is really the Java EE central transport. However, for several cases, it may be needed to use some customization of the threading for WebSocket needs (long connections). This part highly depends on the container. The last thing is that some custom WebSocket threads may be needed to handle connection evictions and things like that, but it has less impact on the end user and performance.
JSON-P 1.1 / JSON-B 1.0	No	No	This specification (JSON low-level API and JSON binding) does not have any thread-related operations and simply executes in the caller context.
Concurrency Utilities for Java EE 1.0	Yes	Yes	Concurrency utilities mainly have the ability to define *Java EE thread pools* and, indeed, they manage custom threads. It also transparently facilitates (through `ContextService`) the propagation of some contexts, such as security, JNDI context, transaction, and so on. Note that, however, the propagation is not standard and you may need to check out your server documentation to know what it does precisely.
Batch 1.0	Yes	No	JBatch is asynchronous by design. When you launch a batch, the invocation returns before the batch is done, as it can be very long. To handle such behavior JBatch has its own thread pools.
JAXR 1.0	No	No	This specification is rarely used and has become old (before Java introduced nio). Being a client, it doesn't use custom threads.
Java EE Management 1.1 (or 1.2)	Yes/No	No	This specifications allows you to interact with the server and its definitions (resources and applications). It uses another transport technology, so it generally needs dedicated threads.

JACC 1.5	No	No	This is a specification linking an authorization policy with the Java EE container. It is contextually executed.
JASPIC 1.1	No	No	This is a security specification, also contextually executed.
Java EE Security API 1.0	No	No	This is the last security API of Java EE, making it pretty usable, but it stays contextual to the caller.
JSTL 1.2	No	No	Inherits from the servlet model.
Web Service Metadata 2.1	No	No	This mainly involves annotations for web services, so there's no particular threading model.
JSF 2.3	No	No	Inherits from the servlet threading model (this is a simplification but good enough for this book's context).
Common annotations 1.3	No	No	Just a set of APIs reused by other specifications, no particular behavior directly bound here.
Java Persistence 2.2 (JPA)	No	No	Inherits from the caller context.
Bean Validation 2.0	No	No	Inherits from the caller context.
Interceptors 1.2	No	No	Inherits from the caller context.
Contexts and Dependency Injection for Java EE 2.0 (CDI)	Yes	Yes	CDI 2.0 supports asynchronous events, which rely on a dedicated thread pool. CDI being about *contexts*, also binds contextual data to threads such as the `@RequestScoped` context.
Dependency Injection for Java 1.0 (@Inject)	No	No	This is mainly a set of annotations of CDI, so there's no real thread-related behavior here.

If we review all the thread usages, we can distinguish between some categories:

- Asynchronous usages: the specification using threads not to block the caller execution (such as JAX-RS client, Batch API, CDI asynchronous events, and so on)
- Network-related implementations that need threads for the selector (partly accepting the connections) and request handling

In terms of code context, this is generally related to the outbound layers of the code. Indeed, the network is an outbound of the application, but asynchronous usages are also in the sense that they split the execution into two branches: the caller context that continues and a new branch that is no more linked to the caller.

What does it mean for you? When you take the lead on an application, at least from a performance or configuration point of view, you need to be clear about the thread execution path of the application (when the application uses a different thread from the one it got affected by, when the request entered into the system). This is also true for inter-system architectures, such as microservices, where you need to track the execution context breakdowns.

Thread data and consistency

Before getting Java EE-specific, it is important to step back a moment and understand the implications of concurrency on the programming model.

Concurrent data access

When a single thread accesses data, then the access is always thread-safe, and it is not possible for a thread to mutate data while another one is reading it. When you increase the number of threads and multiple threads can access the same data structure instances, it is possible for a thread to read the data that's currently being modified, or for two concurrent modifications to happen, leading to an inconsistent result.

Here is a schema representing this issue with two threads. Keep in mind that a Java EE server often handles around 100 to 1000 threads, so the effects are more impacting:

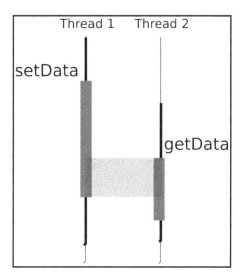

In this simple example, we have a thread (**Thread 1**) setting data that is supposed to be a complex structure. In parallel, we have another thread (**Thread 2**) accessing the data. In the preceding diagram, the very thin black line represents the thread life, whereas the bold black line represents the method execution in the thread's context. The blue box represents the data setter/getter execution time and the red zone represents the overlap of both threads on the data usage. In other words, you can consider that the vertical unit is time.

To understand what can be the impact of such a code without any protection, let's materialize the data structure with this simple code:

```
public class UnsafeData {
    private boolean initialized = false;
    private String content;

    public void setData(String value) {
        content = value;
        initialized = true;
    }

    public String getData() {
        if (!initialized) {
            throw new IllegalStateException("structure not initialized");
        }
        return content;
    }
}
```

This simple structure aims to store a `String` value and handle a state (`initialized`), which allows the structure to prevent access to the data if uninitialized.

If we apply this structure on our previous picture timeline, it is possible that **Thread 2** calls `getData` and fails with `IllegalStateException`, whereas the `setData` method is called and sets the `initialized` variable. In other words, the structure (`getData`) was accessed while it was changing and, thus, the behavior was not consistent with the complete state of the data. In this case, the error is not dramatic, but if you take another example summing some values, you will just get the wrong data:

```
public class Account {
    private double value; // + getter

    public void sum(double credit, double debit) {
        value += credit;
        value += debit;
    }
}
```

If the execution of `sum` is done and `value` is accessed at the same time, then the account value will be wrong, the reporting will potentially be inconsistent, and the validation (which likely considers *credit+debit=0*) will fail, making this account erroneous.

If you look one step further and integrate some EE features, you will quickly understand that the situation is even worse. Let's take the case of a JPA entity, such as `Quote`, and assume that two threads are differently modifying the entity: one thread modifies the price and the other one modifies the name. What will happen when each thread updates the entity? The database can't handle both the updates at the same time, so if there is no failure, then the last update will win and only one of the two updates will be taken into account.

 JPA provides optimistic and pessimistic locking to properly solve the aforementioned problem. As a general rule, try to use optimistic locking until you really need pessimistic locking. In fact, it will give you a better performance even if it will require you to potentially handle a retry logic if relevant.

Java and thread safety

This section doesn't intend to explain all the solutions that Java provides to ensure the thread safety of your code but just to give you some highlights on Java Standalone API, you can reuse in Java EE application if needed.

Synchronized

Surely the oldest solution, but still available in Java, the synchronized keyword allows you to ensure that methods are not concurrently executed. You just need to add it in your method definition as follows:

```
public class SafeData {
    private boolean initialized = false;
    private String content;

    public synchronized void setData(String value) {
        content = value;
        initialized = true;
    }

    public synchronized String getData() {
        if (!initialized) {
            throw new IllegalStateException("structure not
            initialized");
        }
        return content;
    }
}
```

This is the exact same structure as the one we just saw. But now, thanks to the synchronized keyword added to each method, the call to a method would enforce concurrent calls to other synchronized methods to wait for the first one to end before being executed. Concretely, it will chain method execution like in a single thread.

The synchronized keyword is linked to an instance, so two different instances that are synchronized will not lock each other. It is also possible to use synchronized as a block and pass the instance to synchronize on. If you do so and pass a static instance, then you will lock all the instances that can prevent the application from scaling if on a common code path.

Locks

Java 1.5 introduces the Lock interface with its java.util.concurrent package, which contains a lot of concurrency-related classes. It achieves the same goal as that of synchronized but allows you to control manually the scope of the synchronized code.

The performance of `Lock` and `synchronized` differs between Java versions, but recent versions have progressed a lot. And generally, if you don't optimize a computing algorithm, choosing one or the other will lead to something close. However, it is generally better to use `Lock` if the number of concurrent threads accessing the instance is high.

As `Lock` is an interface, it needs an implementation. The JRE comes with a default implementation called `ReentrantLock`. Replacing a `synchronized` block is done in the following way:

```
final Lock lock = new ReentrantLock();
lock.lock();
try {
    doSomeBusinessLogic();
} finally {
    lock.unlock();
}
```

The lock instantiation is directly done through the `new` keyword. We will note here that `ReentrantLock` can take a Boolean parameter to request it to respect a fair order for the lock invocations (the default is `false` and generally good enough in terms of performance). Once you have a locked instance, you can call the `lock()` method to ensure that you are the only one executing the code. Once you are done with your protected code, you can call `unlock()` to release the current thread and let another one execute its code. Also, note that all this locking logic assumes that the lock is shared across the thread. Thus, the instantiation is generally done once per instance (in the constructor or in a `@PostConstruct` method).

It is vital to call the `unlock()` method; otherwise, other locked threads will never be released.

A more common usage of the Lock API is to split the lock and unlock calls into two. For instance, to take Java EE usage, you can lock an instance when a request starts and unlock it when the request ends in order to ensure that a single request is accessing it. This is feasible with Servlet 3 through a listener, even for asynchronous requests. But you will not have a block that you can surround; instead, you will have multiple callbacks, which you need to integrate with the following:

```
public class LockAsyncListener implements AsyncListener {
    private final Lock lock;
```

```
        public LockAsyncListener(Lock lock) {
            this.lock = lock;
            this.lock.lock();
        }

        @Override
        public void onStartAsync(AsyncEvent event) throws IOException {
            // no-op
        }
        private void onEnd() {
            lock.unlock();
        }

        @Override
        public void onComplete(AsyncEvent event) throws IOException {
            onEnd();
        }

        @Override
        public void onTimeout(AsyncEvent event) throws IOException {
            onEnd();
        }

        @Override
        public void onError(AsyncEvent event) throws IOException {
            onEnd();
        }
    }
```

With this listener added to `AsyncContext`, the lock will follow the request's life cycle. The usage will probably look as follows:

```
public class SomeServlet extends HttpServlet {
    @Override
    protected void service(HttpServletRequest req, HttpServletResponse
    resp)
        throws ServletException, IOException {
        final AsyncContext asyncContext = req.startAsync();
        final SomeInstance instance = getInstance();
        asyncContext.addListener(new
        LockAsyncListener(instance.getLock()));
        execute(asyncContext, instance)
    }
}
```

Once `AsyncContext` is obtained, we add the lock listener onto it and execute the request. The lock will be released when the request ends because of a timeout, an exception, or, simply, a normal termination.

This sort of implementation with a synchronized block is quite hard and often requires some workarounds. This is an example where the Lock API is more powerful.

 We will not detail it here, but the `ReadWriteLock` API gives you a holder for two locks: one is used to protect read accesses, and the other one for write accesses. The goal is to let read accesses be done in parallel and ensure that write accesses are done only when a single thread accesses the data.

java.util.concurrent

Although a detailed coverage of the Java Standalone is beyond the context of this book, it is important to know that Java 7 and Java 8 got a lot of enhancements in this area. So don't hesitate to go through its packages. Among the interesting classes, we can note the following:

- `CountDownLatch`: This is a simple and efficient way to ensure that N threads are waiting a condition owned by another thread (a bit like a starter in a race).
- `Semaphore`: This allows you to represent and implement permission *buckets*. The most interesting part is that you can increase and decrease the associated counter. It can be a simple way to implement a bulkhead solution.
- `CyclicBarrier`: This is a way to synchronize multiple threads in some points of the code. Its API is interesting because it allows you to add shared logic that can be executed on all the threads. It can be seen as the opposite of `CountDownLatch`.
- `Phaser`: This is a more flexible barrier implementation than `CyclicBarrier` and `CountDownlatch`.
- `Atomic*`: This is a way to update a data instance atomically.

The volatile data

Finally, to conclude this part of the Java Standalone concurrent programming, it is necessary to keep in mind why the `volatile` keyword is important. This keyword allows you to request the JVM to refresh the value it reads every time it accesses the data.

It is very simple to use; just add the `volatile` keyword on the field declaration:

```
public class SomeData {
    private volatile int value;
}
```

To understand why this keyword changes everything, you need to keep in mind that the JVM can have some thread-related *caching* of the field values (this is very low-level caching and has nothing to do with what we'll see in the next section). Adding this keyword as in the previous snippet forces us to bypass this cache. It is supposed to be a bit slower. However, the usage is often fast by itself, so it is generally worth it.

Java EE and threads

As we saw at the beginning of the chapter, Java EE can silently use threads. Any thread usage is important to identify even if it is good to rely on the Java EE implementation, because it is code that you don't have to maintain. The issue with not identifying the thread is that you can come across cases where your context (`ThreadLocal`) will not be available or will be available with the wrong values. The other pitfall of not identifying the thread is that you may end up abusing the thread and consuming way more resources on the machine than you need. Let's review a few representative cases of such usages.

CDI asynchronous events

CDI 2.0 introduces the notion of asynchronous events. It is a manner of asynchronously firing an event for the caller. Here is a sample usage:

```
public class AsyncSender {
    private static final Logger log =
    Logger.getLogger(AsyncSender.class.getName());

    @Inject
    private Event<MyEvent> sender;

    public void send(final MyEvent event) {
        final CompletionStage<MyEvent> cs = sender.fireAsync(event);
        cs.thenRun(() -> {
        // some post processing once all observers got notified
        });
    }
}
```

This code snippet sends an asynchronous event, thanks to `fireAsync`. The interesting part of this API is that it returns `CompletionStage`, which enables you to chain some logic after the event has notified all the asynchronous observers.

 Asynchronous events notify only asynchronous observers. It uses a new observer marker: `@ObserverAsync`. Here is a signature sample:
`public void onEvent(@ObservesAsync MyEvent event);`

The way the CDI handles the submission of this kind of events is by using `CompletionFuture.all` or by chaining the asynchronous observers in a single asynchronous thread (this is configurable in Weld; OpenWebBeans only supports the first solution). In any case, it submits individual futures to a CDI thread pool. The pool configuration is not yet completely standard, though it is important to know that it is feasible in all the containers and is an important tuning configuration for your application if you rely on it.

Several containers will default to the common fork join pool of the JVM, which doesn't scale a lot. So, you will probably want to provide a custom thread pool dedicated to your application usage.

In terms of the user code, it is important to prefer the signature taking a `NotificationOptions` instance to `fireAsync` (which generally falls back on the default container pool). Doing so will allow you to give a custom pool:

```
sender.fireAsync(event, NotificationOptions.ofExecutor(myExecutor));
```

This signature enables you to pass a custom pool and to properly tune it (using EE concurrency utilities for Java EE, for instance). It will also enable you to specify the pool you are using by event and to avoid putting them all in the same bucket. In fact, it can potentially lead to locking your application if there are some dependencies between the usages!

 Last tip on this API is to make sure that you synchronize the event if you mutate it, to get a new state after through `CompletionStage`. You can use any of the Java Standalone techniques we talked about previously.

EJB @Asynchronous

EJB was one of the earliest Java EE specifications. At that time, it was the specification getting the most attention and features. Now, it is slowly being replaced by CDI and integrations, with other specifications such as JTA, JPA, and so on. However, it still contains a set of useful features that you don't find elsewhere in Java EE.

EJB also has an asynchronous solution. It is more direct compared to CDI, since you can mark a method as asynchronous:

```
@Asynchronous
public Future<MyResult> execute() {
    return new AsyncResult<>(getResult());
}
```

@Asynchronous requests the server to execute the task in the EJB thread pool. The method can return void, but if it needs to return a value, it must return Future. With Java 8, it is easy to return CompletionFuture. However, since this API was designed before that, the easiest way was to return AsyncResult, which was provided by the specification, and pass it the actual value you want to return. Note that the container will wrap the returned Future value to add a particular specification handling, so you will not be able to cast it to CompletionFuture, even if that is the implementation you choose in your code.

Here again, the pool configuration is highly dependent on the server, but it is generally workable and important, depending on the usage of this API in the application. If your application uses it a lot but the container provides only two threads and a small pool queue, then you will not scale very far.

EE concurrency utilities for Java EE

Java EE 7 introduces a new specification called EE concurrency utilities for Java EE. The main target is not only to provide a way to work with threads from your EE application, but also to handle EE context propagation, including security, transaction, and so on.

 When using this API, remember that the propagated context highly depends on the container. This API is, however, a very good choice compared to a custom thread pool management because the configuration is outside the application and *standard* for the container, and also because it gives you the ability to benefit from the API that we will see in this section.

What is very clever to do at the specification level is to reuse the standard APIs, such as `ExecutorService`, `ScheduledExecutorService`, and so on. This gives the developers the ability to use them as a replacement for the SE API. In particular, it enables you to integrate transparently with third-party libraries.

For example, you can integrate with RxJava (`https://github.com/ReactiveX/RxJava`), as you would do with any thread pool:

```
@ApplicationScoped
public class RxService {
    @Resource(lookup = "java:global/threads/rx")
    private ManagedExecutorService mes;

    public Flowable<String> getValues() throws Exception {
        final WebSocketContainer container =
        ContainerProvider.getWebSocketContainer();
        final WebSocketPublisher publisher = new WebSocketPublisher();

        container.connectToServer(new Endpoint() {
            @Override
            public void onOpen(final Session session, final
            EndpointConfig config) {
                session.addMessageHandler(publisher);
            }

            @Override
            public void onClose(final Session session, final
            CloseReason closeReason) {
                publisher.close();
            }
        },      URI.create("ws://websocket.company.com"));

        final Scheduler eeScheduler = Schedulers.from(mes);
        return Flowable.fromIterable(publisher)
        .debounce(1, MINUTES, eeScheduler);
    }
}
```

This code integrates the Java EE WebSocket API with the RxJava Flowable API. The global idea is to let the consumers handle the WebSocket messages, without knowing it comes from WebSocket. This makes it easier to test (replacing the WebSocket layer by a mock) and it decouples the code from the WebSocket layer.

In our service, we inject `ManagedExecutorService`, which is mainly `ExecutorService` managed by the container, and we wrap it in the thread pool API of RxJava through the `Scheduler` API. Then we are done; we can use any asynchronous operation of RxJava relying on the Java EE threads and, therefore, the context. In the previous code snippet, it allowed us to debounce the messages (limit the number of messages emitted per unit of time) in one simple line.

Technically, we implement `Iterator<>` to integrate with RxJava, but we could use `Future` or any other type supported by the Flowable API. The iterator is the part integrating with RxJava. However, to integrate with the WebSocket API, we can also implement `MessageHandler`, which allows us to see the incoming message and register it at our endpoint in the previous snippet. Here is a potential handler implementation:

```
public class WebSocketPublisher implements
        Iterable<String>, Iterator<String>, MessageHandler.Whole<String> {
    private final Semaphore semaphore = new Semaphore(0);
    private final List<String> messages = new ArrayList<>();
    private volatile boolean closed;

    public void close() {
        closed = true;
        semaphore.release();
    }

    @Override
    public void onMessage(final String message) {
        synchronized (messages) {
            messages.add(message);
        }
        semaphore.release();
        // it case we are currently locked in hasNext()
    }

    @Override
    public boolean hasNext() {
        if (closed) {
            return false;
        }
        try {
            semaphore.acquire();
            synchronized (messages) {
                return !closed && !messages.isEmpty();
            }
        } catch (final InterruptedException e) {
            return false;
        }
    }
```

```
        }

        @Override
        public String next() {
            synchronized (messages) {
                return messages.remove(0);
            }
        }

        @Override
        public Iterator<String> iterator() {
            return this;
        }
    }
}
```

Our publisher stacks the received messages and then serves them through the `Iterator<>` API. It requires some synchronization, as we saw in the previous section, to make sure we are able to correctly answer the iterator contract. Concretely, we cannot return anything in `hasNext()` if the connection was not closed or if we did not receive any message. Otherwise, it will stop the iterations.

ManagedExecutorService

As a quick reminder, `ExecutorService` is the standard Java Standalone abstraction for a thread pool. `ManagedExecutorService` is the Java EE flavor. If you compare both the APIs, you will notice that it inherits from all the features of its standalone siblings, but it gets enriched with an auditing: a submitted task (`Runnable`) can implement the ManagedTask API, which will associate a listener to the task, which will be notified of the task's phase (`Submitted`, `Starting`, `Aborted`, and `Done`).

ManagedTask globally gives the following to the container:

- The listener that ManagedTask uses
- A set of properties to customize the behavior of the execution. Three main standard properties are defined and portably usable on all the containers:
  - `javax.enterprise.concurrent.LONGRUNNING_HINT`: This allows the container to change the thread setup for a long time, taking the tasks to complete (using other thread priorities or potentially using dedicated threads)

- `javax.enterprise.concurrent.TRANSACTION`: This can take the `SUSPEND` value that will suspend the current transaction (if any) and resume it after the task is completed
- `USE_TRANSACTION_OF_EXECUTION_THREAD`: This propagates the transaction of the calling thread

If you cannot make your task implementing ManagedTask, then you also have *bridge* adapters to link a normal task to a listener through the `ManagedExecutors` factory:

```
Runnable runnable = ManagedExecutors.managedTask(myTask, myListener);
```

This simple invocation will create `Runnable` and you can therefore submit to `ManagedExecutorService`, which also implements `ManagedTask` with the `myListener` listener. Indeed, there are wrapper factory methods for `Callable`, with the properties we mentioned earlier, to ensure it covers all the `ManagedTask` API's features.

In terms of the overall platform consistency, it is important that this API tends to make EJB `@Asynchronous` legacy.

ManagedScheduledExecutorService

`ManagedScheduledExecutorService` is `ScheduledExecutorService` Java EE API. Like `ExecutorService`, it integrates with the ManagedTask API.

However, this scheduling-related API goes a bit further, providing two new methods to schedule a task—`Runnable` or `Callable` —based on a dedicated API (`Trigger`). This API enables you to handle the scheduling programmatically and it avoids relying on a constant time interval or delay.

Even if, theoretically, this scheduling API can be distributed and was designed to support it, it is generally implemented with local support only. However, it is a good alternative to EJB `@Schedule` or `TimerService` when clustering is not mandatory, which is actually often the case in practice.

Java EE threads

The EE concurrency utilities also provide a Java EE ThreadFactory, which creates `ManageableThread` instead of a plain thread. The main difference is that they provide an `isShutdown()` method, allowing you to know whether the current thread is shutting down and, thereby, exit the process if it is indeed shutting down. `ManagedExecutors.isCurrentThreadShutdown()` allows you to directly test this flag, handling the casting of the thread automatically. This means that a long running task can be implemented as follows:

```
while (running && !ManagedExecutors.isCurrentThreadShutdown()) {
    process();
}
```

You may think that testing only the thread state would be enough, but you still need an application state to ensure that you integrate with the application life cycle. Don't forget that the thread can be bound to the container and not the application deployment time. Also, depending on the strategy you define for the threads, you can evict them at runtime, potentially through the administration API of the container.

ContextService

The last interesting API of the EE concurrency utilities is `ContextService`. It allows you to create proxies, based on interfaces, inheriting from the context propagation of the `Managed*` API. You can see it as a way of using managed thread pool features in the standalone thread pools that you don't control:

```
Runnable wrappedTask = contextService.createContextualProxy(myTask,
Runnable.class);
framework.execute(wrappedTask);
```

Here, we wrap our task in a contextual proxy and we submit the wrapped task through a framework that we don't control. However, the execution will still be done in the EE context of the caller (same JNDI context, for instance), and using another framework is not much affecting.

This `ContextService` is limited to proxy interfaces and doesn't support subclass proxying like CDI does for instance. Java EE understands that modern development is composed of motley frameworks and stacks and that it can't control everything and anything. This trend is traduced by the introduction of a new sort of API to easily integrate with others and enable any use case, rather than introducing a lot of new APIs, which will not evolve very well.

It is important in terms of performance and monitoring—it not only allows you to easily trace invocations and application behavior but also to optimize the application with caching, as we will see in the next chapter.

EJB @Lock

The previous part showed that EJB @Asynchronous and @Schedule can be replaced with the new EE concurrency utilities in some measure. However, there are still some EJB APIs that are not easy to replace without coding them yourself. The @Lock API is one of them.

The global idea is to ensure that the data owned by the EJB (@Singleton) is accessed in a thread-safe context.

Indeed, this API is limited to the singleton EJB, since without a single instance usable in a concurrent environment, it doesn't make sense to lock.

The usage is straightforward, as you just decorate a method or the bean with @Lock, passing READ or WRITE in the parameter, depending on the kind of access:

```
@Singleton
public class MyLocalData {
    private Data data;

    @Lock(READ)
    public Data get() {
        return data;
    }

    @Lock(WRITE)
    public void set(Data data) {
        this.data = data;
    }
}
```

If you remember the part about Java Standalone, it is very close to the synchronized usage, as we define a lock on a block. However, the semantic is closer to the ReadWriteLock API. This was a will of the API design as this is the way it is often implemented. Now, why mix both the styles (block and read/write API)? It enables you to scale on the read, keeping the API very simple (bound to blocks). However, it already fits a lot of cases!

In terms of the performance, it is important to know that you can mix it with a timeout through `@AccessTimeout`:

```
@Singleton
@AccessTimeout(500)
public class MyLocalData {
    // as before
}
```

Here, we request the container to fail with the `ConcurrentAccessTimeout` exception if the lock (read or write) is not acquired after 500 milliseconds.

For a reactive application, correctly configuring the timeouts is crucial and important to ensure that the application doesn't start with a huge response time because of all the threads waiting for a response. This means that you have to define a fallback behavior in the case of a timeout. To say it differently, you need to define a timeout to ensure you match your SLA, but you also need to define what to do when you get a timeout in order to avoid 100% of errors in case the server is overloaded.

 The microprofile initiative has been created by most Java EE vendors and is mainly based on the CDI. So, even if it is not part of the Java EE, it integrates very well with it. Its primary targets are microservices, and, therefore, they define a bulkhead API and other concurrent solutions. However, it is an interesting solution if the `@Lock` is too simple for your needs.

HTTP threads

HTTP layers (server and client) are about network and connections. Therefore, they require some threading to handle the client connections on the server side and, potentially, the reactive processing on the client side. Let's go through these particular settings, which directly impact the scalability of your application.

Server side

The entry point of any web request is the HTTP container. Here, the server configuration is always server-dependent, but most of the vendors will share the same concepts. It is important to tune that part to make sure that the outbound of your application is not unintentionally throttling it too much; otherwise, you will limit the scalability of your application for no reason.

For instance, for GlassFish, you can configure the HTTP connector in the UI administration or the corresponding configuration file. Here is what it looks like:

This page is really about the tuning of the HTTP connector (not the binding address, port, or the supported SSL cipher algorithms). The corresponding configurations are summarized in the following table:

Configuration name	Description
Max connections	This is the maximum number of requests per client in the keep-alive mode. This is not the maximum number of connections the server supports, compared with the other Java EE servers.
Timeout	This is the timeout after which the connection can be dropped in the keep-alive mode if still idle. Here again, it is a client-based configuration and not a request timeout like in most of the other servers.
Request timeout	This is the duration after which the request will timeout and fail from the client point of view.
Buffer size/length	Buffers are used to read the incoming data in the input streams. Adjusting this size to avoid memory overflows will significantly increase the performance, since the server will no longer have to create a new volatile buffer to read the data. This tuning can be hard to do if the application does lots of things. The trade-off is to not use too much memory and to avoid unexpected allocations. Thus, the closer you are to the most common requests in terms of size (a bit more than this value actually), the better you will behave.
Compression	Compression is mainly for browser-based clients (supporting GZIP). It will automatically compress the content of the configure mime types if the size of the resource is more than the minimum configuration size. Concretely, it can, for instance, affect a JavaScript of 2MB (which is no longer rare today). This will use some CPU resources to do the compression, but the space gain on text-based resources (HTML, JavaScript, CSS, and so on) is generally worth it, as the network duration will be reduced a lot.

These parameters are mainly about the network optimization but are crucial to ensure that the application stays responsive. They are also influencing the way the HTTP threads are used, because bad tuning can imply more work for the server. Now, you also have an HTTP thread pool in GlassFish (as in most servers) that you can configure. Here is the corresponding screen:

Edit Thread Pool

Modify an existing thread pool

[Load Defaults]

Configuration Name: default-config

Name: http-thread-pool

Class Name: org.glassfish.grizzly.threadpool.GrizzlyExecutorServic

The name of the class that implements the thread pool

Max Queue Size: 4096

The maximum number of threads in the queue. A value of -1 indicates that there is no limit to the queue size

Max Thread Pool Size: 5

The maximum number of threads in the thread pool

Min Thread Pool Size: 5

The minimum number of threads in the thread pool

Idle Thread Timeout: 900   Seconds

The maximum amount of time that a thread can remain idle in the pool. After this time expires, the thread is removed from the pool

The configuration of GlassFish is very common for a thread pool—its sizes (maximum/minimum), the queue size (the number of tasks that can be added even if the pool is full), and the timeout (when a thread is removed from the pool if not used).

When you are benchmarking your application, ensure that you monitor the CPU usage of your application and the thread stacks (or profiling, depending on the way you monitor your server/application) to identify bad configuration. For instance, if you see a CPU usage of 50% and a few active threads, then you may need to increase the pool size. The overall goal is to make the CPU usage very high (85-95%) and the response time of the server almost constant. Note that it is not recommended to go up to 100% for the CPU usage because, then, you'll reach the limitations of the machine; the performance won't be relevant anymore and you will just see the response time increasing boundlessly.

This is a general rule for any thread pool that can become very important when going reactive. So, always try to name the threads of the application with a prefix that corresponds to the role that they have in order to ensure that you can identify them in the thread dumps.

Client side

Since JAX-RS 2.1, the client has been made to be reactive. As a quick reminder, here is what it can look like:

```
final Client client = ClientBuilder.newClient();
try {
    CompletionStage<Response> response =
    client.target("http://google.com")
        .request(TEXT_HTML_TYPE)
        .rx()
        .get();
} finally {
    client.close();
}
```

This is normal JAX-RS client API usage, except for the call to `rx()`, which wraps the response into `CompletionStage`. The only interest is to become asynchronous; otherwise, it will just be another layer with poor gain in terms of user experience.

The way the implementation handles asynchronous invocations is up to the implementation, but with Jersey (the reference implementation) and in a Java EE container, you will default to the managed executor service. Note that outside an EE container, Jersey will create a very big thread pool.

This kind of configuration is the key to your application, since each client is supposed to have a different pool to ensure that it doesn't affect the other parts of the application, and also because thread usages can be different and may need different constraints. However, it is not yet standardized and, thus, you will need to check which implementation your server uses and how the configuration can be used. In general, the client-side configuration is accessible through the client's properties, so it is not that hard. However, sometimes, you may be limited by container integration. In such a case, you can wrap the invocation into your own pool and not use the `rx()` API to fully control it.

To conclude this section, we can expect in some time (Java EE 8 and this new JAX-RS 2 API) that this `rx()` method will be implemented directly using the NIO API, and therefore, it becomes really reactive at the network level and not just through another thread pool.

We just saw that Java EE brings solutions to handle your application threading properly, but modern developments often require new paradigms. These modifications require a small change in the way the application is developed. Let's go through one of these new patterns.

Reactive programming and Java EE

Reactive programming lets your code be called instead of calling your code. You can visualize it as being event-based instead of procedural. Here is an example to compare both the styles:

```
public void processData(Data data) {
    if (validator.isValid(data)) {
        service.save(data);
        return data;
    }
    throw new InvalidDataException();
}
```

This is a very simple and common implementation of a business method where we call two services: `validator` and `service`. The first one will validate the data by checking whether it exists in the database, the values are in the expected ranges, and so on, while the second one will actually process the updates (a database, for instance).

The issue with this style is that the data validation and persistence are bound in a single `processData` method, which defines the entire execution environment (threading, context, and so on).

In the reactive style, it can be rewritten to replace the synchronous calls by a *chain*:

```
public Data processData(Data data) {
    return Stream.of(data)
        .filter(validator::isValid)
        .peek(service::save)
        .findFirst()
        .orElseThrow(() -> new InvalidDataException("..."));
}
```

In this example, we used the Java 8 stream API, but using a reactive library such as RxJava generally makes more sense; you will understand why in the next paragraph. This code does the same thing as the previous one, but it orchestrates the calls through the definition of a chain, instead of making the calls directly.

What is interesting with this pattern is that you split your logic (`validator`, `service`) from the way it is used (the stream in the previous example). It implies that you can enrich the way the calls are orchestrated, and if you think about the example of RxJava that we saw earlier, you can immediately think about executing each method in different threads.

One common use case of such a pattern is when the response time is more important than the resources used. In other words, if you don't care about consuming more CPU cycles if it helps reduce the time you need to respond to your client, then you can put this pattern in place. If you are working with multiple concurrent data providers, or if you need to contact multiple remote services to process the data, then you will do the three invocations concurrently upfront. And once you have all the responses, you will execute the actual processing.

To illustrate this, you can assume that the data has a contract identifier, a customer identifier, and an account identifier associated with the corresponding entities through three different remote services. The synchronous implementation of such a case will be something like the following:

```
Customer customer = findCustomer(data);
Contract contract = fincContract(data);
Account account = findAccount(data);
process(customer, contract, account);
```

This will work. However, assuming that a remote call is about 10 ms, your method will then take more than 30 ms to process the data.

You can optimize it a bit by doing the three requests concurrently:

```
public void processData(Data data) {
    final CompletableFuture<Customer> customer = findCustomer(data);
    final CompletableFuture<Contract> contract = findContract(data);
    final CompletableFuture<Account> account = findAccount(data);
    try {
        CompletableFuture.allOf(customer, contract, account).get();
        processLoadedData(customer.get(), contract.get(), account.get());
    } catch (final InterruptedException | ExecutionException e) {
        throw handleException(e);
    }
}
```

In this case, you will reduce the invocation duration to 10 ms, more or less. However, you will block the thread for 10 ms (the three parallel invocations).
The `CompletableFuture.allOf(...).get()` line waits for all the three asynchronous operations (`CompletableFutures`) to complete, keeping the thread unusable for other requests/processing.

The direct implication is that you will not scale and will not be able to process many concurrent requests even if your CPU is probably doing nothing (that is, you are waiting on I/O if you obtain a thread dump at that time).

The way to enhance this is to ensure that the main thread is not blocked and that the processing is triggered only when all the data is received:

```
public void processData(Data data) {
    final CompletableFuture<Customer> customer = findCustomer(data);
    final CompletableFuture<Contract> contract = findContract(data);
    final CompletableFuture<Account> account = findAccount(data);
    CompletableFuture.allOf(customer, contract, account)
        .thenRun(() -> {
            try {
                processLoadedData(customer.get(), contract.get(),
                account.get());
            } catch (final InterruptedException | ExecutionException
                e) {
                throw handleException(e);
            }
        });
}
```

In this case, we still execute our three remote invocations in parallel—potentially, in a managed executor service if you need to access EE features—and, then, we wait for all three results to be retrieved in order to do our processing. However, we just register our processing to be done once the entire data is readable, and we don't block the thread waiting for this *ready* state; thus, we will be able to serve more requests simultaneously.

What is important in going reactive is to try to avoid synchronizations as much as possible in order to ensure any thread time is active processing. Of course, it has limitations, like some JDBC drivers, which are still synchronous, it will block a thread waiting for I/O operations. Yet, with microservices becoming common, it is easy to add a lot of latency to your code and reduce the application scalability if you don't take care of it.

A way to represent this kind of programming mentally is to visualize the CPU usage as a big queue and each element of the queue as some active computing time consumer (that is, a task). Then, your program is just a big event loop polling this task queue and executing the tasks. What is the result?—almost no passive time, only active time!

Indeed, being asynchronous implies that all the work will become asynchronous (thread handling, context switching, queue management, and synchronization). Even if most of these tasks are hidden and done for you by the stack, it may make the CPU busy and slow down the application, compared with the same code executed in a single thread. This is true and means that you can't use this pattern for every single invocation. You need to ensure that you use it when relevant and when there is potentially a passive usage of the CPU (blocking time, sleep, and so on). Though, if you respect this pattern, you should be able to work with concurrency better than staying synchronous everywhere. Of course, this is a compromise because if you have a background task (a scheduled task executed once a day, for instance), you will not care about the waiting time since it concerns a single thread. This type of programming will only pay when used in accurate places, but if you respect this usage, you will really get a saner final behavior. However, don't forget that it brings more complexity because tracking is no more natural in Java (stack traces are almost no more useful since you don't have the full stack if you don't use a thread-tracing solution).

Message passing and Java EE

Message passing pattern refers to several theories, but in this part, we'll mainly care about the asynchronous flavor. One illustration of this pattern is the actor flavor. An actor is *something* that can receive messages, send messages to other actors, create other actors, and designate the behavior for the next received message.

It is important to understand the basis of the underlying concepts:

- Global communication relies on an asynchronous bus
- *Current* message processing of an actor is based on a state (a bit like an internal state machine)
- An actor can create other actors to process a message

With such a pattern, it is highly recommended to have immutable messages to avoid any concurrency issues and hard-to-debug behavior (or non-deterministic behavior) going across the actor flow.

Java EE doesn't allow you to handle everything of this pattern out of the box, but most of it is already here:

- CDI provides a bus
- CDI (asynchronous) observers are beans, so you can have a state machine
- The delegation chain (new actors) can be handled through a CDI context bound to the messages

Of course, this stays a poor man's implementation, compared with real actor systems, but it already gives you a solid pattern to avoid passive usage of threads, and, by the way, you should think about it when creating an internal architecture for your application.

Summary

In this chapter, you saw how Java EE ensures that you can parallelize the computing of your applications, and make your applications scale better and process multiple concurrent requests.

Using Java Standalone synchronization mechanisms, Java EE threading management solutions and API will let you get the best out of your hardware and integrate with third-party libraries very easily.

Now that we have seen what is related to the CPU, we need to go through the machine's other main resource that you can exploit to make your application's behavior better: the memory. When processing can't be optimized and is too impacting on the application, the solution is often just to skip it as much as possible. The most common—and probably, efficient—way of doing so is to make sure that the data is computed once and reused while valid. This is where the caching enters into the game and this is what our next chapter will be about.

6
Be Lazy; Cache Your Data

In the previous chapter, we saw how to parallelize the processing of our requests and reduce our response time using our processor more accurately.

However, the best way to be efficient and fast is, obviously, not doing anything. This is what caching tries to do, allowing you to use the memory to keep track of the already processed results and read them fast when needed later on.

In this chapter, we will go through the following topics:

- What caching is, how it works, and when it is interesting
- Which kind of cache to use: local versus remote caching
- JCache – a standard API for Java EE

Caching challenges

To ensure that we keep in mind the pattern we target when we put caching in place, let's use a simple example taken from our quote manager application. Our goal will be to make our *find by symbol* endpoint go faster. The current logic looks like this pseudo code snippet:

```
Quote quote = database.find(symbol);
if (quote == null) {
    throw NotFoundException();
}
return convertToJson(quote);
```

We only have two operations in this code snippet (find it in the database and convert the database model into a JSON model). Wonder what you're caching: the database lookup result, the JSON conversion, or both?

We will come back to this part later, but to keep it simple, here, we will just cache the database lookup. Therefore, our new pseudo code can look like the following:

```
Quote quote = cache.get(symbol);
if (quote == null) {
    quote = database.find(symbol);
    if (quote != null) {
        cache.put(symbol, quote);
    }
}
if (quote == null) {
    throw NotFoundException();
}
return convertToJson(quote);
```

This is pretty much the same logic as before, except that we try to read the data from the cache before reaching the database, and if we reach the database and find the record, then we'll add it to the cache.

Indeed, you can also cache if you did not find the quote in the database, in order to avoid issuing a query to the database which will not return anything. It depends on your application whether it encounters these kind of requests often or not.

So, we now have a cache layer with the data from our database to consider in our application. We can visualize this structural change with the following diagram:

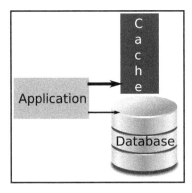

This image represents the fact that the **Application** goes through the **Cache** and **Database**. The fact that the connection (the arrow) to the **Cache** is bolder than the one to the **Database** represents our assumption that **Cache** access is faster than **Database** access. Therefore, it is cheaper to access the **Cache** than the **Database**. This implies that we want to go more often to the **Cache** than to the **Database** to find our quotes. Finally, this picture represents the **Cache** and the **Database** in the same *layer*, since with this kind of solution—and even if the **Cache**, access should be very fast—you now have two data sources.

How does the cache work?

What is cache? The word *cache* is actually very generic and hides a lot of different flavors, which don't target the same needs.

However, all cache implementations share a common basis in terms of principles:

- The data is accessible by key
- The cache provides some eviction mechanisms representing the validity of the stored values
- The cache relies on memory storage *first*

The cache key

Most cache APIs are very close to a map in terms of their behavior—you can put some data with `put(key, value)` and retrieve it back with the same key through a `get(key)` invocation.

This means that a poor man's cache can be implemented with `ConcurrentMap` of the JRE:

```
private final ConcurrentMap<Long, Optional<Quote>> quoteCache = new
ConcurrentHashMap<>();

@GET
@Path("{id}")
public JsonQuote findById(@PathParam("id") final long id) {
    return quoteCache.computeIfAbsent(id, identifier ->
    quoteService.findById(identifier))
            .map(this::convertQuote)
            .orElseThrow(() -> new
WebApplicationException(Response.Status.NO_CONTENT));
}
```

In this implementation, we wrapped the database access in a concurrent map access, which triggers the database access only if the data is not already in the cache. Note that we cached `Optional`, which also represents the fact that we do not have the data in the database. Thus, we will bypass the SQL query, even if the data is absent.

This kind of implementation works, but as it doesn't have any eviction policy, you will keep the same data during the application's lifespan, which means that updates in the database are completely bypassed. Don't use it in production if your data is not constant.

The important part of the usage of such structures (let's call them *maps*) is the choice of the key. Cache implementations will try to limit the locking as much as possible. They can even be lock-free, depending on the implementation. So, you can assume that caches will scale by themselves, but the key is yours and you need to ensure that it is well implemented.

The usage of key by the cache generally has multiple strategies, but the most known and used are the following:

- **By reference**: The equality is tested using a reference equality, which means that you need to use the same key instance to find the value. It is, by design, limited to local caches.
- **By contract**: This uses `equals` and `hashCode` of the key.
- **By value**: This is the same as *by contract*, but it also copies the key when putting it into the cache. It ensures that if the key is mutable and has somehow been mutated after having put the data into the cache, it doesn't affect the cache, which will potentially be corrupted by a wrong `hashCode` affectation.

The `hashCode` usage is generally needed to affect the key/value pair of a cell in the cache storing structure. It enables the distribution of data in a structure, which will then be faster to access. If the key's `hashCode` changes after the key has been affected to a cell, then the data won't be found, even if `equals` is correctly implemented.

Most of the time, you will use the *by contract* solution (or *by value*, depending on the implementation), since the *by reference* rarely works in web applications because the key's reference is often bound to the request and changes with each request. This implies that you must define what the key of your data is and that you must implement `equals` and `hashCode`.

With such a constraint, you need to take care of two very important consequences:

- These methods must be fast to execute
- These methods must be constant once the data is put into the cache

To understand what this means, let's put a computing result in our cache, based on our Quote entity, as a natural key of the computation (we cache some news related to the quote, for instance). As a reminder, here is our entity structure:

```
@Entity
public class Quote { // skipping getters/setters
    @Id
    @GeneratedValue
    private long id;

    @NotNull
    @Column(unique = true)
    private String name;

    private double value;

    @ManyToMany
    private Set<Customer> customers;
}
```

If you use your IDE to generate the equals and hashCode methods, you will probably get something like the following implementation:

```
@Override
public boolean equals(Object o) {
    if (this == o) {
        return true;
    }
    if (o == null || getClass() != o.getClass()) {
        return false;
    }
    Quote quote = (Quote) o;
    return id == quote.id && Double.compare(quote.value, value) == 0 &&
    Objects.equals(name,
            quote.name) && Objects.equals(customers, quote.customers);
}

@Override
public int hashCode() {
    return Objects.hash(id, name, value, customers);
}
```

It is a very common implementation, but it takes all the fields into account. For a JPA entity, it is a disaster because of the following:

- What happens if the identifier is not affected? If the entity is persisted after the entity is put into the cache, you will lose the cache benefit or cache it again (with another hash value).
- What happens when `customers` is accessed? This is a lazy relationship, so if not touched before the `hashCode` or `equals`, then it will load the relationship, which is surely something we do not want.
- What happens if `value`—any state of the entity unrelated to the identifier—changes? The cache usage will also be missed.

JPA is a case where the identifier is really important, even without caching. But with caching, it is more obvious. All these observations lead to the fact that each key of the cache must be based on a natural identifier, which should be immutable, or you must ensure that you evict the cache entry if you receive an event mutating the key hypothesis. In the case of JPA, the natural identifier is the JPA identifier (`id` for `Quote`), but it must also be affected from the first usage. This is why, most of the time, good technical identifiers are based on UUID algorithms and affected when a newly created entity is instantiated. Corrected, our `equals` and `hashCode` methods will look as follows:

```
@Override
public boolean equals(Object o) {
    if (this == o) {
        return true;
    }
    if (o == null || getClass() != o.getClass()) {
        return false;
    }
    Quote quote = (Quote) o;
    return id == quote.id;
}

@Override
public int hashCode() {
    return Long.hashCode(id);
}
```

These implementations take into account the `id` value only, and assuming that it is affected early, it is safe to use as the key in a cache.

Several databases rely on the key/value paradigm to ensure good performance and efficient storage. However, the main difference from a cache will be the volatility of the data that a cache is not intended to store, whereas a database will ensure the persistence of the data, even if it is an eventually consistent database.

Eviction policy

The eviction policy is what makes the cache different from a database or `Map`. It enables you to define how the data is automatically removed from the cache storage. This is very important because if you cache some reference data taken from a database, then the database storage can be bigger than the memory storage you have available on the machine and, thus, without any eviction, you will end up filling the memory and getting `OutOfMemoryException` instead of the performance boost you were expecting from the cache addition.

There are several kinds of eviction policies, but there are few mainstream categories:

- **Least Recently Used (LRU)**
- **First In First Out (FIFO)**
- Random
- **Least Frequently Used (LFU)**

Only LRU, FIFO, and *Expire* are really mainstream; the other ones highly depend on your provider capabilities.

Least Recently Used (LRU)

The LRU strategy is based on the usage of cache elements. Some statistics are maintained to be able to *sort* elements by the last usage date, and when eviction is needed, the cache just goes through the elements in order and evicts them in the same order.

You can imagine it as the cache maintaining a map of data (storage) and a list of the usage of the data (or keys). Here is a sequence to help you visualize it:

Action	Cache storage (unsorted)	Eviction list (sorted)
-	[]	[]
add key/value E1	[E1]	[E1]
add key/value E2	[E1, E2]	[E1, E2]
add key/value E3	[E1, E2, E3]	[E1, E2, E3]
read E2	[E1, E2, E3]	[E1, E3, E2]

What is important to notice here is that each usage (*put*, *get*, and so on) will first put the element in the eviction list. This means that when the eviction is executed, it will remove this element last. In terms of behavior, LRU leads to keeping the most used elements in the cache for the longest possible time, which is exactly when a cache is the most efficient. However, this also means that the cache has to maintain an eviction list state that can be done in several manners (through a list, sorting at eviction time, dynamic matrix, and so on). Since it has additional work to do, it will impact the performance or memory usage, which will no longer be here for the application/cache.

First In First Out (FIFO)

The FIFO algorithm is a simplistic flavor of the LRU algorithm aiming to avoid the drawback of the LRU algorithm at the cost of a little less accurate behavior. Concretely, it will bypass the statistics on the usage and just rely on the time of entry into the cache—a bit like when you are waiting in a supermarket line.

Here is an illustration similar to the one we used to depict the LRU algorithm:

Action	Cache storage (unsorted)	Eviction list (sorted)
-	[]	[]
add key/value E1	[E1]	[E1]
add key/value E2	[E1, E2]	[E1, E2]
add key/value E3	[E1, E2, E3]	[E1, E2, E3]
read E2	[E1, E2, E3]	[E1, E2, E3]

The main difference here is the last entry, which doesn't impact the eviction order between E2 and E3. You can see it as *updates don't change the eviction time.*

Random

As you can guess from its name, this eviction policy randomly selects entries to remove. It looks inefficient because there's a higher probability of removing most used entries and thereby decreasing the cache efficiency. However, there are a few cases where it can be a good choice. The main advantage of this strategy is that it doesn't rely on any eviction order maintenance and is, thus, fast to execute.

Before using it, make sure that it is really less efficient than the others: almost 20% less efficient than LRU, experimentally.

Least Frequently Used (LFU)

The last common algorithm you can meet in caches is the LFU algorithm. Like the LRU algorithm, this flavor also maintains statistics on the cache access.

The main difference with LRU is that, instead of using a time-based statistic, it uses a frequency statistic. It means that if E1 is accessed 10 times and E2 is accessed 5 times, then E2 will be evicted before E1.

The issue with this algorithm is that if you have a fast access rate during a small period of time, then you may evict a more regularly used element than the one often used during a very short period of time. So, the final cache distribution may not be that optimal.

Cache eviction trigger

The previous algorithms define how to select the items to evict when the eviction is triggered. It means that if the eviction is not triggered, they are pointless. Eviction triggers can be of multiple types, but the main ones are the following:

- **Size**: The *size* of the cache can be of several types, such as the actual number of objects of the cache or the memory size (in bits or bytes).
- **Expiration**: With each element, you can associate an *end of life*. When the *end of life* is reached, then the element should be evicted (removed) from the cache. Note that this parameter is not strict, and the element can stay in memory and be removed during access if the cache doesn't use a background thread to evict the element fast enough. However, you shouldn't notice it as a client (cache user).

This is the high-level configuration. However, every cache implementation has a lot of different flavors, mixing a bit of everything. For instance, you can configure a cache to support keeping 1 million objects in memory with a cache memory of the maximum size of 10 MB, and if the objects don't fit in memory, then you can use 1 GB of disk space (overflow on disk strategy). This kind of advanced configuration may affect a different *end of life* to each element, and the cache can thus remove elements from the cache when this *end of life* is reached. Finally, you can associate this *per-element end of life* with a global maximum *end of life* policy of 10 minutes.

If you browse your cache implementation provider, you will identify a lot of configuration options, and what is important is to not try to copy-paste a cache configuration from an existing application without ensuring you are in a similar scenario.

The idea is to start simple and complicate the configuration if your application requires it, or if you get a performance benefit from it. For instance, activating the disk overflow of the data can decrease your performance compared with going to your backend, especially if your backend connection is pretty fast and the disk is highly used already.

Starting from a simple LRU strategy with a max memory size or object size is generally the most pragmatic choice.

Cache storage – memory or not

The idea of caching is to keep the instances in order to serve them faster than rebuilding them or fetching them from a *slow* backend. The first-citizen storage is the heap because it is a fast-access solution. However, several cache vendors allow other strategies. Most of the time, it will allow to be pluggable through a **Service Provider Interface** (**SPI**), so you will often see a lot of implementations. Here is a small list of the ones you can find:

- Hard disk
- RDBMS database (MySQL, Oracle, and so on)
- NoSQL database (MongoDB, Cassandra, a specific cache server kind of storage, *network cache*, and so on)

Before discussing the usage of these extensions, don't forget that it is generally a cache-specific way to use backends. For example, it is not rare for hard-disk implementation to keep keys in memory, store the values on the disk to keep a fast lookup of the data, and ensure that memory usage is respectful of the configuration. This means that you will not always be able to use these *overflow* strategies to persist cached data.

The question is that if the overflow leads to using yet another backend, why is it useful and not more efficient to just go to the main backend, where the data is? This has several answers and they become more and more accurate with the microservices trend that we see nowadays.

The two main reasons for going through this kind of caching are as follows:

- Provide a more reliable access to the data, even if the main backend is not reliable (and owned by another application you don't control).
- Work around an access limitation (like a rate limit) without having to entirely rewrite the application to take it into account. For example, if you access the GitHub API, you will not be able to do more than 30 requests per minute on some endpoints, so if your application requires to do 1,500 accesses per minute, you will need to store the corresponding data on your side. Here, a cache can be fancy because it allows to put an eviction adapted to the rate limit, time unit, and your own application through output.

Using a distributed solution (such as a centralized RDBMS or distributed database such as NoSQL) will allow you to share the data between nodes and avoid doing as many queries on the main backend as you have nodes. For instance, if you have 100 nodes of your application in your cluster and you cache the key, *myid*, then you will request the backend 100 times for the *myid* data by using in-memory storage. Whereas, using a distributed storage, you will cache it once from one node, then just read it from this distributed storage, which is still faster than the main backend.

 Even though using the overflow can be very tempting, don't forget that it is generally slower than in-memory caching (we often say that in-memory access time is one, disk access time is 10, and network access time is 100). There are alternative strategies that allow you to push data eagerly in memory instead of relying on overflow (lazy) reads, which may pay off if your cluster load balancing doesn't use any affinity.

Consistency of the data

We can now set up our caching on all our cluster nodes; the question, however, is whether our application is still working. To answer this, we will take a very simple case where two requests are executed in parallel:

Node 1	Node 2
put data1 in cache at time t1	-
	put data1 in cache at time t1
access data1 at time t3	access data1 at time t3

With this simple timeline, we can immediately see that using a local in-memory cache can lead to inconsistencies, since nodes will likely not cache the data at the same time (cache is generally lazy, so the cache is populated at the first request or when the machine starts, if eager, which may lead to potentially inconsistent data in both cases).

If the data is cached, it generally means it is okay to not have the most up-to-date data. Is it really an issue?—It can be. In fact, if you load balance without affinity (randomly in terms of business logic, which is the case with a *by load* or *round-robin* load balancer), then you can fall into such a situation:

Node 1	Node 2
put data1 in cache at time t1	
	update data1 at time t2
	put data1 in cache at time t3
get and put data2 in cache at time t4	
	put data2 in cache at time t5
access data1 at time t6	access data1 at time t6
access data2 at time t7	access data2 at time t7

We are exactly in the same case as the previous one, but we can now use two kinds data (data1 and data2) in our business logic and cache both. Then, to identify the issue, we must consider that data1 and data2 are *logically* linked (for instance, data1 is an invoice and data2 is a contract with a price). In this situation, if you validate the data (data1 and data2), the processing may fail because the data is cached at different times and in different nodes, which would give more guarantees on the data consistency (since a single node will access a single cache and, therefore, be consistent with its current state).

In other words, it is very important to cache the data in a way that guarantees whether your application still works even with the server's concurrency. The direct implication of this statement is to resist putting the cache everywhere during benchmarks, and adding it only when proven useful, while avoiding breaking the application.

> The same thing exists in a worse manner with an overflow storage, since the overflow can be local to a node (hard disk, for instance), leading you to use three sources of truth for your data.

Generally, *reference data* is the first type of data we cache. It is the data that rarely changes, like a contract that is not supposed to change every day. This helps the application to go faster, since part of the data will have fast access. However, it will not break the application, since the *dynamic* data is still looked up from the main source (a database, for instance). Globally, you will end up with a hybrid lookup setup, where part of your data is read from the cache and the other part is read from the main backend.

HTTP and caching

Implementing an HTTP server is one of the main purposes of Java EE. Using the Servlet API, JAX-RS, or even JAX-WS, you can easily expose data over HTTP without caring for the transport.

However, HTTP defines a caching mechanism that is interesting to take into account in order to optimize the client's behavior.

The common communication with your server will look as follows:

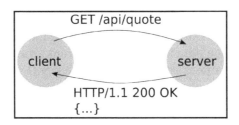

The server makes a request and the client sends back some data in headers and a payload (which can be huge). On the previous schema, it is a JSON payload, but don't forget that your web applications will probably also serve images and other sorts of resources, which get big very quickly.

To avoid having to do it each and every time, even when nothing is changed (a picture will not change very often in general), the HTTP specification defines a set of headers that help identify the resource that didn't change. Thus, the client doesn't need to read the payload, but can just reuse the one it already has.

Even if this way of caching the data is mainly intended to be used with resources and browsers, nothing prevents you from reusing these same mechanisms in a JAX-RS client to avoid fetching the data you access frequently, to ensure you are always up-to-date.

Cache-Control

`Cache-Control` is a header that helps to deal with the cache. It defines the policy to use for the request/response. Used on a response, it defines how the client should cache the data; on a request, it defines what the server can send back in terms of policy.

This header supports multiple values, which can be concatenated when compatible, separated by a comma. Here are the values you can use to define the way data is cached on the client:

Value	Description
public/private	This defines whether the cache is public or private. A private cache is dedicated to a single client whereas a public cache is shared by several clients.

no-cache	This defines the cached entry as outdated and enforces the loading of data once again from the server.
no-store	This prevents the not volatile storage—no disk or persistent storage.
no-transform	This requests additional network layers, such as proxies, to keep the payload *as it is* .
max-age=<duration in seconds>	This defines how long the data can be cached (0 meaning never), for example, `max-age=600` for a 10-minute cache.
max-stale=<duration in seconds>	This notifies the server that an outdated response is acceptable while in this range. For instance, `max-stale=600` allows the server to serve data from 9 minutes ago, even if the server policy is 5 minutes.
min-fresh=<duration in seconds>	This requests a response that will be valid during N seconds. Note that this is not always possible.
min-vers=<value>	This specifies the HTTP protocol version to consider for caching.
must-revalidate	The cached data will contact the server back (associated with an `If-Modified-Since` header) to validate the cached data.
proxy-revalidate	This is same as `must-revalidate` but is used for proxies/gateways.

Here is an example of the header value you can use to not cache the data:

```
Cache-Control: no-cache, no-store, must-revalidate
```

This is the type of configuration you can use for sensitive data to avoid keeping them and reuse them transparently. A *login* endpoint often does it.

ETag

The `ETag` header presence is important for this header more than its value, which is not supposed to be read by the browser. However, its value is often `W/<content length>-<last modified>`, where `content length` is the size of the resource and `last modified` is its last modified timestamp. This is mainly because it is easy to generate and stateless for the server, but it can be anything, including a random string.

This header value can be used as a strong validator. The presence of `W/` at the beginning marks it as a weak validator, which means multiple resources can have the same value.

The value is used with other headers as an identifier, for instance, `Other-Header: <etag>`.

Used with `If-None-Match`, the header takes a list of `Etag` values, potentially `*` for uploads as well, in a comma-separated fashion. If the server doesn't match any resource (or already uploaded payload for *PUT/POST*), then the request will be processed; otherwise, it will return an HTTP 304 response for the read methods (*GET, HEAD*) and 412 (precondition failed) for others.

An interesting header linked to this kind of logic is `If-Modified-Since`. It will allow you to do almost the same, but based on a date if you don't have `Etag` for the resource. It is often associated with the `Last-Modified` value sent back by the server.

Vary

The `Vary` header defines how to decide whether a cached response can be used or not. It contains a comma-separated list of headers, which must not change, in order to decide whether the cache can be used.

Let's take these two HTTP responses, for example:

```
HTTP/1.1 200 OK              HTTP/1.1 200 OK
App-Target: desktop          App-Target: mobile
....                         ....
```

Both the responses are the same, except the `App-Target` header. If you add caching, a desktop or mobile request will lead to the same payload being served if cached.

Now, if the responses are modified, like in the following snippets, to add the `Vary` header, each kind of `App-Target` will not reuse the cache of the other one:

```
HTTP/1.1 200 OK              HTTP/1.1 200 OK
App-Target: desktop          App-Target: mobile
Vary: App-Target             Vary: App-Target
....                         ....
```

This way, both *desktop* and *mobile* experiences can use different resources. For instance, the server can use a different folder depending on the `App-Target` value.

HTTP caching and the Java EE API

Java EE doesn't define a dedicated API (or specification) for HTTP caching, but it provides a few helpers.

The more direct (and low level) way to configure it is by using the Servlet specification, which abstracts the HTTP layer:

```
public class NoStoreFilter implements Filter {
    @Override
    public void doFilter(ServletRequest request, ServletResponse
    response, FilterChain filterChain)
            throws IOException, ServletException {
        final HttpServletResponse httpResponse =
        HttpServletResponse.class.cast(response);
        httpResponse.setHeader("Cache-Control", "no-store");
        filterChain.doFilter(request, response);
    }
}
```

With this filter, the `Cache-Control` value will prevent the cached data from being persistently stored. To activate it, just add it in your `web.xml` or in the server if you don't want to modify your application:

```
<web-app xmlns="http://xmlns.jcp.org/xml/ns/javaee"
         xmlns:xsi="http://www.w3.org/2001/XMLSchema-instance"
         xsi:schemaLocation="
           http://xmlns.jcp.org/xml/ns/javaee
           http://xmlns.jcp.org/xml/ns/javaee/web-app_4_0.xsd"
         version="4.0">

    <filter>
        <filter-name>NoCacheFilter</filter-name>
        <filter-class>com.company.NoCacheFilter</filter-class>
    </filter>
    <filter-mapping>
        <filter-name>NoCacheFilter</filter-name>
        <url-pattern>/*</url-pattern>
    </filter-mapping>

</web-app>
```

Using this XML declaration, and not the `@WebFilter` one, allows you to reuse the same filter on different mappings (URLs) without having to redeclare it or modify the code. The previous declaration put this filter on all the web applications. It can be good for an application that has secured only web services, for instance.

If you want a bit higher level API, you can use the JAX-RS API, which provides a `CacheControl` API. But for some particular headers, you will still go to a lower level, even while using JAX-RS `Response` instead of `HttpServletResponse`:

```
@Provider
public class NoStoreFilter implements ContainerResponseFilter {
    @Override
    public void filter(ContainerRequestContext containerRequestContext,
    ContainerResponseContext
            containerResponseContext)
            throws IOException {
        containerResponseContext.getHeaders().putSingle("Cache
        -Control", "no-store");
    }
}
```

This JAX-RS filter will do the same as the previous Servlet filter, but in a JAX-RS way. Now, if you return a `Response` in your endpoint, you can directly use the `CacheControl` API:

```
@GET
public Response get() {
    CacheControl cacheControl = new CacheControl();
    cacheControl.setNoCache(true);

    return Response.ok("...")
                    .cacheControl(cacheControl)
                    .build();
}
```

This code associates a cache control strategy with the response, which will be converted to headers in the actual HTTP response.

HTTP 2 promise

Servlet 4.0 specification brings HTTP/2 support, which is new for Java EE and for a lot of applications. The idea is to be able to eagerly push some resources to the client. Here is a basic example to give you a high-level picture in mind:

```
@WebServlet("/packt")
public class PacktServlet extends HttpServlet {

    @Override
    protected void doGet(HttpServletRequest req, HttpServletResponse resp)
            throws ServletException, IOException {
        PushBuilder pushBuilder = req.newPushBuilder();
        pushBuilder
                .path("images/packt.png")
                .addHeader("content-type", "image/png")
                .push();

        // serve the response which can use images/packt.png

    }
}
```

This Servlet will start pushing the resource `images/packt.png` upfront. This will enable the browser to rely on it in the response it serves after (likely an HTML page), without having the client to load the image later on.

This will enable the applications to be more reactive since it is all done in a single connection. Thus, it is faster than opening multiple connections to get multiple resources, but it doesn't mean you don't need caching. As you can see in the preceding code snippet, the headers are supported per resource, so you can still use what we previously saw per resource to make the resources load faster, even on HTTP/2.

JCache – the standard cache of Java EE

JCache was added to Java EE to enable the application and libraries to interact in a standard manner with the caching. Therefore, it has two types of APIs and features:

- A programmatic Cache API to write/read data
- A CDI integration to automatically put data in the cache

Setting up JCache

To use JCache, you may need to add it to your application—or to your server, depending on how you want to deploy it—since not all servers add it in their distribution(s). To do it with maven, you can add this dependency:

```
<dependency>
    <groupId>javax.cache</groupId>
    <artifactId>cache-api</artifactId>
    <version>1.0.0</version>
</dependency>
```

Then the only thing you will need to do is select an implementation and add it as well. The most common ones are the following:

- Apache Ignite
- JBoss Infinispan
- Apache JCS
- Ehcache
- Oracle Coherence
- Hazelcast

As often, the choice of the provider is a multicriteria choice and you will probably want to take the following into account:

- The performances
- The dependency stack the provider enforces you to adopt (it can conflict with your other libraries for the biggest ones)
- The extensions the provider has (some of them don't even support CDI)
- The community and support you can get from it

However, using the JCache API, the provider implementation should not impact your code. So, it doesn't impact you and you can start setting up JCache and change the provider later.

 If the provider you choose doesn't support CDI, JCS provides a *cdi* module, which allows you to add CDI integration without using the JCS cache implementation, but using the one you provide.

Programmatic API

A JCache cache can be very quickly accessed using the `Caching` factory:

```
Cache<String, Quote> quotes = Caching.getCache("packt.quotes",
String.class, Quote.class);
quotes.put(symbol, quote);
```

The `getCache` method directly gives you back a `Cache` instance, which allows you to write/read data. The API is then close to a plain `Map` semantic. However, this only works if the cache already exists; otherwise, the `getCache` call will fail.

To understand how JCache works, we need to look at how the instances are managed. This design is pretty common in Java EE and is quite efficient in general:

- A factory method gives you a provider instance (a link between the API and implementation)
- The provider gives you a manager, which stores instances and avoids creating them for every request
- The manager allows you to create and get cache instances

Here is what it looks like in terms of code:

```
final ClassLoader loader = Thread.currentThread().getContextClassLoader();
// Caching.getDefaultClassLoader()

final CachingProvider cachingProvider = Caching.getCachingProvider(loader);

final CacheManager cacheManager =
cachingProvider.getCacheManager(cachingProvider.getDefaultURI(), loader,
new Properties());

final Cache<String, Quote> cache = cacheManager.createCache("packt.quotes",
new MutableConfiguration<String, Quote>()
    .setTypes(String.class, Quote.class)
    .setStoreByValue(false));

cachingProvider.close();
```

The caching factory will give a provider on line 2, but we passed a classloader as a parameter to load the provider for potential future uses. We could use `Caching.getDefaultClassLoader()`, but depending on the environment, you can get a classloader other than the one in your application. So, it is generally saner to manually pass your own application's classloader. Then, we'll create `CacheManager` from the provider we just retrieved. The `getCacheManager` method takes three parameters, which are mainly about how to configure the cache. The URI can default to the provider default value using the provider `getDefaultURI()` method. It is the path (URI, actually) to the vendor-specific configuration file. The loader is the classloader to use for the manager/caches usages and the property is a list of key/values used to configure the cache in a vendor-specific manner. Then, once we have a manager, `createCache()` allows you to define a cache name and its configuration.

Note that we have two types of configurations here:

- The implementation-specific configuration passed through the URI and properties to the manager
- The JCache configuration passed through the `createCache()` method

JCache configuration

The JCache configuration implements `javax.cache.configuration.Configuration` or, more often, `javax.cache.configuration.CompleteConfiguration`. This specification provides the `MutableConfiguration` implementation, which provides a fluent DSL to configure the configuration. Here are the main entry points:

Configuration	Description
key type/value type	Allows to enforce the keys/values to respect a typing. If a key or value doesn't respect the configuration type then it will be rejected (the `put` will fail).
store by value	If true, it will copy the values to prevent them from being mutable (which is the case in store by reference mode). It is faster to store by reference, but in such a case, it is recommended to ensure the key/value pair is immutable in your application.

cache entry configuration listeners	JCache provides several listeners for all cache events (entry created, updated, deleted, expired) and registering a configuration listener allows to register such a listener and define its behavior—which entry to trigger the event for (the listener event filter), is the listener synchronous, and should the listener provide the old value of the data if it exists. This last parameter intends to avoid triggering a network communication if not needed for distributed caches.
cache loader/writer factory	JCache provides loader and writer mechanism. The goal is to be able to populate the cache from an external source (like a database) if the data is not in the cache yet, and to synchronize the cache with the same - or another - external storage. In your application, it means you only access the cache, but your data can be persisted. This is a paradigm change in terms of code where the cache is the source of truth for your data.
management enabled	Registers a JMX MBean for each cache exposing the cache configuration.
statistics enabled	Registers a JMX MBean for each cache exposing the cache statistics (hits, misses, removals, and so on) and allows to reset the statistics. This is very helpful to validate your cache is useful (if you only get misses then the cache just adds an overhead and is never used as intended).
read/write through	Activates the reader/writer if configured.

CDI integration

The JCache specification (and, therefore, complete implementations) comes with a CDI integration. The idea is to enable you to cache your data without having to deal with all the glue of `Cache`.

The CDI integration provides four operations usable with CDI:

- `@CacheResult`: This is probably the most useful feature that will cache a method result and serve it from the cache for later invocations.
- `@CacheRemove`: This removes data from the cache.
- `@CacheRemoveAll`: This removes all the data of the referenced cache.
- `@CachePut`: This adds data to the cache. It relies on `@CacheValue`, which marks a parameter to identify the value to cache.

If we want to cache our quotes in our service, we can just decorate our finder method with @CacheResult:

```
@CacheResult
public Quote findByName(final String name) {
    return ...;
}
```

Adding the @CacheResult annotation will allow you to use the cache from the second invocation of this method and bypass the JPA lookup we used to do.

Note that here we are not caching an optional, as it was our original signature, which will work but is not serializable. Being part of the JDK, we could have trouble making it serializable if our cache needs that constraint to distribute the values into the cache cluster. In practice, try not to cache optionals, and never cache streams that are lazily evaluated and not reusable.

Cache configuration

All these annotations share the same type of configuration where you can define if the corresponding action is done before/after the method execution, how the cache behaves in case of an exception (is the cache operation skipped?), what the cache name is and how to resolve the cache and key to use.

While the first set of parameters is simple to understand, let's focus on the cache resolution, which is a bit peculiar with CDI, as you don't bootstrap the cache yourself but simply reference it.

In the programmatic approach, we saw that the cache configuration is done through a CompleteConfiguration instance. How do you provide it in a CDI context?

All these annotations take two important parameters:

- cacheName: This represents the cache name to use for the operation. Note that by default it is based on the qualified name of the method if not explicitly set.
- cacheResolverFactory: This is the way a cache instance will be retrieved.

A cache resolver factory provides access from the method metadata to the cache resolver to do the operation associated with the annotation, or a cache resolver for the exception if an exception is thrown and the configuration of the annotation requires to cache it if CacheResult#exceptionCacheName is set.

The cache resolver is just a contextual factory of cache. Here is a simplistic implementation:

```
@ApplicationScoped
public class QuoteCacheResolver implements CacheResolver {
    @Inject
    private CacheManager manager;
    @Override
    public <K, V> Cache<K, V> resolveCache(CacheInvocationContext<?
    extends Annotation> cacheInvocationContext) {
        try {
            return
    manager.getCache(cacheInvocationContext.getCacheName());
        } catch (final CacheException ce) {
            return
    manager.createCache(cacheInvocationContext.getCacheName(), new
    MutableConfiguration<>());
        }
    }
}
```

This implementation is a CDI bean that allows you to reuse the CDI power and tries to retrieve the existing cache from the contextual cache name; if it doesn't exist, it creates a new instance. This is done in this order to avoid passing in the catch block at runtime—it will happen only once.

Indeed, to make this implementation work, you need to produce the cache manager somewhere:

```
@ApplicationScoped
public class JCacheConfiguration {
    @Produces
    @ApplicationScoped
    CacheManager createCacheManager() {
        return ....;
    }

    void releaseCacheManager(@Disposes CacheManager manager) {
        manager.close();
    }
}
```

This is a plain CDI producer and the associated code can reuse the code we saw in the programmatic API part.

The interesting thing using CDI and extracting the resolver is that you can easily integrate with any configuration. For instance, to read a configuration from ${app.home}/conf/quote-manager-cache.properties, you can use this implementation of the cache resolver factory:

```
@ApplicationScoped
public class QuoteManagerCacheResolverFactory implements
CacheResolverFactory {
    private Map<String, String> configuration;

    @Inject
    private CacheManager manager;

    @Inject
    private Instance<Object> lookup;

    @PostConstruct
    private void loadConfiguration() {
        configuration = ...;
    }

    @Override
    public CacheResolver getCacheResolver(final CacheMethodDetails<?
    extends Annotation> cacheMethodDetails) {
        return doGetCache(cacheMethodDetails, "default");
    }

    @Override
    public CacheResolver getExceptionCacheResolver(final
    CacheMethodDetails<CacheResult> cacheMethodDetails) {
        return doGetCache(cacheMethodDetails, "exception");
    }

    private CacheResolver doGetCache(final CacheMethodDetails<? extends
    Annotation> cacheMethodDetails, final String qualifier) {
        final MutableConfiguration cacheConfiguration =
        createConfiguration(cacheMethodDetails, qualifier);

        return new CacheResolver() {
            @Override
            public <K, V> Cache<K, V> resolveCache(final
            CacheInvocationContext<? extends Annotation>
            cacheInvocationContext) {
                try {
                    return manager.getCache(cache);
                } catch (final CacheException ce) {
                    return manager.createCache(cache,
```

```
                    cacheConfiguration);
                }
            }
        };
    }
}
```

With this skeleton, we can see that the cache resolver factory getting injections as any CDI bean, that it read the configuration in a `@PostConstruct` method to avoid reading it each time (but this is not mandatory, it just shows that it really can leverage CDI features), and that when a cache needs to be provided, it is created using the strategy we saw previously (see the simplistic implementation).

To be complete, we need to see how we read the configuration. It can be as simple as reading a `properties` file:

```
final Properties cacheConfiguration = new Properties();
final File configFile = new File(System.getProperty("app.home", "."),
"conf/quote-manager-cache.properties");
if (configFile.exists()) {
    try (final InputStream stream = new FileInputStream(configFile)) {
        cacheConfiguration.load(stream);
    } catch (IOException e) {
        throw new IllegalStateException(e);
    }
}
// potentially create defined caches
configuration = cacheConfiguration.stringPropertyNames().stream()
                        .collect(toMap(identity(),
cacheConfiguration::getProperty));
```

The code is not very complicated and quite common, but the trick is to convert `Properties` into `Map`, which avoids being synchronized at runtime and would potentially slow down the runtime a little bit while different caches are getting created for no reason.

The last missing thing for having a functional implementation is how to create the cache configuration. It is mainly just a matter of converting the configuration into a cache configuration instance. Here is a potential implementation:

```
private MutableConfiguration createConfiguration(final String
configurationPrefix) {
    final MutableConfiguration cacheConfiguration = new
    MutableConfiguration<>();
    cacheConfiguration.setStoreByValue(Boolean.getBoolean(
            configuration.getOrDefault(configurationPrefix +
            "storeByValue", "false")));
```

```
cacheConfiguration.setStatisticsEnabled(Boolean.getBoolean(
        configuration.getOrDefault(configurationPrefix +
        "statisticsEnabled", "false")));
cacheConfiguration.setManagementEnabled(Boolean.getBoolean(
        configuration.getOrDefault(configurationPrefix +
        "managementEnabled", "false")));

final String loader = configuration.get(configurationPrefix +
"loaderCdiName");
if (loader != null) {
    cacheConfiguration.setReadThrough(true);
    CacheLoader<?, ?> instance = lookup.select(CacheLoader.class,
    NamedLiteral.of(loader)).get();
    cacheConfiguration.setCacheLoaderFactory(new
    FactoryBuilder.SingletonFactory<>(instance));
}
final String writer = configuration.get(configurationPrefix +
"writerCdiName");
if (writer != null) {
    cacheConfiguration.setWriteThrough(true);
    CacheWriter<?, ?> instance = lookup.select(CacheWriter.class,
    NamedLiteral.of(writer)).get();
    cacheConfiguration.setCacheWriterFactory(new
FactoryBuilder.SingletonFactory<>(instance));
}
return cacheConfiguration;
}
```

To create the cache configuration, we rely on `MutableConfiguration` and just read the values from the properties we loaded. The trick is to get instances like the reader or writer. This can be done using CDI `Instance<Object>`, which can be seen as a generic CDI lookup; you can also use `BeanManager` directly if you prefer. In this implementation, we look up the reader/writer from their CDI name, so we need to provide the `@Named("...")` literal. Since CDI 2.0, you can use the `NamedLiteral` API, which will create the corresponding annotation instance for you. Finally, readers/writers need to be passed to the JCache runtime through a factory, but JCache provides a singleton factory implementation, preventing you from creating your own.

@CacheDefaults

`@CacheDefaults` allows you to define at the cache level, the cache name, the resolver factory, and the key generator to use. It prevents having to do it on all the methods if they all share the same setup:

```
@ApplicationScoped
@CacheDefaults(
    cacheName = "packt.quotes",
    cacheResolverFactory = AppCacheResolverFactory.class,
    cacheKeyGenerator = QuoteCacheGenerator.class
)
public class CachedQuoteService {
    @Inject
    private QuoteService service;

    @CachePut
    public Quote create(final Quote newQuote) {
        return service.create(newQuote);
    }

    @CacheRemove
    public Quote delete(final Quote quote) {
        return service.delete(quote);
    }
}
```

This class, which delegates the logic to a dedicated service, has two methods using JCache CDI integration. Both are using the same shared configuration relying on the `@CacheDefaults` setup done at the class-level. It prevents having to code it this way:

```
@ApplicationScoped
public class CachedQuoteService {
    @Inject
    private QuoteService service;

    @CachePut(
        cacheName = "packt.quotes",
        cacheResolverFactory = AppCacheResolverFactory.class,
        cacheKeyGenerator = QuoteCacheGenerator.class
    )
    public Quote create(final Quote newQuote) {
        return service.create(newQuote);
    }

    @CacheRemove(
        cacheName = "packt.quotes",
```

```
            cacheResolverFactory = AppCacheResolverFactory.class,
            cacheKeyGenerator = QuoteCacheGenerator.class
        )
    public Quote delete(final Quote quote) {
        return service.delete(quote);
    }
}
```

In a more simplistic flavor, cache configuration was duplicated by method, which is less readable.

Cache key

Now, we are able to control our cache and activate our cache operations on our methods; what did we miss?—A way to control the key used for the cache. For instance, let's take the following method:

```
@CacheResult
public Quote findQuote(String symbol)
```

Here, the natural key is the symbol, so it would be nice if JCache could do it automatically, right? It is the cache, but the rule is a bit more complicated because if you apply the same reasoning for a `create` method, then it doesn't work:

```
@CacheResult
public Quote create(String symbol, double price)
```

Here, we want the result to be cached, but if `findQuote()` must match the `create()` method, then we must have a way to ask JCache to use only `symbol` in the key.

To do so, JCache relies on the `@CacheKey` API. The following are the rules:

- If there is no `@CacheKey`, then use all parameters
- If there is `@CacheValue` used on some parameter but no `@CacheKey`, then use all the parameters except the one decorated with `@CacheValue`
- If some parameters (>= 1) are decorated with `@CacheKey`, then use them

In other words, our `create` method should look like the following:

```
@CacheResult
public Quote create(@CacheKey String symbol, double price)
```

This way, and due to the previous rules, the `findQuote` and `create` methods use the same key, based on the symbol—*based* because the key of the cache is not directly the value you pass as the parameter. This is mainly because it can be a key composed of multiple parameters, so you need to wrap them in a single object. The actual key type is `GeneratedCacheKey`, which just enforces the implementation to be serializable and to implement `equals` and `hashCode` for the reason we mentioned at the beginning of the chapter.

The JCache implementation will, by default, provide an implementation respecting these rules, but in some cases, you can optimize or want to customize the key. In our case, a plain string key, we can optimize `GeneratedCacheKey` to fully rely on the String specifics, which allows to cache `hashCode`. Here is the implementation:

```
public class StringGeneratedCacheKey implements GeneratedCacheKey {
    private final String value;
    private final int hash;

    public StringGeneratedCacheKey(final String value) {
        this.value = value;
        this.hash = value.hashCode();
    }

    @Override
    public boolean equals(final Object o) {
        return this == o ||
                o != null && getClass() == o.getClass() &&
                Objects.equals(value,
StringGeneratedCacheKey.class.cast(o).value);
    }

    @Override
    public int hashCode() {
        return hash;
    }
}
```

Since a cache access is an access to a storage cell through the hash index, optimizing the hash can be worthy if the delegate parameters' hash code computing is long or needs to go through a complex graph. The same kind of logic can apply to `equals`.

Now, we have an *optimized* flavor of our key; we need to enable it. This is done through the cache annotation (`@CacheDefaults`) and the `cacheKeyGenerator()` member. It allows us to reference a *key generator*. Here, again, it can be a CDI bean, and it gives you the contextual information of the method, so you can instantiate the key:

```
@ApplicationScoped
public class SingleStringCacheKeyGenerator implements CacheKeyGenerator {
    @Override
    public GeneratedCacheKey generateCacheKey(final
    CacheKeyInvocationContext<? extends Annotation> context) {
        return new StringGeneratedCacheKey(String.class.cast(
            context.getKeyParameters()[0].getValue()));
    }
}
```

This a very simple implementation; directly extract the (assumed) single key parameter of the method and cast it to a string to instantiate our optimized generated cache key. Then, to use it, we just reference this class in the cache annotation:

```
@CacheResult(cacheKeyGenerator = SingleStringCacheKeyGenerator.class)
public Quote findByName(final String name) {
    return ...;
}
```

It is very important to ensure that the generator implementation matches the method signature. Typically, in this last snippet, if we change our `name` parameter to `long`, then we need to change the key generator; otherwise, it will fail. However, it is not rare to have generators assuming the type of key parameters, since it is generally coupled to optimize their usage.

Cache once

If we look back at our quote manager application, we have the following layers through which a request goes:

- Servlet
- JAX-RS
- Service layer (`@Transactional`)
- JPA

You can add some caching (such as JCache, not HTTP, which is more a client data management solution) to all the layers. On the Servlet side, you can cache the responses using the requests as key. In JAX-RS, you can do the same, but in a more business-oriented manner. In the service layer, you can use CDI JCache integration. And in JPA, you can use level 2 caching, which can be implemented with JCache or a provider-specific implementation—this generally just requires configuration to be set up so that the API is not very crucial.

However, if you configure the caching on all layers, it is likely that a part of the cache will be useless, and since all the layers will not have access to the same information, you will duplicate the caches for a poor gain or for nothing. To use an extreme example, if you cache the response from the request in the Servlet layer, the JAX-RS/service/JPA layer will never be called once the data is in the cache and, therefore, setting up caching in these layers is useless. It doesn't mean that the caching in these layers should be avoided because using some caching in the service layer can benefit some background tasks as well (such as a batch developed with JBatch using some reference data).

Nonetheless, caching the closest of the outbound of your application will give you the best performance boost, as it will bypass more layers. For instance, caching the response in the Servlet layer will bypass JAX-RS and, thereby, JAX-RS routing and serialization steps, where caching the same data in the service layer will keep executing these steps through the JAX-RS layer.

There is no general rule here, since it is a trade-off between the memory it takes (closer to the data you are). The less memory you use in general, the simpler the key handling will be (since you don't accumulate other data such as HTTP headers in Servlet layer). The best you should do is to think about your application and how it uses data and then validate the cache setup by a comparative benchmark.

Summary

At the end of this chapter, you have all the keys you need to enhance your application performance. We saw how to send the right data to a browser to not have to load cached data, how to set up a cache using Java EE API (JCache), and the caching challenges you need to think about to not decrease the performance.

Being able to cache data in a distributed system is important, since any network call is very impacting on performances. Now that we know how to cache, we can go to the next level about distributed systems and see how to control the performance in a wider system. This is what our next chapter will be about—how to be fault-tolerant and avoid impacting all the applications of a system when one is starting to fail or running slower than usual.

7
Be Fault-Tolerant

For years, Java EE has been about putting the maximum number of applications inside a single application server, but it has been changing for a few years now. It has become more common to deploy a single application in a container instance and to reduce the application size to handle a single responsibility. The direct implication of such a paradigm change is that a system, as a whole, is now composed of far more applications than before, and we rely more and more on remote communications.

In such a context, the performance of one application directly depends on another application, and it is important to be able to limit the side effects between applications. To ensure that your applications identified the impact of its environment and can work with such constraints, we will cover the following topics in this chapter:

- Load balancing on clients and servers
- Fail-overs
- Circuit breaker
- Bulkhead usage
- Timeout handling

It will fail, no doubt!

When developing an application, we often spend most of the time on the *passing* code path, as the code path gives the application its actual feature. However, it is important to not forget all the unexpected cases. It can sound weird to try to solve something we don't control but, here, the idea is to follow the Murphy's law which is often summarized as follows: *anything that can go wrong, will go wrong*. It doesn't mean that the system will never work, but it means that if there is a potential issue, it will become your reality one day or another.

In terms of a modern system and, more particularly, Java EE deployment, the typical consequence is that you can lose the connectivity to a related resource or application. Another common failure case you can desire to address is about the JVM failing (no more memory, OS issue, and so on), but this is linked to the infrastructure (potentially Kubernetes), and it is beyond the scope of this book.

We will illustrate this with a very simple system where three Java EE applications are chained:

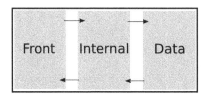

With such an architecture, we can assume that a front layer exposes some customer features or API. Then, the front application delegates the actual logic to an internal system owned by another team. Finally, the internal system relies on a data system which is again owned and developed by another team.

 It is not rare to use the same sort of architecture, but with external systems. In such a case, you often have a support phone number, but it is rarely as efficient as calling a colleague, which makes you even more dependent on this system/company in the case of a failure.

What is important with such systems is that if the data fails (because the data engineers did an upgrade that didn't work as expected), then all the internal systems will start failing because the data doesn't answer anymore. Transitively, the front system will fail because the internal system fails.

You may think that this will just make the system inefficient and that there is no link with the performance. This is not really the case. In the previous schema, the data system looks quite central. If the company adds a second internal system (let's call it *internal2*), then we can assume that the load on the data store will be multiplied by two. Nonetheless, if the data is not sized for the load increase, it will be slower to answer and will potentially return more errors. Here again, all consumer services, including transitive services, will start being slower, as they depend on the data system.

This is not something you can actually avoid. You can limit the effect of an unexpected failure, but it is almost impossible to guarantee that it will not happen. If you are in a big company with an operation team in charge of all the applications, this kind of issue will likely be sorted by priority and performance degradation will be less important than a failing system. When a distributed system like this starts to fail, each brick often fails slowly, just because of the relationships. Thus, all the applications will be seen in *red* by the monitoring team, which doesn't help them to solve the issue, when only one part of the whole system is failing (our data system in this example). This is why ensuring that your system is ready to fail will make sure that your system is fixed faster if there is an issue, and that the performance impact on the other parts of the system will be reduced if some related application go uncontrolled.

Load balancing – pick the best one

Load balancing is about defining how to select the backend node that will process the request. It can be done on the server or client side, but strategies are globally the same. The fact that it is **Client** or **Server** is mainly a deployment concern because when the **Load Balancer** is an instance (software), then you actually add a **Client** in the chain between the final clients and your middlewares.

At very high level, a **Load Balancer** can be schematized as follows:

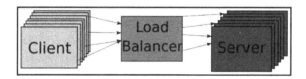

The global idea is to add a layer in between the **Client** and the **Server**, which will orchestrate the way the requests are distributed to the servers depending on different strategies. This picture represents four clients calling the same application through a **Load Balancer**, which will delegate the request processing to three servers (one server will process two of the four client requests).

This is a common representation of server-side load balancing, but it can also be applied on the client side. The only difference is that the **Load Balancer** will be *deployed* inside the JVM of the client and, instead of taking the incoming requests through a network protocol (websocket, HTTP, and so on), it will take it from the inside of the JVM (normal method invocation).

Transparent load balancing – client versus server

The main advantage of using a server load balancer is that the clients don't really care about a load balancer. Concretely, all the clients will use the same endpoint (let's say, *quote-manager.demo.packt.com*) and the load balancer will distribute the requests without requiring any knowledge of the clients. This is very important in terms of the infrastructure, since you can update your infrastructure without notifying or updating the clients (which can be impossible if not owned by your own system).

For instance, if you start with two machines and decide to add a third one a month later because you get more load or to support the *black friday* additional load, then you will just register this third machine against the load balancer and it will distribute the work load against the three machines instead of only two. It is also true for the opposite way: if you need to do some maintenance on a machine, you can remove it from the cluster behind the load balancer, assuming that removing one machine still supports the load, but it should be taken into account during the sizing phase of the infrastructure. Then, do your maintenance offline, and once done, just add back the machine into the cluster.

So, this analysis makes it sound like server load balancing is the best solution and the one to choose. However, modern systems have efficient client-side load balancers if you own the clients (which is often the case for microservice-oriented systems). What makes server load balancing strategy better than client load balancing?—The fact that the server can be updated without notifying the clients. This means that if the clients are autoupdated from the server/backend changes, then we achieve the same on the server side. In practice, this is done using a service registry that can enumerate the list of URLs that you can use to contact a service. In practice, the client load balancer will contact this registry service to get the list of endpoints it can use for a particular service and update this list from time to time with a configuration policy close to the pool ones that we saw in the previous chapter. It sill means that this *registry* service must be reliable and should likely use a server load balancer solution, but then, all other services can use point-to-point connection (without an intermediate load balancer instance). In terms of application impact, it means that adding (or removing) a server must imply (de)registration against the registry instead of the load balancer, but it is the same sort of work in both the cases.

At this point, we see that both the client and server load balancing can achieve the same sort of features, so what can be differentiating? There are two main criteria you can use to choose between both:

- Who is responsible for the infrastructure and load balancing? If it is the dev(ops) team, both the solutions will work well. However, if you are working in a company that splits development and operations into teams, you will likely prefer to delegate the part to the operations team and, thus, use a server load balancer, which they will fully control without impacting the application development.
- What kind of logic do you want to put in place inside the load balancer? Server-side load balancers have the most common strategies already implemented and, often, a small scripting language that you can use to customize. However, if you have a very custom strategy (potentially depending on your application state), then you will want to code the load balancing strategy inside the client.

To summarize, client-side load balancing is more impacting in terms of development because you need to handle it on the client side, which means in all the clients instead of a single instance for the server side, but it gives you really more power for very advanced needs.

Common strategies

How to distribute the request is the central piece of a load balancer. In this section, we will go through the most common solutions that you will encounter while configuring a load balancer.

The round-robin algorithm

The round-robin algorithm is certainly the most known of all the strategies. It considers the list of available members of the cluster (the *servers*) as a ring and continuously iterates over this ring each time a request comes.

For instance, if you have three servers
(`server1.company.com`, `server2.company.com`, `server3.company.com`), here is how
the first requests will be served:

Request number	Selected server
1	`server1.company.com`
2	`server2.company.com`
3	`server3.company.com`
4	`server1.company.com`
5	`server2.company.com`
6	`server3.company.com`
7	`server1.company.com`
...	...

You will note that to have a *fair* distribution, the load-balancer strategy must lock or
synchronize the list every time it selects a server. There are other flavors of this algorithm
where the implementation is lock-free but the fairness of the distribution is not fully
guaranteed. However, keep in mind that it is rarely something you'd really care about, as
you want to have something that looks like being fair.

Random load balancing

Random load balancing also takes a list of servers to target but every time a request comes,
it picks one randomly. If random implementation is equally distributed, it leads to a
distribution close to the round-robin solution. However, it can potentially scale better, since
it doesn't need to synchronize the list to pick the *current* server to use.

Link to failover

We will talk more about failover in the next section, but it is important here to mention that load balancing can be used to implement a failover strategy. Here, the goal will be to try the request against another machine if the *current* one fails. This can be sort of seen as round-robin, but instead of using each request as a trigger for the iteration over the hosts (to change targeted instance), a failure would be the trigger. Here is an example sequence using the failover strategy, considering that we have the same three hosts as in the round-robin part:

Request number	Selected server	Status
1	`server1.company.com`	OK
2	`server1.company.com`	OK
3	`server1.company.com`	OK
4	`server1.company.com`	OK
5	`server1.company.com`	*OK*
6	`server2.company.com`	OK
7	`server2.company.com`	OK
...	...	

As you can see in the preceding table, each request is using the same host (`server1.company.com`) until a request fails (request #5), in which case, the algorithm iterates over the host list and starts using `server2.company.com`.

Indeed, there are some variants to this algorithm. For instance, the failed request can be retried (or not) with the *next* host in the list, or you can configure a number of failures to wait before switching the host or even configure what failure means (the default is generally a 5xx HTTP status, but you can also configure it to be any HTTP status > 399, or base this choice on a header or any other part of the response).

Sticky session

Sticky session routing is generally used because of a business use case. The idea is to always route a client to the same backend server if a session is started. Java EE defines three session modes through `SessionTrackingMode`:

- **COOKIE**: The session is tracked through its identifier (`JSESSIONID`) inside cookies, so it hits the browser (client) and is sent with each request in the cookies.
- **URL**: The `JSESSIONID` is sent to the client through the URL.
  Example: `http://sample.packt.com/quote-manager/index.html;jessio nid=1234`
- **SSL**: This uses the HTTPS native mechanism to identify sessions.

Each time, the tracking works by passing a shared *identifier* between the client and the server. If you add a load balancer in between, the communication can be broken if you don't target the same host. Here is a diagram representing this statement:

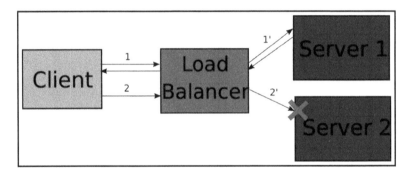

This diagram represents a **Client** serving two requests. The first request (**1**) will hit the **Load Balancer**, which will redirect the request to **Server 1** (**1'**) and the request processing will create a session on **Server 1**. It implies that the response of this first request will create a `JSESSIONID` (or its SSL replacement). Now, the client issues a second request (**2**) and, here, the **Load Balancer** redirects the request, respecting the stickiness of the strategy, to the second server (**2'**). During the processing on **Server 2**, the application tries to access back the session information created during the first request (the identified user for instance), but since we switched the node, the session is not here. So, the request processing fails (red cross).

To ensure that this workflow works, there are two main solutions:

- Ensure that the session state is distributed and shared across all the nodes. This solution sets up a kind of distributed storage space between the servers. It generally either implies a lot of latency (if synchronously done), or some potential miss (failure) if asynchronously done, which can lead to the same issue as the previous schema. It also implies to configure a solution other than the server's default session handling, which is local only out of the box.
- Ensure that the load balancer always hits the same backend node once a session is created. This is what we call the *sticky session* mode. The load balancer will check if a `JSESSIONID` (or an SSL connection) exists and, if so, will store which node created it. If it sees again this identifier in a request, it will redirect the request to the same node ignoring any distribution strategy.

This means that the sticky session mode is often coupled with another strategy, which will define the distribution, since the sticky session only applies once a request has already been served for a client.

The scheduling algorithm

The scheduling algorithm is a wide category of strategies based on some statistical criteria. The idea here is to be more accurate about the way load distribution is done regarding the available resources in the backend servers. The most common criteria are as follows:

- **By request**: The distribution is based on the number of requests served by the node. Note that each server node can have a weight associated with this distribution to bias the distribution if a machine is less powerful than the other.
- **By traffic**: This is the same sort of distribution as the previous one, but instead of counting the requests, it uses the transmitted bytes.
- **By busyness**: This is also based on the number of requests, but only the live number. The least *busy* node is selected.
- **Heartbeat**: This is not a distribution solution per se but is more of an alternate evaluation solution. It uses a heartbeat or *agent* to evaluate the load a node has and, based on this information, it distributes to the node that can handle the most load. It is generally a time statistics, which is, therefore, dynamic and autoadaptive.

Load balancing or proxy – additional features

Even if you set up a load balancing to distribute the load with one of the previous strategies, a load balancer solution is often a full proxy and, therefore, also provides additional features. It generally concerns the server middlewares more than the client ones, but it remains very interesting. Part of the features that you can get from the backend (servers) point of view are as follows:

- **Compression:** Your backend server can serve plain text and the load balancer/proxy layer will automatically add GZIP compression on text resources (HTML, JavaScript, CSS, and so on). Since the client (browser) to load balancer communication is generally slower than the load balancer to server/backend communication, it will allow you to save precious time for these requests.
- **TCP buffering:** Here, the idea is to buffer the response sent by the backend server in the load balancer layer to free the backend from this load and let it serve other requests. This is useful for slow clients that would hold a connection on the backend but not imply any processing/computing work.
- **HTTP caching:** We saw, in the previous section, that HTTP defines some caching. The proxy layer can handle it for you for free without having to request the backend server. This generally concerns only static resources that are moved to the proxy layer in this condition.
- **Encryption:** The proxy layer can encrypt a part of the request to prevent the end users from knowing enough about the backend to understand how it works or even access some sensitive data.

When the load balancer layer adds features more business-oriented than communication/network-oriented, we often call it a *gateway*. However, technically, it is pretty much the same sort of middleware. Here are the features you can find in gateways:

- **Security handling**: The load balancer layer can authenticate and validate the permissions from the request (generally from a header).
- **Version handling:** Depending on the incoming request, the route (requested endpoint of the backend) can change, allowing us to automatically handle the versioning of the backend points.
- **Rate limiting:** This limits the access to the backend with a particular rate, either by application or per user, if the authentication is associated with the rate limiting. It is generally expressed as the number of allowed requests per unit time, for example, 1,000 requests per minute.

- **Concurrent limiting:** This controls the number of requests that can be sent in parallel/concurrently. As for rate limiting, it can be done for the entire application or per user (or other units if relevant). For example, 512 requests.

As you can see there are several features and all are not related to the performance. However, most of them will have performance impacts depending on your final environment. HTTP caching, for instance, will allow your backend server to handle more actual load and, therefore, will scale more easily. The rate/concurrent limiting features can enable you to control the performances and ensure that they are not degraded under unexpected load circumstances, but other features such as the security ones can have a very strong impact on your performance if the gateway layer can use a hardware encryption solution instead of a software encryption, like you would generally do in a Java EE application.

What is important to keep in mind here is to think of the application as a system solution and not to try to put everything inside the application just because it is easier or more portable. Relying on well-optimized hardware solutions will yield good performance compared with optimizing a software solution, which can lead you to use native integration, particularly, when it comes to security and cryptography, and will affect the portability of your application.

Failover

In a distributed system, it is very important to ensure that you know how to handle failures. Java EE applications being more and more connected to other systems, they face this challenge more and more, so it is important to know how you will deal with failover when it happens.

The first meaning of failover is, indeed, to fail over. It can be rephrased as *the capability to switch to a backup system when the primary system fails*. In Java EE applications, there are lots of places where this can be set up, but they are all related to external systems:

- **Databases**: If a database connection fails, how to still handle the requests?
- **JMS**: If a broker fails, what to do?
- **Other network API (such as SOAP or REST API)**: If the remote server is down, what to do?
- **WebSocket**: If the target server closes the connection or fails, what to do?

In general, each time your application relies on something it doesn't control (a.k.a. external systems), it can need a plan B to still be functional if the primary solution is no more responding or working.

There are several ways to handle the failovers, which either rely on selecting another system or are based on some default/caching implementation.

Switching to another system

The easiest implementation of a failover is switching to another system when an error occurs. This is what we saw in the previous section with load balancing. The only condition for us to be able to implement a failover is to be able to identify the error encountered by the system.

Here is an example using the JAX-RS client API of Java EE to illustrate this logic:

```
@ApplicationScoped
public class ExternalServiceClient {
    @Inject
    private Client client;

    public Data get() {
        return Stream.of("http://server1.company.com",
        "http://server2.company.com")
                .map(server -> {
                    try {
                        return client.target(server)
                                .path("/api/quote")
                                .request(APPLICATION_JSON_TYPE)
                                .get(Data.class);
                    } catch (final WebApplicationException wae) {
                        if (supportsFailover(wae)) {
                            return null;
                        }
                        throw wae;
                    }
                })
                .filter(Objects::nonNull)
                .findFirst()
                .orElseThrow(() -> new IllegalStateException("No
                available target
                server"));
    }
}
```

This snippet replaces the direct call to the remote API with Stream. The usage of Stream is fancy here compared with the usage of Collection, since the leaf of the stream will trigger the flow to be executed (but by element) and will enable us to stop the *iteration* if we encounter a final condition early. Concretely, it prevents us from iterating over all the elements if irrelevant, which is exactly what we want for failover. In terms of implementation, here is the flow:

- From a server, we invoke the endpoint we want.
- We process the response of the server. If it requires a failover, we return null; otherwise, we keep the default behavior of the invocation.
- We remove the null response from the flow, since the previous step defines null as a failover condition.
- We use the first available response as being valid, which will avoid doing the invocation for all servers.
- If all the servers fail, then we throw IllegalStateException.

What is missing in the previous snippet is the way to evaluate that we want a failover. In the previous code, we are basing this decision on WebApplicationExceptinon, so the client can throw in the case of an error. A default implementation of supportsFailover() will just be to return true, but we can be more fancy:

```
private boolean supportsFailover(final WebApplicationException wae) {
    final Response response = wae.getResponse();
    if (response == null) { // client error, no need to retry
        return false;
    }
    return response.getStatus() > 412;
    // 404, 412 are correct answers we don't need to retry
}
```

This is still a simple implementation but we use the HTTP status code to retry only if its value is more than 412, which means we will not retry if we get HTTP 404 (not found) or HTTP 412 (precondition failed), since both the cases will lead to sending the same request to another server and getting the same response.

Of course, you can customize a lot of this logic (and this can even be service-dependent), but luckily, Java EE provides you with all you need to do.

Local fallback

The previous failover implementation was considering that there is an alternative system to contact if the primary one fails. This is not always the case and you may desire to replace a remote invocation by a local default in the case of an error. This sort of solution is available in the hystrix framework, which can be integrated with Java EE using the concurrency utilities that we saw earlier.

The high-level logic of defaulting is as follows:

```
try {
    return getRemoteResponse();
    } catch (final UnexpectedError error) {
    return getLocalResponse();
}
```

This is actually a generalization of the previous implementation. Instead of seeing a list of hosts to contact, you need to consider the remote invocations that you can do as a list of tasks. Concretely, we can rewrite this as follows:

```
@ApplicationScoped
public class ExternalServiceClient {
    @Inject
    private Client client;

    public Data get() {
        return Stream.<Supplier<Data>>of(
                () -> getData("http://server1.company.com"),
                () -> getData("http://server1.company.com"))
            .filter(Objects::nonNull)
            .findFirst()
            .orElseThrow(() -> new IllegalStateException("No
            available remote
            server"));
    }
    private Data getData(final String host) {
        try {
            return client.target(host)
                .path("/api/quote")
                .request(APPLICATION_JSON_TYPE)
                .get(Data.class);
        } catch (final WebApplicationException wae) {
            if (supportsFailover(wae)) {
                return null;
            }
            throw wae;
```

```
        }
    }

    // supportsFailover() as before
}
```

Here, we just moved the client invocation to a method and we replaced our stream of hosts by a stream of invocations. The stream logic is exactly the same—that is, it will take the first working result of the list.

The direct gain of such a solution is that, since you are passing tasks to the failover logic and not hosts, you can implement every task as you wish. For instance, if you want to default to a hardcoded value, you can do this:

```
Stream.<Supplier<Data>>of(
            () -> getData("http://server1.company.com"),
            () -> new Data("some value"))
```

With this definition, we will first try to contact `http://server1.company.com`, and if it fails, we will just create a `Data` instance locally.

Before seeing what type of strategy can be used for these fallbacks, let's just take a moment to see what it can mean in terms of code organization.

Fallback code structure

When you were just handling a failover across servers, it was not very complicated, as you would probably have the list of hosts in the `Client` class, and iterating over them was almost natural. Now that we iterate over different implementations, it is less natural and we need an *orchestrator* bean. Concretely, for the previous example, which first calls a remote service and then falls back on a local hardcoded instantiation, we would need the following:

- A remote client
- A local *mock* implementation
- A facade (orchestration) service, which is used everywhere, so we can leverage this failover logic

When you start integrating lots of services, it is not very convenient.

Microprofile to the rescue

Microprofile includes in its scope a specification helping you to handle your fallback logic in a "standard" way. The specification allows to define a fallback method reference or handler on a method in case this last one fails. Here what it can look like:

```
@Fallback(method = "getDataFallback")
public Data getData() {
    return client.target("http://server1.company.com")
                .request(APPLICATION_JSON_TYPE)
                .get(Data.Class);
}

private Data getDataFallback() {
    return new Data(...);
}
```

Here, you will call `getData` from all the consumers of the enclosing service, and if the method fails, the microprofile fallback handling will automatically call `getDataFallback`.

This implementation also supports `@Retry`, which allows you to define how many times you execute the primary method (`getData` in the previous example) before falling back on the fallback handling/method.

This API is nice and straightforward but couples the different implementations together, since the primary and secondary methods are linked with the `@Fallback` API.

Failover extension

With CDI, you can define a small extension, which will automatically handle the failover, exactly as we did with streams previously, without much effort. The extension will be composed of two main parts:

- It will identify all the implementations of a particular logic
- It will register a bean for chaining the implementations in the right order with the failover logic

To do so, we need a few API elements:

- To find a service implementation, we will mark an interface method with @Failoverable to identify that we need to create a failover implementation for this interface; we will also use this annotation to mark the implementations.
- To sort the services, we will use @Priority. We will just use the priority value as a sorting order for the sake of simplicity.

In terms of what it will look like from a user's point of view, here is the previous example:

| ```
@Failoverable
public interface
GetData {
    Data fetch();
}
``` | ```
@ApplicationScoped
@Priority(0)
@Failoverable
public class RemoteGetData
{
    @Inject
    private Client client;

    @Override
    public Data fetch() {
        return client.
        ....
        get(Data.class);
    }
}
``` | ```
@ApplicationScoped
@Priority(1000)
@Failoverable
public class LocalGetData {
    @Override
    public Data fetch() {
        return new
Data(...);
    }
}
``` |

The interface defines the methods that we want to support failover. Then, we have two different implementations with their priority. Such an organization will allow us to add another strategy and insert it into the chain, easily and automatically, without having to modify all other implementations and respecting CDI loose coupling. Now, any user can just inject the GetData bean into any service and call fetch() with automatic failover.

 This example doesn't define any parameter to the method, but this is not a limitation and you can use this strategy with any method, even very complex ones.
```

In terms of caller code, it really looks like any CDI bean invocation:

```
public class MyService {
    @Inject
    private GetData dataService;

    public void saveData() {
        final Data data = dataService.fetch();
        doSave(data);
    }

    // implement doSave as you need
}
```

And that's it! No need to implement the `GetData` failover for the end user; it is done by the extension.

Now that we saw how the API looks, let's see how the CDI allows us to do it easily.

The first step is to define our API; the only API that is not in Java EE is `@Failoverable`. It is a plain annotation without anything special, except that it must be usable on an interface:

```
@Target(TYPE)
@Retention(RUNTIME)
public @interface Failoverable {
}
```

Then, we just need an extension identifying the implementations of the interfaces decorated with this annotation, sorting them, and defining a bean for each interface:

```
public class FailoverExtension implements Extension {
  private final Map<Class<?>, Collection<Bean<?>>> beans = new
  HashMap<>();
  private final Annotation failoverableQualifier = new
  AnnotationLiteral<Failoverable>() {
  };

  // ensure our @Failoverable annotation is qualifying the beans who
  used this
  annotation
  // to avoid any ambiguous resolution during the startup
  void addQualifier(@Observes final BeforeBeanDiscovery
  beforeBeanDiscovery) {
    beforeBeanDiscovery.addQualifier(Failoverable.class);
  }

  // find all API we want to have support for failover
```

```
void captureFailoverable(@Observes
@WithAnnotations(Failoverable.class) final
ProcessAnnotatedType<?> processAnnotatedType) {
  final AnnotatedType<?> annotatedType =
  processAnnotatedType.getAnnotatedType();
  final Class<?> javaClass = annotatedType.getJavaClass();
  if (javaClass.isInterface() &&
  annotatedType.isAnnotationPresent(Failoverable.class)) {
    getOrCreateImplementationsFor(javaClass);
  }
}

// find all implementations of the failover API/interfaces
void findService(@Observes final ProcessBean<?> processBean) {
  extractFailoverable(processBean)
      .ifPresent(api ->
      getOrCreateImplementationsFor(api).add(processBean.getBean()));
}

// iterates over all API and create a new implementation for them
which is
added
// as a new CDI bean with @Default (implicit) qualifier.
// to do that we use the new CDI 2.0 configurator API (addBean())
which allows
// us to define a bean "inline".
void addFailoverableImplementations(@Observes final
AfterBeanDiscovery
afterBeanDiscovery, final BeanManager beanManager) {
  beans.forEach((api, implementations) ->
      afterBeanDiscovery.addBean()
        .types(api, Object.class)
        .scope(ApplicationScoped.class)
        .id(Failoverable.class.getName() + "(" + api.getName() + ")")
        .qualifiers(Default.Literal.INSTANCE, Any.Literal.INSTANCE)
        .createWith(ctx -> {
          final Collection<Object> delegates =
          implementations.stream()
              .sorted(Comparator.comparingInt(b -> getPriority(b,
              beanManager)))
              .map(b -> beanManager.createInstance()
                  .select(b.getBeanClass(),
                  failoverableQualifier).get())
              .collect(toList());
          final FailoverableHandler handler = new
          FailoverableHandler(delegates);
          return Proxy.newProxyInstance(api.getClassLoader(), new
          Class<?>[
```

```
            ]{api}, handler);
          }));
    beans.clear();
  }


  // helper method to extract the priority of an implementation
  // to be able to sort the implementation and failover properly
  // on lower priority implementations
  private int getPriority(final Bean<?> bean, final BeanManager
  beanManager) {
    final AnnotatedType<?> annotatedType =
    beanManager.createAnnotatedType(bean.getBeanClass());
    return
  Optional.ofNullable(annotatedType.getAnnotation(Priority.class))
        .map(Priority::value)
        .orElse(1000);
  }


  // if the api doesn't have yet a "bucket" (list) for its
  implementations
  // create one, otherwise reuse it
  private Collection<Bean<?>> getOrCreateImplementationsFor(final Class
  api) {
    return beans.computeIfAbsent(api, i -> new ArrayList<>());
  }


  // if the bean is an implementation then extract its API.
  // we do it filtering the interfaces of the implementation
  private Optional<Class> extractFailoverable(final ProcessBean<?>
  processBean) {
    return
  processBean.getBean().getQualifiers().contains(failoverableQualifier)
    ?
        processBean.getBean().getTypes().stream()
          .filter(Class.class::isInstance)
          .map(Class.class::cast)
          .filter(i -> i.isAnnotationPresent(Failoverable.class))
          .flatMap(impl -> Stream.of(impl.getInterfaces()).filter(i ->
          i !=
          Serializable.class))
          .findFirst() : Optional.empty();
  }
}
```

This extension has four main entry points:

- `captureFailoverable`: This will ensure that any `@Failoverable` interface is registered and will automatically get a default implementation even if there is no service implementing it. It avoids having a `bean not found` error at the time of deployment and will instead throw our failover implementation exception to ensure a consistent exception handling for all our beans. Note that it only works if the scanning mode of the module containing the interface includes interfaces (that is, not `annotated`). If not, we may get `UnsatisfiedResolutionException` or equivalent during deployment.

- `findService`: This captures all the implementations of a `@Failoverable` interface.

- `addFailoverableImplementations`: This adds a bean with the `@Default` qualifier implementing the `@Failoverable` interface.

- `addQualifier`: This just adds our `@Failoverable` API as a qualifier to avoid ambiguous resolutions, since all the services (implementations) will implement the same API and we want to use the `@Default` qualifier (implicit qualifier) for our facade. Note that we could have added `@Qualifier` on the annotation as well.

Also, to register this extension, don't forget to create a `META-INF/services/javax.enterprise.inject.spi.Extension` file containing the fully qualified name of the class.

The implementation of the facade bean is done with a proxy. All the failover logic will be passed to the handler, which takes, as input, a list of delegates that are actually the implementations we identified in `findService`:

```
class FailoverableHandler implements InvocationHandler {
    private final Collection<Object> delegates;

    FailoverableHandler(final Collection<Object> implementations) {
        this.delegates = implementations;
    }

    @Override
    public Object invoke(final Object proxy, final Method method, final Object[]
    args) throws Throwable {
        for (final Object delegate : delegates) {
            try {
                return method.invoke(delegate, args);
            } catch (final InvocationTargetException ite) {
```

```
            final Throwable targetException =
            ite.getTargetException();
            if (supportsFailover(targetException)) {
                continue;
            }
            throw targetException;
        }
    }
    throw new FailoverException("No success for " + method + "
    between " +
    delegates.size() + " services");
}

private boolean supportsFailover(final Throwable targetException) {
    return
targetException.getClass().isAnnotationPresent(Failoverable.class);
    }
}
```

This implementation is probably the most straightforward:

- The list of delegates is already sorted (see the previous extension).
- It iterates over the delegate and tries to do the invocation for each of them; the first one to succeed provides the returned value.
- If no invocation succeeds, then `FailoverException` is thrown, which includes the case where no implementation was provided (that is, the `delegates` list is empty).
- If an exception is thrown, it is tested to see if the failover should occur and the next delegate should be used. In this implementation, it is done by ensuring that the exception has `@Failoverable` on it, but it could also test some well-known exceptions such as `WebApplicationException` or `IllegalStateException`, for instance.

Fallback handling – caching, an alternative solution

In the previous subsection, we saw how to handle a fallback using another strategy, which can be a hardcoded default value, or can be an alternative way to compute the service, including how to contact another service from another provider potentially. This is the straightforward implementation of a failover.

However, if you step back and think about why you set up some failover mechanisms, you'll realize that it was to ensure your service can run even if an external system is down. Therefore, there is another solution, which is not a failover, strictly speaking, but fulfills the same goal, that is, caching. We saw in a previous section how JCache can help your application go faster, enabling you to bypass computation. Caching data from external systems also allows you to be more resilient and can potentially prevent you from implementing a failover mechanism for them.

Let's take a very simple case to illustrate this. In our quote application (`Chapter 1`, *Money – The Quote Manager Application*), we grab the list of symbols to use from CBOE and query Yahoo!Finance to get the price of each quote. If one of the two services is down, then we don't get any price update. However, if we've already executed this logic once, then the price and the list of symbols will be in our database, which is a sort of *persistent caching*. This means that our application, which serves the price of quotes through our JAX-RS endpoint, will still work for clients even if the background update process fails. If we want to go one step further, we can update this logic to fall back on selecting all the symbols of the database if the CBOE service is no more available, which will allow the application to at least get price updates and still be more accurate than if we fail the whole update process because CBOE is down but not Yahoo!Finance.

More generally, if a remote system is not fully reliable and data can be cached, which implies that the data is regularly (re)used and can be a bit outdated for your business, then caching is a very good alternative to failover.

In terms of implementation, you have two main options:

- Manually handle the cache and the fallback (not recommended)
- Use the cache as a data source and fall back on the external system if the data is outdated or missing

The first option is plain failover handling but the fallback implementation is based on cache access. This solution, indeed, considers that you'll fill the cache when the primary source works; otherwise, the fallback will just return `null`.

The second option can be implemented through the solutions we saw in the previous part, either using JCache CDI integration or the `Cache` API as the primary source manually in your application. You will note that this reverses the failover paradigm, as the primary source (remote system) becomes secondary because the cache is checked first. But that's how caching works and if the remote system supports caching, you will, most of the time, get more benefit from it.

To provision the cache, you can use the `@CacheResult` API but don't forget to add `skipGet=true` to just provision the cache and not bypass the logic. For instance, here is what it can look like:

```
@ApplicationScoped
public class QuoteServiceClient {
    @Inject
    private Client client;

    @CacheResult(skipGet = true)
    public Data fetch() {
        return client.target(....)....get(Data.class);
    }
}
```

Enforcing JCache to skip the get phase of the interceptor associated with `@CacheResult` enables you to put the result in the cache when the method succeeds, but to not use the cached data if it is already in the cache. Therefore, if this service is chained with a fallback service reading the data from the cache, it will correctly implement the failover based on the cached data.

However, note that there is a trick here—you need to use the right cache name and key. To do so, don't hesitate to just use another method relying on JCache as well:

```
@ApplicationScoped
public class QuoteServiceCache {

    @CacheResult(cacheName =
    "com.company.quote.QuoteServiceClient.fetch()")
    public Data fetch() {
        return null;
    }
}
```

The implementation is quite straightforward; it returns `null` to represent it doesn't have any data if it is not already in the cache. An alternative implementation could be to throw an exception, depending on the caller behavior you want to provide. Then, to ensure that we use the same cache as the previous primary service, we name the cache with the previous method's name. Here, we used the default name for the primary service and set this name to the secondary service but you can also use a more business-oriented cache name through the `cacheName` configuration that we saw in the Chapter 6, *Be Lazy; Cache Your Data.*

Now, if we go back to the caching-first solution, reversing the primary and secondary sources, we can implement it a bit differently. If the cache is the source, we can still use the CDI integration, but the provisioning of the cache (which is the secondary source now) can be done through a native JCache mechanism. Concretely, our service can look as follows:

```
@ApplicationScoped
public class QuoteServiceClient {
    @Inject
    private Client client;

    @CacheResult
    public Data fetch() {
        return client.....get(Data.Class);
    }
}
```

This is the standard way of using it, but there is an alternative way to do it that would also work better with manual cache handling—that is, without CDI integration. Instead of using the method as a fallback and cache its result, we programmatically set the way the cache is lazily provisioned when configuring the cache. In this case, our service can become the following:

```
@ApplicationScoped
public class QuoteServiceClient {
    @CacheResult
    public Data fetch() {
        return null;
    }
}
```

Yes, you saw it correctly: we don't even implement the loading logic into the service! So where does it go? This service will trigger `cache.get(...)`, so we need to inject our data when `get()` is called if the data is not already available. To do so, we can use the `CacheLoader` API, which is initialized on the cache itself.

To configure the cache, you can use a custom `CacheResolver` (see the previous chapter for more details), which will set `CacheLoader` into the cache configuration:

```
new MutableConfiguration<>()
  .setCacheLoaderFactory(new FactoryBuilder.SingletonFactory<>(new
QuoteLoader()))
```

The loader implementation can now be the following:

```
@ApplicationScoped
public class QuoteLoader implements CacheLoader<QuoteGeneratedCacheKey,
Quote> {
    @Inject
    private QuoteClient client;

    @Override
    public Quote load(QuoteGeneratedCacheKey generatedCacheKey) throws
    CacheLoaderException {
        return client.load(key.extractSymbol());
    }

    @Override
    public Map<QuoteGeneratedCacheKey, Quote> loadAll(final Iterable<?
  extends
    QuoteGeneratedCacheKey> iterable) throws CacheLoaderException {
        return StreamSupport.stream(
            Spliterators.spliteratorUnknownSize(iterable.iterator(),
            Spliterator.IMMUTABLE), false)
                .collect(toMap(identity(), this::load));
    }
}
```

The `loadAll` method just delegates to the `load` method, so it is not very interesting, but in some cases you can bulk-load multiple values at once and it makes sense to have a different implementation. The `load` method delegates the loading to a CDI bean. We can consider that we call the remote service here without any failover.

The important point for this solution is to have a custom `GeneratedKey` key to be able to unwrap it and extract the business key (`extractSymbol()` in the previous example) to be able to execute the actual business. As a quick reminder of the previous chapter, `GeneratedKey` is the key deduced from the method signature in JCache CDI integration, so you need to ensure you can work with such a key using `@CacheResult`. As we saw in Chapter 6, *Be Lazy; Cache Your Data*, using a custom `CacheKeyGenerator` allows you to fulfill this requirement for this solution.

In terms of usage, when should you use `CacheLoader` instead of a method implementation that behaves as an implicit cache loader after all? The cache loader makes more sense when you don't use the CDI integration because, in such a case, you manipulate a more natural key (such as a string for symbols) and get the same behavior:

```
Cache<String, Quote> quotes = getNewQuoteCacheWithLoader();
Quote pckt = quotes.get("PCKT");
```

If the cache is set up to load the data from a remote service if not already present in the cache, then the second line of this snippet will call the remote service and transparently initialize the cache with the data.

 This kind of caching usage also works in the case of a remote service, which is rate-limited. It will allow you to rely on its data more than you would be allowed to without a cache. For instance, if the service accepts only 1,000 requests per minute with your credentials, you can, with the cache, call it 10,000 times per minute.

Circuit breaker

The circuit breaker involves allowing the application to disable a code path if it is known or estimated as failing.

For instance, if you call a remote service and this service has failed 10 times already, then you can say: *don't call this service anymore for 5 minutes*. The main idea is to bypass errors when possible.

A circuit breaker generally has three states:

- **CLOSED**: The system is considered to be working, so use it (default case).
- **OPEN**: The system is considered not working, so bypass it.
- **HALF-OPEN**: The system must be reevaluated. Try an invocation: if it fails, go back to the OPEN state; otherwise, go to the CLOSED state.

Then, all the conditions to go from a state to the other are configurable. For instance, what triggers a CLOSED state depends on the way you configure it (it can be an exception, an HTTP status, a timeout, and so on). The same applies for when the system enters into the HALF-OPEN state—it can be a timeout, a number of requests, and so on.

There are multiple available implementations of circuit breaks but the most known ones for Java EE are in these projects:

- Hystrix
- Failsafe
- Microprofile fault-tolerant specification
- commons-lang3 project.

Using a circuit breaker is important for the system health to ensure that your system is always healthy even if one functionality is not. However, it can also be used for performance because it will keep them under control if the system starts failing and avoid a domino effect where each connection between a failing system and another system implies the other system to fail too. To ensure that the impact of the circuit breaker is as expected, you need to associate two solutions with it:

- A failover solution to ensure that your system behaves correctly (as much as possible, since it is not always feasible)
- A monitoring solution to ensure that you properly report that you are no more fully functional to let the support/operation team efficiently work and enable your circuit breaker to automatically recover once the failing system is fixed

Bulk head

Bulk head is a pattern designed to ensure that no part of the system deeply impacts other system areas. The name comes from a common solution used in ships to ensure that if there is a hole in the hull, it doesn't lead to the boat sinking.

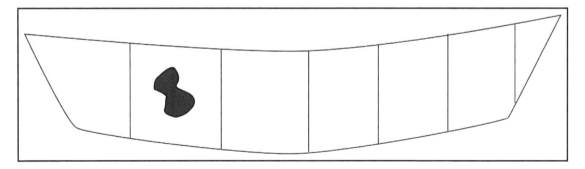

Here, for instance, the second area has a hole and the water is coming into the section but the boat will not sink, as the other sections are isolated.

The Titanic used this technique but the isolation was not fully done from down to top for passengers and crew members comfort. And we all know the outcome of that choice. That is why, if you go with isolation, it is important to make sure that it is complete; otherwise better not do anything.

What does it mean for an application? It means that each service that can sink your application should be isolated from the other ones. This isolation is mainly about the execution and, therefore, the execution environment of the service invocation. Concretely, it is generally about which pool (thread, connection, and so on) and which context to load. To be able to isolate services, you need to be able to identify which service you are calling. If we take our quote manager application, we can identify the *quote finder* service, which can be isolated from the *quote update* service, for instance. This is a business criteria for the isolation, but in practice, you will often want to go further to isolate the execution of your services, including the use of the tenants. It is not rare to want to use a different pool for different tenants. This is actually often even related to different contracts clauses.

To illustrate this concept in a Java EE application, we will update our `QuoteResource#findId` method to apply this pattern. The first step will be to isolate the invocation from the servlet container context/threads. To do so, we will make the method asynchronous, using the JAX-RS `@Suspended` API and a Java EE concurrency utilities thread pool:

```
@Resource(name = "threads/quote-manager/quote/findById")
private ManagedExecutorService findByIdPool;

@GET
@Path("{id}")
public void findById(@PathParam("id") final long id,
                     @Suspended final AsyncResponse response) {
    findByIdPool.execute(() -> {
        final Optional<JsonQuote> result = quoteService.findById(id)
              .map(quote -> {
                    final JsonQuote json = new JsonQuote();
                    json.setId(quote.getId());
                    json.setName(quote.getName());
                    json.setValue(quote.getValue());
                    json.setCustomerCount(ofNullable
                    (quote.getCustomers())
                    .map(Collection::size).orElse(0));
                    return json;
              });
        if (result.isPresent()) {
            response.resume(result.get());
        } else {
```

```
        response.resume(new
        WebApplicationException(Response.Status.NO_CONTENT));
    }
});
}
```

Here, we created and configured, into the container, a dedicated pool for a part of the application called `threads/quote-manager/quote/findById`. The `findById` method executes its original logic in a task submitted to this dedicated pool. Using the JAX-RS asynchronous API, we manually `resume` the request response, since the container doesn't handle the execution of the logic anymore, but we do it ourselves.

This implementation works only if the thread pool has a maximum size to ensure that the execution is controlled. If you use an unbounded thread pool, this will not help control your application at all.

There are other ways to implement a bulkhead not relying on different threads, such as using `Semaphore` as we saw in the threading chapter, but they don't allow you to isolate the application logic from the container threads. Thus, it can have side-effects on the overall application (or even cross-applications if you use the same HTTP container thread pool). The main advantage of using a no thread-related implementation is that it is generally faster even if it doesn't isolate the executions as well as the thread-based implementation. Here again, make sure to benchmark your application to know which implementation best fits your case.

Timeouts

The last and very important criteria to ensure control over the performance and to ensure that the performance is bounded (your application doesn't start being very slow) is related to timeouts.

An application has timeouts everywhere even if you don't always see them:

- The HTTP connector, or any network connector in general, has timeouts to force the release of clients connected for too long.
- Databases generally have timeouts as well. It can be a client-side (network) timeout or a server-side setting. For instance, MySQL will cut any connection that lasts for more than 8 hours by default.
- Thread pools can handle timeouts if an execution is too long.
- The JAX-RS client supports vendor-specific timeout configuration to avoid blocking the network later.

Configuring timeouts enables you to ensure that if something starts being wrong in your system, including a remote system being slow or unresponsive, you will be able to respond in a correct (or, at least, bounded) duration. Of course, you will cumulate all the timeouts in the worst case, considering you use them synchronously and not concurrently, but at least, you will know the maximum duration a request can take in your system.

Timeouts for code without timeouts

A trick for adding timeouts to methods that weren't designed to handle timeouts is to use a thread pool. A thread pool allows you to execute tasks and wait for them for a certain duration. Of course, it means that you will block the calling thread, but you will block it for a certain amount of time:

```
return threadPool.submit(() -> {
    // execute your logic
    }).get(10, TimeUnit.SECONDS);
```

This code will compute some value or throw `TimeoutException` if it lasts for more than 10 seconds. Wrapping any code inside such a block will allow you to handle a timeout for any sort of code. However, this doesn't mean that the wrapped code ends after 10 seconds; it just means that the caller doesn't wait for it anymore. The task, however, is still submitted and can last forever taking a thread. To stop you from needing to keep a reference on `Future`, the `submit` method will return and cancel the task, allowing you to interrupt the execution thread:

```
Future<?> task = null;
try {
    task = threadPool.submit(() -> {
        // some logic
    });
    task.get(10, TimeUnit.SECONDS);
} catch (final TimeoutException te) {
    if (task != null) {
        task.cancel(true);
    }
}
```

Now, if we get a timeout, we can cancel the running task, so as to not leak tasks, and potentially fill the thread pool even if we have timeouts.

If you want to handle some failover on a timeout, you can add it in a block that catches `TimeoutException`.

Summary

In this chapter, we saw that properly handling faults in an application is the key to ensuring that you can still control the response time of your system and keep it under control in any circumstance. This is true for any system but with the spreading of microservices, it is even more true for systems using this architecture.

Well, defining how your Java EE application is deployed and what is needed to ensure you control all the potential failures of your system is a full time job; we often forget to work on the *main* codepath of our applications, but doing so ensures that the production deployment and behavior are sane.

This chapter showed you some common patterns used to handle fault tolerance more or less transparently and reliably.

Logging is another important factor when issues start popping up in a system. It will allow you to investigate what happened and identify the issue to fix it. However, logging too much or without reflection can be very costly. This is what our next chapter will be about: ensure that you are correctly leveraging your logging regarding the performance factor.

8

Loggers and Performances – A Trade-Off

Logs are probably one of the most important parts of an application, whatever technology it uses. Why is that? Because without logs, you have no idea what your application is doing or why your application is behaving in a particular way.

Of course, we saw in `Chapter 3`, *Monitor Your Application*, how to instrument the application to get some monitoring information about the JVM and application, but it was very technical and mainly performance or tracking oriented. This is important but rarely enough and generally not helpful enough for operation and support teams who generally prefer a higher level view of application tracing. This is where logging enters into the game. However, it is important that you correctly use it and configure it, so that you do not impact your application performance.

You may think that Java EE and logging are not directly related, but actually it is probably way more important to ensure you understand what logging is doing in an EE context. The main things you get from an EE container are services. Services are code and therefore have the same kind of constraints as your own code. You can take any Java EE library, and most services, if not all, will use some logger to let you understand what happens without having to look into the code. There are even some coding practices of some vendors that require you to log each time a method starts and stops. Long story short, loggers and log statements are everywhere, whether you wrote it yourself in your codebase or not because they are present in a library codebase.

Therefore, in this chapter, we will cover:

- When to use logging
- The work implied by a logging statement
- Some common and useful performance-related logging patterns
- Some well-known logging libraries and how to configure them in EE land

I log, you log, they log

When do we use logging? This very technically-oriented question should be rephrased this way: *when do we provide information about what the application is doing?* This is exactly what logging is used for; it lets the user know what the application did at some point.

This is something we, as developers, often forget because we are focused on the feature we are implementing. But if the application intends to hit production, it is crucial to not forget to make sure the operation teams can work with it very efficiently as well. Don't forget that if the development takes six months, the production will probably last for some years and the cost of an incident is way higher than a small delay before the production is launched. Therefore, investing in a system communicating enough information is often worth it.

However, logging is not a trivial task to underestimate. All the difficulty is about:

- Designing messages that are meaningful for someone with poor—or without—knowledge of the code
- Ensuring the message is logged, whatever happens
- Log error cases which can be *invisible* in the code by default

Let's just take a moment on this last case to deal with a more and more common use case in EE applications, particularly in microservice environments—an HTTP client in a REST endpoint:

```
@Path("quote")
@ApplicationScoped
public class QuoteEndpoint {
    @Inject
    private Client client;

    @GET
    @Path("{id}")
    public Quote getQuote(@PathParam("id") final String id) {
        return client.target("http://remote.provider.com")
```

```
                .path("quote/{id}")
                .resolveTemplate("id", id)
                .request(APPLICATION_JSON_TYPE)
                .get(Quote.class);
    }
}
```

This is a very common pattern used in microservice infrastructure, a service calling another one. This particular implementation is a flat proxy (no additional logic), but it can be used to hide some machine to machine credential or security mechanisms, for instance. What is important to identify here is that a JAX-RS client is called in a JAX-RS endpoint (getQuote). Now, when you think about error handling, what can happen with such code?

If the client call fails because the server returns an error (let's consider an HTTP 404 as the ID is invalid), then the client get() invocation will throw a javax.ws.rs.NotFoundException. Since there is no exception handling around the client invocation, your endpoint will throw the same exception, which means an HTTP 404 for JAX-RS on the server side, and thus, your own endpoint will throw the same exception.

It can be what you want—in the case of a proxy, for instance—but it is not very good in terms of implementation because when you get HTTP 404 responses on the client side (final client, not the endpoint client), then how do you know whether your endpoint or the remote service is broken?

A way to mitigate that side effect is to change the implementation of the endpoint a bit, as in the following snippet:

```
@GET
@Path("{id}")
public Quote getQuote(@PathParam("id") final String id) {
    try {
        return client.target("http://remote.provider.com")
                .path("quote/{id}")
                .resolveTemplate("id", id)
                .request(APPLICATION_JSON_TYPE)
                .get(Quote.class);
    } catch (final ClientErrorException ce) {
        logger.severe(ce.getMessage());
        throw ce;
    }
}
```

This is not a perfect implementation, but at least now, in the server logs, you will be able to identify that the invocation failed due to an error on the remote service. And that is already better than being silent. In real life, you can notify the final client that the error is not your fault and either use another status code or add a header, allowing the client to identify it depending on the type of service you implement. However, what doesn't change is that, at least, logging the error is allowing your application to give enough information for you to investigate where the issue comes from. Then, all the enrichments you can do on top of it (logging format, MDC, and so on) are mainly about making the information easy to find and fast to analyze.

Logging is a simple way—probably the simplest—to communicate from the JVM to outside of it. This is also probably why it is so widely used in all layers of any application. You can be sure that most (if not all) libraries and containers rely on a logger, somewhere. Generally, this is also the first contact you get with your container. When you start it as *empty*, the first thing you see is this output:

```
[2017-10-26T17:48:34.737+0200] [glassfish 5.0] [INFO] [NCLS-LOGGING-00009]
[javax.enterprise.logging] [tid: _ThreadID=16
_ThreadName=RunLevelControllerThread-1509032914633] [timeMillis:
1509032914737] [levelValue: 800] [[
  Running GlassFish Version: GlassFish Server Open Source Edition 5.0
(build 23)]]

[2017-10-26T17:48:34.739+0200] [glassfish 5.0] [INFO] [NCLS-LOGGING-00010]
[javax.enterprise.logging] [tid: _ThreadID=16
_ThreadName=RunLevelControllerThread-1509032914633] [timeMillis:
1509032914739] [levelValue: 800] [[
  Server log file is using Formatter class:
com.sun.enterprise.server.logging.ODLLogFormatter]]

[2017-10-26T17:48:35.318+0200] [glassfish 5.0] [INFO] [NCLS-SECURITY-01115]
[javax.enterprise.system.core.security] [tid: _ThreadID=15
_ThreadName=RunLevelControllerThread-1509032914631] [timeMillis:
1509032915318] [levelValue: 800] [[
  Realm [admin-realm] of classtype
[com.sun.enterprise.security.auth.realm.file.FileRealm] successfully
created.]]
```

What is important here is not really the content of the output, but more that you can control it from the logging configuration. Java EE containers are not uniform on the implementation they use, but most of them rely on **Java Util Logging** (JUL), which is the Java standard logging solution. We will get back to the logger implementations later. But just to continue giving you an idea of why it is not directly done with console output or file management, we will open the GlassFish configuration.

GlassFish, relying on JUL, uses a `logging.properties` configuration. If you use the default GlassFish domain, you will find it in the `glassfish/domains/domain1/config/logging.properties` file. If you open this file, you will see these lines:

```
handlers=java.util.logging.ConsoleHandler
handlerServices=com.sun.enterprise.server.logging.GFFileHandler
java.util.logging.ConsoleHandler.formatter=com.sun.enterprise.server.loggin
g.UniformLogFormatter
com.sun.enterprise.server.logging.GFFileHandler.formatter=com.sun.enterpris
e.server.logging.ODLLogFormatter
com.sun.enterprise.server.logging.GFFileHandler.file=${com.sun.aas.instance
Root}/logs/server.log
com.sun.enterprise.server.logging.GFFileHandler.rotationTimelimitInMinutes=
0
com.sun.enterprise.server.logging.GFFileHandler.flushFrequency=1
java.util.logging.FileHandler.limit=50000
com.sun.enterprise.server.logging.GFFileHandler.logtoConsole=false
com.sun.enterprise.server.logging.GFFileHandler.rotationLimitInBytes=200000
0
com.sun.enterprise.server.logging.GFFileHandler.excludeFields=
com.sun.enterprise.server.logging.GFFileHandler.multiLineMode=true
com.sun.enterprise.server.logging.SyslogHandler.useSystemLogging=false
java.util.logging.FileHandler.count=1
com.sun.enterprise.server.logging.GFFileHandler.retainErrorsStasticsForHour
s=0
log4j.logger.org.hibernate.validator.util.Version=warn
com.sun.enterprise.server.logging.GFFileHandler.maxHistoryFiles=0
com.sun.enterprise.server.logging.GFFileHandler.rotationOnDateChange=false
java.util.logging.FileHandler.pattern=%h/java%u.log
java.util.logging.FileHandler.formatter=java.util.logging.XMLFormatter

#All log level details
javax.org.glassfish.persistence.level=INFO
javax.mail.level=INFO
org.eclipse.persistence.session.level=INFO
```

We will not enter into the way JUL is configured here, but what we can identify from this snippet is that the logging abstraction allows us to:

- Configure where the logs (messages) are going. We can see that `GFFileHandler` is pointing to the `server.log` file for instance, but that the `ConsoleHandler` is also set, which is consistent with the fact that we see the logs in the console.
- Configure the log level, which is something we will detail a bit more later; very high level, it allows you to select the logs you want to keep or not

If the implementation didn't use a logger abstraction, you wouldn't have the choice of the output (handler) and the level selection would be per case (not standardized), which would make the work of the operation teams way harder.

Logging frameworks and concepts

There are lots of logging frameworks and this is probably one challenge integrators have, since the more you integrate libraries, the more you will need to ensure loggers are consistent and potentially go to the same output. However, they all share the same basic concepts, which are important to understand to know how to properly use loggers and how they can impact the application performance in a bad way if you don't take care of their usages.

These concepts can be differently named depending on the framework, but to identify them, we will use the JUL names in this book:

- Logger
- Logger Factory
- LogRecord
- Handler
- Filter
- Formatter
- Level

Logger

The logger is the entry point of the logging framework. This is the instance you use to *write* messages. The API has, generally, a set of helper methods but the requisite API elements are:

- To allow passing a level with the message.
- To allow passing a precomputed message of what is needed to compute a message (it can be a pattern with some variables or a `Supplier<>` as of Java 8). In this last case, the goal is to not evaluate/interpolate the message if not needed and avoid paying the cost of that computation if the message is *hidden*.
- To allow association with an `Exception` (mainly for error cases) to the message.

The most common example of a logger usage will probably be:

```
logger.info("Something happent {0}", whatHappent);
```

This logger invocation is equivalent to the following line, but avoids the concatenation if not needed:

```
logger.info("Something happent" + whatHappent);
```

Then, it will also trigger the sending of the message (`String`) to the final output (console, file, and so on). It may not look that important, but think how many logger invocations you can have in a single request with the multiple and complex layers we saw in `Chapter 2`, *Looking Under the Cover – What is This EE Thing?*. It can be important to avoid all these small operations, particularly because in general, you don't have just a simple concatenation but multiple ones on complex objects.

Logger Factory

The Logger Factory is generally a utility method (`static`) giving you a logger instance.

Most of the time, it looks like this:

```
final Logger logger = LoggerFactory.getLogger(...);
// or
final Logger logger = Logger.getLogger(...);
```

The Logger Factory is either a specific class or the `Logger` class itself depending on the logging framework, but in all cases, it gives you a `Logger` instance. The parameter of this factory method can change, but generally leads to a `String` (a lot of libraries allow a `Class` shortcut) which can be used to configure the log level as we saw earlier in the JUL configuration file.

Why do logger frameworks need a factory and why don't they allow you to instantiate the logger yourself with a plain `new`? Because the way the logger instance is resolved can depend on the environment. Don't forget that most of the logger consumers (the code using a logger) can be deployed in a lot of environments, such as:

- A standalone application with a flat classpath
- A JavaEE container with a hierarchic classloader (tree)
- An OSGI container with a graph classloading

It is always possible, in all logging frameworks, to configure the way the configuration is resolved and thus how the loggers are instantiated. Specially, as soon as you have a container, you will want to handle a global—container—configuration and a *per application* configuration to be able to make one application configuration more specific than the default one. To do that, containers (or logging frameworks when the implementation is generic enough) will implement a custom configuration resolution and let the logging framework instantiate a logger with this configuration.

Typically, in an EE container, you will get a different logging configuration per application. And if the application doesn't provide any configuration, then the container configuration will be used. If you take Apache Tomcat implementation for instance, it will read `conf/logging.properties` by default, and for each application, it will try to read `WEB-INF/logging.properties` if the file exists.

LogRecord

The `LogRecord` is the logging message structure. It encapsulates more data than just the `String` message you passed, allowing you to get the information we often see in the log messages, such as:

- The log level
- Optionally, a log sequence number
- The source class name
- The source method name

- The message indeed
- The thread (often identified by its identifier rather than its name but this last one is not always unique)
- The logger invocation date (often in milliseconds as of 1970)
- Optionally, an exception associated with the logger invocation
- The logger name
- Optionally, a resource bundle if the logger supports internationalization
- Optionally, a call context such as a set of contextual data based on custom values (MDC) or the current HTTP request, for instance

In this list, we find the information we see (such as the message) but also all the metadata associated with the logger call such as the caller of the logger (class and method), the call context (its date and thread for instance), and so on.

Thus, it is this *record* which is passed into the logging chain, as we will see next.

Handler

Sometimes called `Appender`, the handlers are the output implementations. They are the ones receiving the `LogRecord` of the previous part and doing *something* with it.

The most common implementations are:

- The `FileHandler` : Outputs the messages in a file.
- A `MailHandler` : Sends the messages by mail. This is a particular handler that should not be used for a high volume of messages but it can be used with a *particular* logger dedicated to sending some messages under specific circumstances.
- The `ConsoleHandler` to output messages into the console.
- There are more, such as `JMSHandler`, `ElasticsearchHandler`, `HTTPHandler`, and so on.

In any case, the handlers are sending data to a *backend* which can be anything, and the logging framework always ensures you can plug in your own implementation if you need to extend the default handlers.

Filter

A `Filter` is simply a class allowing you to let the `LogRecord` be passed or not. In the Java 8 ecosystem, it can be seen as a `Predicate<LogRecord>`; this class has been in Java since its 1.4 version, far before `Predicate` was created.

It is often bound to a particular `Handler`.

Formatter

A `Formatter` is a class taking a `LogRecord` and converting it into a `String`. It is the one responsible for preparing the content to be sent to the backend. The idea is to separate the *writing* and *formatting* concerns, allowing you to reuse one part without having to create a new `Handler`.

Again, it is often bound to a particular `Handler`.

Level

`Level` is a simple concept. It is the metadata of the log record but also most of the logging components we just looked at. The main idea is to be able to compare the log record level to the level of the component the record goes through to skip the message if it is not compatible. The common (sorted) logging levels are:

- `OFF`: Not directly used by the log record, but generally used only by other components, it disables any log message.
- `SEVERE` (or `ERROR`): The highest log level. It is intended to be used when something bad occurs. A record is logged if the component level is not `OFF`.
- `WARNING`: Generally used when something wrong happened (but is not preventing the application to work); a record is logged if the level of the components is not `OFF` or `SEVERE`.
- `INFO`: The default logging level of a lot of applications, it is used to notify us that something normal but interesting happened.
- `CONFIG`: Not the most used level, it is intended to be used for messages related to the configuration. In practice, applications and libraries often use `INFO` or `FINE` instead.

- `FINE,FINER,FINEST,DEBUG`: These levels are intended to give low granularity information about the application. The message computing can be costly and it is not intended to be turned on in production in general. However, it can be a very useful piece of information when investigating an issue.
- `ALL`: Not used for the log record itself but only for component levels, it lets any message be logged.

The log levels are sorted (associated with an integer) and a log record level is *active* if all the component levels are lower than the log record level. For instance, a `WARNING` message will be logged if the component levels are `INFO` or `FINE`.

Logging invocations

Before looking at how to properly integrate loggers into your application using some common patterns, let's see what a logger invocation will trigger.

A simple logger invocation, like `logger.info(message)`, can be inspected to be represented as equivalent to the following steps:

- Check if the level of the logger is active; if not, exit
- Create a log record (set the message and level, initialize the source of the log, class, method, and so on)
- Check if the message is filtered with a `Filter`; if the filter filters it, then exit
- For all handlers, publish the log record to the handler:
    - Check the level of the handler versus the log record level, if not compatible then exit (note: this check is often done multiple times; it is fast because it is just an integer comparison)
    - Format the log record (convert it to a `String`)
    - Write the formatted message to the actual backend (file, console, and so on)

This high-level drilling down of a single logger invocation shows many interesting things about the loggers. The first one is that using a logger and having levels in all logging components allows the logging framework to bypass a lot of logic if the levels are not compatible. This is true at the logger level, and potentially at the filter level, and finally at the handler level. Then, we can identify that there are two layers where the logic depends on the configuration, and the processing time will be the function of the complexity of these elements, the filtering and the formatting. Lastly, the actual work—and generally the slowest part of the chain—is the backend interaction. Concretely, writing a line in a file is slow compared to the rest of the chain as it interacts with some hardware (your hard disk).

Filters

In JUL, there is no default filter implementation. But some common filters you can find in other frameworks or JUL extensions are:

- A time-based filter:
    - If the log message is outside a time range, then skip it
    - If a log message is older than some configured duration, then skip it (can be useful depending on the work done before the filter in the chain and if the machine has a hot peak)
- A **Mapped Diagnostic Context** (**MDC**) based filter: Typically, if an MDC value is matched (for example if MDC['tenant'] is *hidden_customer)*, then skip the message
- Throttling: If you know you use a handler that can't support more than 1,000 messages/seconds—or if the actual backend, such as a database, can't support more—then you can use a filter to enforce that limitation
- Regex-based: If the message doesn't (or does) match a regex, then it is skipped

These examples are just a short list of potential filters you can encounter, but it illustrates the fact that the complexity can be more or less important and thus the execution duration of the filter layer can be more or less fast.

Formatters

As for filters, there are several formatters, and since it is really about how to convert the log record—the logging API—to the backend representation (String), then it can be more or less pricey. To get a high-level idea about that, here are some examples:

- XML: Convert the log record to an XML representation; it generally uses string concatenation and logs all the record information (logger, thread, message, class, and so on).
- Simple: Just the log level and the message.
- Pattern: Based on a configured pattern, the output is computed. Generally, the logging frameworks allows you to include, in this pattern, the thread identifier or name, the message, the log level, the class, the method, the exception if there is one, and so on.

The default JUL pattern is `%1$tb %1$td, %1$tY %1$tl:%1$tM:%1$tS %1$Tp %2$s%n%4$s: %5$s%6$s%n`. This pattern leads to this sort of output:

```
oct. 27, 2017 6:58:16 PM com.github.rmannibucau.quote.manager.Tmp main
INFOS: book message
```

We will not detail the syntax here, but it reuses the Java `java.util.Formatter` syntax behind the `SimpleFormatter` which was used for that output. This implementation passes, to the formatter, the following parameters:

- Date of the log event
- Source of the log event (`class method`)
- Logger name
- Level
- Message
- Exception

What is interesting with this last type of formatter is that it lets you customize the output and change its formatting depending on your needs. For instance, instead of using the default format on two lines, you could set the format to be `%1$tb %1$td, %1$tY %1$tl:%1$tM:%1$tS %1$Tp %2$s %4$s: %5$s%6$s%n`, then the output would be:

```
oct. 27, 2017 7:02:42 PM com.github.rmannibucau.quote.manager.Tmp main
INFOS: book message
```

The big advantage is to really customize the output to your needs and potentially match a log forwarder like Splunk or Logstash.

To activate this pattern with JUL, you need to set the system property `"-Djava.util.logging.SimpleFormatter.format=<the pattern>"`.

Using handlers

When dealing with performance, it is important to define the trade-off you want in terms of logging. An interesting metric can be to compare the application without any active logging statement versus the ones you want to keep (for production). If you identify that the performance drastically decreases with logging activated, then you probably have a configuration issue, either in one of the logging layers or—more commonly—with the backend usage (such as overusing a remote database).

The handler, being the part *exiting* the application, is the one requiring most of the attention. This doesn't mean other layers are not important, but they are generally faster to check since they often lead to a constant evaluation time.

There are several implementations of handlers, but it is not rare to have specific ones in companies because you want to target a specific backend or you want custom integration. In these cases, you have to make sure it doesn't introduce some bottleneck or performance issues. To illustrate that statement, we will use a case where you want to send the log records to an HTTP server in JSON format. For each message, if you send a request, then you can send many requests as threads in parallel and you will pay the HTTP latency for each logger invocation. When you think that a method can have multiple logger invocations and that a logger can have multiple handlers (you can log the same messages in the console and a file and a server), then you quickly understand this synchronous *per message* first implementation will not scale for very long.

This is why all the backend integrations, which are implying remote operations, are using alternative implementations and generally support some bulking of the messages to send them in chunks (multiple messages at once). Then, the handler reception of the message just triggers an addition in a *stack*, and later, another condition will trigger the actual request (HTTP request in our previous case). In terms of performance, we converted a high latency implementation in a low latency operation, as the operation is as fast as adding an object to a queue.

Logging components and Java EE

It can be tempting to reuse Java EE to implement logging components. It is not impossible, but there are some points to consider before doing so:

- JUL doesn't always support the loading of classes with the container or application classloader, so you may need a facade implementation that contextually loads the container or application classes. In other words, you will not always be able to programmatically depend on CDI, but you may need some reflection which has a cost you want to minimize. So, make sure to keep the results of your CDI lookup if you can.
- In the first chapters, we looked at the Java EE layers. Make sure you don't rely on something too heavy for a logger implementation to avoid being impacted by all this work and to avoid hiding the fact that you have *an application under the application* through your loggers.
- Logging context is not controlled. Generally, you don't know when a logger is used. So, if you implement a component using CDI, make sure you use features available only in all contexts. Concretely, don't use `@RequestScoped` if you don't use the `RequestContextController` to activate the scope yourself. Also, ensure you have configured the *EE* component on a logger only, used in an EE context.

It is not impossible to do a logging-EE bridge, but for logging, we generally want to be very efficient and as raw as possible. See it more as a potential fallback if you can't modify the application than the opposite by default. In a realistic manner, it is better to send an EE event you observe and call a logger from an observer, than the opposite.

Logging patterns

There are but a few important logging patterns you can utilize to try to minimize the logging overhead implied, without any benefit from a functional point of view. Let's go through the most common ones.

Testing your level

The most important thing about a log message is its level. It is the information allowing you to efficiently ignore the messages - and their formatting/templating - if they will be ignored later anyway.

For instance, take this method that relies on loggers at different levels:

```
public void save(long id, Quote quote) {
    logger.finest("Value: " + quote);
    String hexValue = converter.toHexString(id);
    doSave(id, quote);
    logger.info("Saved: " + hexValue);
    logger.finest("Id: " + hexValue + ", quote=" + quote);
}
```

This method is mixing *debug* and *info* log messages. Nevertheless, it is very likely that the *debug* messages will not be activated in production, but *info* messages will be if you use the *info* level as optional messages, then do the same reasoning with the *warning* level. For that reason, it is pointless to log the *debug* messages in most cases. It is also useless to compute the concatenations of these messages as they will not be logged.

To avoid these computations—and don't forget a `toString()` can be complex in some cases or at least `long` to compute—a common pattern is to test the log level in the application yourself, instead of waiting for the logging framework to do it:

```
public void save(long id, Quote quote) {
    if (logger.isLoggable(Level.FINEST)) {
        logger.finest("Value: " + quote);
    }

    String hexValue = converter.toHexString(id);
    doSave(id, quote);
    logger.info("Saved: " + hexValue);

    if (logger.isLoggable(Level.FINEST)) {
        logger.finest("Id: " + hexValue + ", quote=" + quote);
    }
}
```

Simply wrapping the rarely logged messages in a `isLoggable()` conditional block will do a quick test against the logger level and bypass the message computation, and all the logging chains most of the time, ensuring the performance is not too affected by debug statements.

Since Java 8, there has been an alternative to that pattern which is quite interesting: using `Supplier<>` to create the message. It provides a way to compute the message rather than the message itself. This way, the code is more condensed thanks to the lambda which is compatible with the related signatures. But the cost of the string evaluation is not paid anyway:

```
logger.finest(() -> "Value: " + quote);
```

Here, we passed a lambda computing the actual message only if the log statement passed the first test, which is about the log level of the logger. This is really close to the previous pattern but still a bit more costly than an integer test which is generally the `isLoggable()` implementation. Yet, the overhead is not that significant and the code is less verbose, but generally efficient enough.

> If you use the same log level multiple times, it can be worth factorizing the log level check a single time at the beginning of the method, instead of calling it multiple times in the same methods. The more you use a logger abstraction, and therefore go through layers, the more it will be true. Since it is a very simple optimization—your IDE can even suggest you to do it for you—you shouldn't hesitate to do it. Though, don't do it at class level (such as storing the loggable test in a `@PostConstruct`; since most logger implementations support dynamic levels; you could break that feature).

Using templates in your messages

In the previous section, we looked at how to bypass the logging of a message. With JUL, it is often done with the methods called log levels, but there is a more generic log method called `log`, which can take the level, the message (or a key in a resource bundle if you internationalize the messages), and an object array parameter. This type of method exists in all frameworks and most of them will also provide some particular signatures with one, two, or more parameters to make it smoother to use.

In any case, the idea is to use the message as a pattern and the parameters to valorize some variables of the message. This is the feature this log pattern uses:

```
logger.log(Level.INFO, "id={0}, quote={1}", new Object[]{ id, quote });
```

This log statement will replace the `{i}` templates with the ith value in the `Object[]` array.

Using this pattern is interesting as it avoids computing the actual string value if not needed. This solution seems better than the previous `isLoggable()` check in terms of code impact, right? It actually depends on the logger implementation. JUL doesn't support it. But for the frameworks supporting parameters without arrays, they can have some optimization, which would make this assumption right. However, for JUL or all the cases where you have enough parameters to require an array creation, it is not right. The fact that you have to create an array is impactful and therefore it is better to skip it if you don't need it, which means to fallback on the previous pattern or the `Supplier<>` based API.

Asynchronous or not?

Due to modern requirements in terms of scaling, the loggers needed to be enhanced to support a higher message rate, but still needed to be less impactful on the application performance itself.

The first step to reduce the latency of a logger is to make the handlers asynchronous. This is not yet standard with JUL but you can find some libraries providing that feature—some containers like Apache TomEE even provide it out of the box. The idea is exactly the one we described in the section about handlers, compute the minimum context for the log record and push the record in a *queue* in the caller thread, then actually *store*/publish the message in another thread (or threads depending on the backend).

This pattern already solves most of the logger impact in terms of performance, but some logging frameworks (such as Log4j2) go further, making the loggers themselves asynchronous. Since the filtering (and sometimes formatting) is now fully asynchronously done, then the caller duration is way smaller and the performance impact is reduced a lot (still, considering, you have enough CPU to handle this additional work as you execute more code in parallel).

If you add some modern implementation to the asynchronous handling, based on the ring buffer pattern, as Log4j2 did using the disruptor (`https://lmax-exchange.github.io/disruptor/`) library, then you have a solution scaling very well. More you will have threads, more the impact of such an implementation will be significative, even compared to an asynchronous handler (appender for log4j2).

Logging implementations – which one to pick

Logging is one of the oldest topics you can encounter in computer science, but it is also one that has been solved many times. Understand that you will find lots of frameworks about logging. Let's have a quick look at them and see how they can sometimes relate.

Logging facade – the good bad idea

Logging facades are frameworks such as SLF4J (`https://www.slf4j.org/`), commons-logging, jboss-logging, or more recently, the log4j2 API (`https://logging.apache.org/log4j/2.x/`). They intend to provide a uniform API usable with any sort of logging implementation. You must really see it as an API (as Java EE is an API), and the logging frameworks as implementations (as GlassFish, WildFly, or TomEE are Java EE implementations).

These facades need a way to find the implementation they have to use. You can encounter several strategies, such as the following ones:

- SLF4J, for instance, will look up a particular class all implementations provide in their distribution (called *bindings* for SLF4J), and once instantiated it will give SLF4J API the link with the final implementation (JUL, Log4J, Logback, and so on). The issue here is that you cannot have multiple implementations in the same classloader and you cannot just configure the one you want.
- Commons-logging will read a configuration file to know which implementation to pick.
- A global system property-based configuration with a hardcoded default allowing to select the implementation to use.

Using a logging facade is generally a good idea as it allows your code, or the code of the libraries you use, to be decoupled from the logging implementation, delegating the choice of that implementation to the application packager or the deployer. It allows you to run it in all circumstances without you having to care about it during development.

Even ignoring the fact that there are multiple implementations of such an API, which makes things complicated already, their usage is not that elegant depending on the implementation you use. Several implementations will need to fill some parameters that are costly to evaluate.

The best example is the computation of the source class and method. In several implementations, it will be done by creating an `Exception` to get its associated stack trace and, after having dropped the known caller of the logging framework, will deduce the business caller. In a Java EE environment, and due to the stacks it uses to provide a simple programming model, the exception stack can be huge and *slow* to compute and fill (allocate the array). This means that each log message will be slowed down a bit to implement the bridge between this facade API and the actual logger implementation you use.

For that reason, it can be worth checking the implementation you use with such a facade. For the most common one, SLF4J, there are two well-known implementations very well integrated with the API:

- Logback: A native implementation of the API
- Log4j2: Has got an SLF4J direct implementation (binding)

Logging frameworks

As mentioned, there are several logging frameworks you can encounter. The most famous, and the ones you have probably already heard about, are:

- Log4j1: The historical standard de facto, slowly replaced by log4j2.
- Log4j2: Probably one of the most advanced implementations today. Supports asynchronous loggers and has a ring buffer integration.
- Logback: The native SLF4J implementation. It was probably the best choice before log4j2 was done.
- Java Util Logging: The JVM standard logging API. Not the most evolved API, but it works and doesn't require any dependency, though, you may need some custom integrations (handlers) for production. Check out your server which can already provide some solutions here.

Each of these share the concepts we just went through, but may have some small differences. To let you work faster with them, we will quickly go through these implementations to define the semantics used by the framework and show you how to configure each of them. When you do some benchmarks, it is very important to know how to configure the logging and guarantee it doesn't slow down your performance due to a bad configuration.

Log4j

Logj4 (1.x) uses the `org.apache.log4j` base package. Here are the logging concepts we talked about adapted to log4j1 semantic:

Concept	Name
Logger	Logger
Logger Factory	Logger
Handler	Appender
Filter	Filter
Formatter	Layout
Level	Level

Most of the concepts are the same as in JUL, but with a few different names.

In terms of usage, it is the same as in JUL, except it uses another package:

```
final Logger logger = Logger.getLogger("name.of.the.logger");
logger.info("message");
```

What is a bit different is the configuration. It uses a `log4j.properties` or `log4j.xml` in the classpath (by default) which looks like this:

```
log4j.rootLogger=DEBUG, stdout

log4j.appender.stdout=org.apache.log4j.ConsoleAppender
log4j.appender.stdout.layout=org.apache.log4j.PatternLayout
log4j.appender.stdout.layout.ConversionPattern=%-4r [%t] %-5p %c %x - %m%n

log4j.com.packt.quote = WARN
```

With this sample configuration the root logger (default) level is DEBUG and it will use a stdout appender. The appender is using ConsoleAppender; it will log the messages on the System.out and uses a pattern layout with a custom pattern (ConversionPattern). The package com.packt.quote log level is set to WARN. So, loggers using this name or a sub-name of this package will only log WARN and ERROR messages.

Log4j2

Log4j2 was obviously inspired by Log4j1 but was completely rewritten. It still has some differences and it is completely different in terms of behavior and performance. Here is the concept mapping for log4j2:

Concept	Name
Logger	Logger
Logger Factory	LoggerManager
Handler	Appender
Filter	Filter
Formatter	Layout
Level	Level

The configuration has some fallbacks, but the default file is looked up in the classpath and is called log4j2.xml. It uses a different syntax than the XML version of Log4j1, based on the new plugin system of Log4j2, to have a nicer syntax (less technical):

```
<?xml version="1.0" encoding="UTF-8"?>
<Configuration status="WARN">
  <Appenders>
    <Console name="stdout" target="SYSTEM_OUT">
      <PatternLayout pattern="%d{HH:mm:ss.SSS} [%t] %-5level %logger{36} -
      %msg%n"/>
    </Console>
  </Appenders>
  <Loggers>
    <Root level="debug">
      <AppenderRef ref="stdout"/>
    </Root>
  </Loggers>
</Configuration>
```

This is the same sort of configuration as the one in the previous section, but it uses this new syntax that relies on the plugin names (`Console` is the name of the console appender in log4j2 for instance). Nevertheless, we still have the same structure where loggers are defined in a loggers block with the specific root logger, and where appenders have their own block linked to the loggers through a reference/idenfitier (`ref`).

Log4j2 has other nice features such as the hot reloading of the configuration, JMX extensions, and so on, which can be worth a look. It can help you change the logging configuration without restarting the application during your benchmarks.

Logback

Logback is a native implementation of SLF4J and an advanced logging implementation. Here is its mapping with the concepts we talked about:

Concept	Name
Logger	Logger (from SLF4J)
Logger Factory	LoggerFactory (from SLF4J)
Handler	Appender
Filter	Filter
Formatter	Encoder/Layout
Level	Level

Note that logback also has the concept of `Encoder` to link the messages to `byte[]`.

The configuration relies, by default, on a `logback.xml` file in the classpath, looking like this:

```
<configuration>
  <appender name="STDOUT" class="ch.qos.logback.core.ConsoleAppender">
    <encoder>
      <pattern>%d{HH:mm:ss.SSS} [%thread] %-5level %logger{36} -
%msg%n</pattern>
    </encoder>
  </appender>

  <root level="debug">
    <appender-ref ref="STDOUT" />
```

```
    </root>
</configuration>
```

This is a configuration close to the previous one (log4j1, log4j2) and recognizes the same kind of configuration, except the `encoder` layer wrapping the `pattern`. This is mainly because the encoder will pass a `byte[]` value to the appender and the pattern will pass a `String` to the encoder, allowing the implementation to be more easily composed, even if rarely used.

JUL

We used JUL to name the concepts we talked about, so we don't need a mapping table for the concept. Yet, it is interesting to see how JUL is configured since it is used in lots of containers.

Very high-level JUL uses a `LogManager`, which is the Logger Factory (hidden behind the `Logger.getLogger(...)` Logger Factory).

The `LogManager` is instantiated from the class passed to the `java.util.logging.config.class` system property. If not set, the default implementation will be used, but note that most EE containers will override it to support additional features such as a configuration per application, for instance, or a custom configuration, generally dynamic and managed through a nice UI.

The configuration is located with the system property `java.util.logging.config.file` or falls back on `${java.jre.home}/lib/logging.properties`—note that Java 9 used the folder `conf` instead of `lib`. The syntax of this properties file is the same as we saw earlier:

```
handlers= java.util.logging.FileHandler, java.util.logging.ConsoleHandler

java.util.logging.FileHandler.pattern = %h/java%u.log
java.util.logging.FileHandler.limit = 50000
java.util.logging.FileHandler.count = 1
java.util.logging.FileHandler.formatter = java.util.logging.XMLFormatter

java.util.logging.ConsoleHandler.level = INFO
java.util.logging.ConsoleHandler.formatter =
java.util.logging.SimpleFormatter

.level = INFO
com.packt.level = SEVERE
```

At the end of the snippet, we identify how to set a level to a package (the key is just suffixed by `.level` and the value is the level name). The same sort of logic applies to the default logger, which has an empty name, so its level is set using the `.level` key directly. The `handlers` key gets a list of handlers to configure (comma separated). It is generally a fully qualified name of a handler. Then, the two blocks in the middle, starting with handler names, are the handler configurations. It generally uses a dotted notation (`<handler class>.<configuration> = <value>`), but there is no obligation since the handler has access to all the properties through the `LogManager`.

> Apache Tomcat/TomEE `ClassLoaderLogManager` allows you to prefix the handler with a custom prefix value starting with a number. It enables you to define N times the same handler with different configuration, which is not supported out of the box by JUL, which can only define a handler once.

Choosing an implementation

If you can choose your implementation, you should check where you want to send your logs and pick the implementation already doing what you need, or the implementation which has a very close feature. Then, if multiple implementations fit your requirements, you need to check which one is the fastest.

Starting from log4j2 or logback is generally a good choice. Yet, in practice, you rarely have the choice and part of your stack is imposed by your environment (dependencies and containers). Thus, it is highly probable you will need to configure JUL as well. In such a case, a good option is to check if you can reuse your container backbone without being dependent on your container in terms of code (that is, you can use the JUL API and delegate, to your container, the JUL configuration for instance). Then, you need to evaluate if JUL will fit your runtime needs in terms of performance. JUL gets lots of bad reviews on the internet, but it is more than sufficient for a lot of applications asynchronously logging into a file. Don't disregard it without evaluating it against your concrete needs. It can avoid configuration headaches and dependencies in a lot of cases.

Another criteria can be the easiness to redirect all logs to the same logging stack. One of the best ones in that area is log4j2, which supports pretty much all integrations (SLF4J, commons-logging, log4j1, log4j2, and so on).

If you use file-based handlers/appenders, probably the most common use case, you should also have a look at the rotation policies. It is generally configurable and the most common strategies are:

- Per day: Each day, you get a new log file for the handler (mylog.2017-11-14.log, mylog.2017-11-15.log, and so on).
- At restart: Each time the server is restarted, a new log file is created. Note this strategy doesn't work well except for batch instances or no long running instances.
- Per size: If the log file size exceeds some disk space, then create a new one.

Note that all these strategies can often be mixed or accumulated. Only JUL will not support it out of the box, but containers often try to fill that gap. It is not because your container uses JUL that you don't have this feature. Don't hesitate to have a look at your container logging configuration and investigate it before rejecting JUL as an API.

Summary

In this chapter, we looked at why logging is important to get a good and easy monitoring level. We also saw that a logging statement must be as minimally impactful on performance as possible so as not to defeat the optimization and coding you may have done elsewhere in your application.

This chapter gave you some common and simple patterns that can help you to rely, as much as possible, on the logging framework to make sure you maintain good performance.

Finally, we saw that several implementations may need to be configured in your applications, but that they will all share the same concepts, and that it is possible to rely on a single API, or even a single implementation from multiple APIs.

At this point of the book, you know what Java EE does and how to code and monitor an application. Now it is time to look at how you should approach a benchmark. This will be the topic of our next chapter.

9
Benchmarking Your Application

In the previous chapters, we saw how to develop a Java EE application to ensure it could scale later using multiple threads, asynchronous handling, pooled resources, and so on. We also saw how to get metrics on the performance and resource (CPU, memory) usage of your application and optimize the performance thanks to JVM or container tuning, as well as more aggressive techniques such as adding caching to your application.

At this point, you should be able to work on the performance. However it does not mean you are safe to get surprises when going into production. The main reason is that the work we talked about previously is rarely done in an environment close enough to the production or final environment the application will be deployed to.

To avoid these surprises, benchmarks can (or should) be organized, but it is not as easy as taking all we previously learned and putting it all together. It, most of the time, requires more preparation that you should be aware of, if you don't want to lose precious time when you go to production.

In this chapter, you will prepare a benchmark, going through the following points:

- What a benchmark is
- Preparing a benchmark
- Iterating during a benchmark
- What to do after a benchmark

Benchmarking – validating your application against your SLA

Benchmarks often enter into play when you have a **Service Level Agreement** (**SLA**) to respect. The SLA can be more or less explicit. Typically, you may have a very blurry definition of your SLA, such as *the application must provide good user experience*, or you may have them in a very precise manner in a contract, such as *the application must support Black Friday weekend and 10 million users a day, and each user action must be executed in less than one second*. There are even some standards to describe the SLA, such as the **Web Service Level Agreement** (**WSLA**) to define how to measure and expose your SLA.

In any case, if an SLA is identified, and even more so if you have some compensation in your contract if it is not met, it is very important to go through a benchmark phase in your project to make sure you increase your performance when going to production.

 The next and last chapter of the book will deal with the continuous evaluation of your performance and will help you to do it continuously and avoid this *phase* effect. Although, it is still common to have a dedicated phase because of the infrastructure constraints required by a benchmark, so we will consider it the case in this chapter.

At this point, you know that you need to validate the performance of your application and your project manager, or you, has planned a benchmark. But what is this task about?

Benchmark, benchmark, benchmark

Working on performance is not uniform work. We saw that in the previous section; there are lots of tools doing that and each of them gives more or less information, but also has more or less impact on the actual performance. For instance, instrumenting all the code of the application to get metrics on all layers will make the application very slow, but the report very rich. On the contrary, instrumenting only some parts—such as the outbounds—will not impact the application that much, yet the report will give you only a very small set of data. This means that depending on the layer you work on, you will not use the same tools to ensure you have the right level of information.

Thus, we can distinguish multiple potential benchmark types:

- The *algorithm benchmark*: You develop some code sections and want to validate the performance is correct or there is no bottleneck.
- The *layer benchmark*: You develop a layer—the persistence layer, front layer, and so on—and want to ensure the performance is correct before adding another layer or integrating it with another part of the application.
- The *sizing* benchmark: You get the figures of the application performance to identify the number of machines to use. This is directly related to horizontal scaling—this doesn't work as smoothly as for a vertical one since the performance can't be linear. Note that this is exactly the same kind of logic big data frameworks are based on to distribute their work.
- The *deliverable benchmark*: This is the benchmark validating that the application (delivery) and the performance of the final application matches expectations (SLA).

Of course, we can split the sort of benchmarks you can do into more precise categories, but these are the three you will encounter in most projects. Each kind of benchmark will use different tools and will have different preparation steps and output. However, each of them will validate criteria (one or more) against expectations.

In previous benchmarks, we can clearly split the criteria into two very high-level categories, but this split will have a huge impact on the way you drive your benchmark:

- The *development benchmark*
- The *deliverable benchmark*

Even if a benchmark is done at delivery, by definition, this split means that the two first categories of benchmarks we identified are about validating the code is correctly done, and therefore it belongs to developer work in general, and it is rarely split from the development itself. The *layer benchmark* is generally done during multiple development iterations; it stays a development benchmark as it is still about validating an application internally, and not something exposed to the end user normally. The *deliverable* benchmark is about ensuring final performance is acceptable for the end user (or contract). It is therefore different from the previous categories of benchmarks because you need to have a deliverable complete enough to be tested.

In terms of implications, the fact you will work on a deliverable benchmark mainly means you will not be able to do it on *your machine*. What you want is to validate your performance against a contract, so you will need to validate the application on the machine it is installed on.

At this point, it is important not to get confused between a benchmark to validate the SLA and a benchmark to size the infrastructure needed for the application. Both will almost look the same and are organized the same way. But in the case of a *sizing benchmark*, you will define an infrastructure (machine power, memory, and so on) and measure performance to then deduce how many machines you need if you horizontally scale. However, the *SLA benchmark* already assumes the infrastructure is fixed and then you just validate the performance to encounter the SLA. In practice, both are often done at the same time which leads to this confusion between both types of benchmarks. This mainly comes from the fact that developers or project managers have an idea of the infrastructure needed for an application, so the starting infrastructure for sizing is close to the target one, and then the game is only to validate the performance to match the expectations. Nonetheless, if you start a sizing benchmark then you will need another benchmark *phase* to validate the SLA, which can be seen as a second benchmark. Never forget the phase you are in; otherwise, you may change too many parameters at the same time and lose track of the current state of the application (it is crucial to be able to compare benchmark iterations, as we will see later).

Preparing your benchmark

Preparing a benchmark is probably the most important task you will have to do. In fact, if you miss it, it is guaranteed the benchmark will be a failure and useless. Even if tasks are not very complicated in general, they will not be done by themselves. So take your time to ensure they are done before the benchmark starts.

Defining the benchmark criteria

A benchmark is always done to make sure we encounter a metric. Therefore, the first step of benchmark preparation is to *clearly* define this metric.

Defining a metric means clearly defining what is measured and how to measure it.

Defining the metric

Defining what is measured means to define the bounds of the measurement. In other words, when the metric starts and when the metric ends. This can sound simple to do, but don't forget we work in a multi-layer environment and that you can miss some layers if your monitoring is not well defined.

Here are some examples, based on our quote-manager application, where not defining the bounds of the metric well enough can lead to incorrectly validating the application:

- Measuring an endpoint execution duration with a CDI interceptor: You miss the JAX-RS layer
- Measuring an endpoint execution duration with a JAX-RS filter: You miss the servlet layer
- Measuring an endpoint execution duration with a servlet filter if the metric is the processing time of the request: You miss the container processing

These examples are all server-side mistakes but illustrate the fact that being explicit about the metrics is not as trivial as it may seem, since the three mentioned solutions are easy and also very tempting ones.

There is a case that is worse: the client side. When the metric is a client-side metric—often the case for an SLA, since in that case we generally don't care about what the server does if it is fast for the clients—then the measurement definition is very important. The client case implies some infrastructure you don't always control. Thus, ensuring the definition is well done will avoid ambiguities and potential disagreements with customers or reviewers of the benchmark. Here are some examples of different interpretations of the same metric:

- The client execution time is measured from a client connected to the application server
- The client execution time is measured from a client connected to the load balancer in front of the application servers
- The client execution time is measured from a client connected to an API gateway that redirects the call to a load balancer
- The client execution time is measured from a client connected to a proxy in another **Wide Area Network** (**WAN**) that routes the request to an API gateway and so on

Each of these lines adds an infrastructure layer on top of the previous one, and thus, adds some latency for the client. They all measure the *client execution time*. This is why precisely defining the infrastructure, and moreover how the metric is designed, is very important, before starting to benchmark the application.

Defining acceptance criteria

Once you have a metric clearly defined, you need to define the criteria based on that metric that will make the benchmark validated or rejected—is your application fast enough to rephrase it at a high level?

Generally, it is a number that can be expressed as a time unit or percentage, depending on the metric. If the measure is lower (or higher) than this number then the benchmark is rejected.

Most of the time, the metric is not self-sufficient and needs some additional parameters to be able to define the acceptance criteria in a measurable way. Here are some common examples:

- The *client execution duration* must be under 1 second for *64 concurrent users*
- The *client latency* must be under 250 milliseconds when *128 messages per second* are received
- The *insertion rate of the data into the database* must be higher than 1,500 records per second for *two connections*

In these examples, the bold expression is the metric we build our criteria on, and the italic one is another potential metric fixed in the context of the defined criteria (the underlined number).

Of course, it is possible to use more than two metrics in the same criteria and even to make them all vary at the same time. However, this leads to complicated acceptance criteria, and it is generally always possible to rephrase them based on acceptance criteria that are using constants. Don't hesitate to rebuild a criteria database from the ones you get in inputs, to ensure they are easy to validate and measure. A very simple example of this sort of rephrasing can be represented by changing *the client execution duration must be under 1 second for a number of concurrent users between 1 and 64* into *the client execution duration must be under 1 second for 64 concurrent users*. This change is not strictly equivalent and you will need to validate the first statement, but the second phrase is easier to work with, in particular, if you need some tuning. It is worth using this simpler one to start work and to get a rough estimate of your metrics and then, once it passes, just validate the original one.

One criteria, which was not mentioned before, is the *time*. Generally, all criteria are defined for an *infinite* duration. This means you will need to make sure that once they are reached they are respected for *long enough* to assume it will not be degraded after some time. This is something to take into account when you prepare your tooling, as lots of factors can degrade the performance:

- A database that slows down after a certain number of records are inserted
- A cache that is wrongly sized and starts being too big for its configuration
- A badly tuned memory, and so on

All these factors will not always prevent you from reaching your performance in a *short* period of time, but they will likely degrade the performance after some duration.

The idea here will be to ensure you can associate the acceptance criteria with some environment metrics, such as the memory behavior. For instance, you can associate the acceptance of your criteria with memory usage and/or a garbage collector profile, such as the following one:

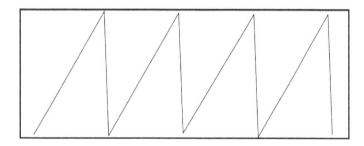

Assuming the X axis is the time and the Y axis the memory used, then this profile shows that the garbage collection is regular (almost each vertical line) and that the memory usage is bounded and regular since it doesn't go over the red line representing the maximum, even after a few cycles.

This sort of definition is rarely self-sufficient as it implicitly defines that this validation happens when the application has already reached the criteria we measure, and that *some time* has passed. Although, it is better than just measuring the criteria and not validating that the result is true for a long-running instance.

Indeed, the best case is to be able to test the application for days, but it is generally costly and not doable. If you can't do it, using this kind of strategy and high-level validation is generally a good fallback.

Defining the scenario

Defining the scenario is linked to the criteria but removes the constant constraint. This allows you to define more complex cases where all metrics can vary at the same time.

A common example is to make the user (client) number a variable moving with the time: *the response time will be constant from 5 users to 1,000 users with an increment of 5 users every 10 seconds*.

A scenario is generally very close to the actual application usage but also harder to work on if you don't encounter it immediately because you are no longer running the application under a constant load. This is why they are seen more as validation checkpoints than work criteria.

Defining the environment

Once you know what you want to test, you will need to set up your application *somewhere* to be able to validate it and potentially optimize it.

It may sound obvious but, here, you have to be very strict on that point and benchmark your application in an environment comparable to your final environment. What does it mean? The same machine, same network setup, same load balancing strategy, same backends/databases, and so on.

Any part of the setup must match where you will run. Otherwise, when deploying in production, you may be surprised by some unexpected factors you should have seen coming and evaluated far before this final deployment. The best case is that the application is not functional, which is generally identified by some smoke tests done after the deployment. The worse case is that the application is functional, but its scalability or performance are affected by an unexpected factor. We rarely run performance tests in a production environment. Thus, limiting the potential error factors due to the environment is very important.

The machines

Before installing any application, you need a machine. From what we just said, the machine must be close to the final one, but what does it mean in the machine's context?

The machine is often seen as its resources:

- The CPU: The computing power the application can use
- The memory: The space the application can use
- The disk space: The local storage the application can rely upon

Your first choice will be to pick the same CPU/memory/disk as the production machine. Yet make sure, before going this way, that the machine is not shared with other services (like another application), which can completely deserve the 1-1 choice in terms of resources (CPU, memory, disk, ...) because the resources would be consumed by the other application. That is to say, if the application is sharing its resources with other software, you will need to find a way to either estimate the available resources for your application and limit them to this amount, or isolate both applications to guarantee each of them will have a well-defined set of resources.

If you rely on Docker/Kubernetes for deployments, these recommendations apply as well, except they are no longer at *machine* level but *pod* level. Also, make sure your JVM is configured to support the pod (or container) settings that require some JVM tuning to use cgroup configuration instead of the whole machine setup—the Java default.

The network

The network is, nowadays, a very important factor in a deployment. If your application is self-sufficient, it is not very crucial, but this is almost never the case. All applications have either an HTTP layer (through a UI or web services), a (remote) database, or are remotely connected to other applications. This is becoming even more crucial in a microservices architecture where some libraries are even designed to handle that part more specifically (with fallbacks, bulhead, and concurrency, as we saw in previous chapters).

In this context, it is very important to be able to rely on a good network. In the same spirit as for the machine selection, you must choose a network comparable to the production network. Assuming the material is almost the same, this means that you will select networks with the same throughput, but this is not enough.

When working with a network, there are two other criteria to take into account very quickly to avoid surprises:

- The *distance* between the machines/hosts: If remote services are *far* then the latency will be increased and the code relying on these services will be *slower*. Ensuring you benchmark in conditions close to the production ones—the same latency and response times—is very important to be able to rely on the figures you obtain.
- The network usage: If the network is used a lot by other applications, the bandwidth available for your *new* application will be reduced, and the performance will be very quickly impacted. A common error in a benchmark is to have a network dedicated to the benchmark, whereas in production it is shared with some other applications. Ensuring you get a consistent setup here will avoid big surprises during your deployments.

Databases and remote services

If your application uses a remote service, which can be a classical **relational database management system** database (**RDBMS**), a NoSQL database, or another application, it is important to make sure you are benchmarking under realistic conditions. Concretely, if we take back our quote-manager application, which uses an RDBMS database, we should not test with local MySQL if our production database will be an Oracle instance. The idea is to get as close to the reality as possible—the latency our production environment will get.

In some cases you (or your company) will own the other services/databases and can tune them to make them scale more. But in some other cases, you use external services you can't optimize, such as CBOE and Yahoo! Finance, in the quote-manager application. In any case, it will always be saner to come to the other node (service/database) manager to ask to make it faster. Realizing you are slow in production because you don't have the same setup as during the benchmark will slow you down and impact you more.

This doesn't mean that *mocking* an external service is stupid. It can be very handy during the optimization phase of your own application, since it will make the external service interaction as fast as is potentially feasible. However, you must ensure you remove the mock when doing your *validation* benchmark.

If you enable the application to be configured to use mocks or fast alternative systems, don't forget to write a log message (in the INFO or WARNING levels) during startup to ensure you can find this information later. It can save you a lot of time and avoid you re-running a benchmark because you are not sure of the *actual* running setup.

During the benchmark, in particular the tuning phase, you will likely configure your pools (connection pools). Thus, it is important to ensure you can rely on the database (or service) scalability. The goal is to avoid successfully passing a benchmark with a pool of 1,024 connections and realizing you can only use 20 connections in production (20 being the maximum number of connections your database accepts).

More than the database/service type, more than the version, more than the environment (OS, machine), you need to make sure the configuration of the database is copied from the production instance (or, if you are in the tuning phase, that the final configuration you used can be copied to the production instance).

The server

We are talking about a Java EE application—but it could be generalized to any application if we talk about *packaging*—so we deploy the application into a server. Even embedded applications are packaging (*bundling*) a server in their deliverable. As with all the previous points, it is important to align it with the target system: the production environment.

Concretely, it means that you shouldn't test against a WildFly server if your production environment is using Apache TomEE or GlassFish.

A server is not far from your application if we talk about the way it is developed and packaged. This means that it embeds several libraries selected by the server vendor. The direct implication is that a server version embeds several library versions. Since Java EE is between ~15 and ~30 specifications, it is at least as important as libraries packed together. Because it is software and you can't avoid some changes between versions—particularly during the early stages of a new specification—you should try to ensure you are using not only the same server as in production but also the same version.

This statement should be extended to all the code that is *outside* of your application. It can include your JDBC drivers, directly deployed in the container, or even some infrastructure/operation team services.

Once you have picked your server, you need to ensure you use a setup (configuration) close enough to the production one. This includes the logging configuration you will need (typically, if you use a log aggregator, you may need a specific log format) and the resources deployed to it. If you auto-deploy resources from an infrastructure service, ensure you deploy them all to have the same thread usage, network usage (if it implies remote resources, such as JMS), and so on.

Finally (and linked to machine selection), ensure the setup is consistent with the production one. If you log on a **Solid State Drive** (**SSD**) disk in production, ensure you log on an SSD during your benchmark.

Automatize your scenarios

Once you have your scenarios, you can just describe them and manually execute them for simple ones you can script or code directly without much effort. But most of the time, you will need to automate them. This is typically the case for load testing scenarios. The advantage of automating them is that you can run them on demand (*in one click*), and thus, it is easy to test and retest them without a huge investment.

There are several tools to automate the scenarios, and they mainly depend on the scenario you need to test. We will go through some mainstream ones you can use if you don't know where to start.

JMeter

Apache JMeter (`http://jmeter.apache.org/`) is a historical solution to load test an application. It supports several modes and is fully written in Java, which makes it easy to integrate and use for most Java developers. It supports main *connections* used by applications:

- HTTP/HTTPS, SOAP/REST for JavaEE, NodeJs, and so on
- FTP
- JDBC

- LDAP
- JMS
- Mail
- TCP and so on

What is immediately interesting for you is that you will be able to test your Java EE application but also your other backends, and thus can compare the performance (of the database and application, for instance) to potentially be able to report that the database is the bottleneck.

It provides a nice UI, which looks like this:

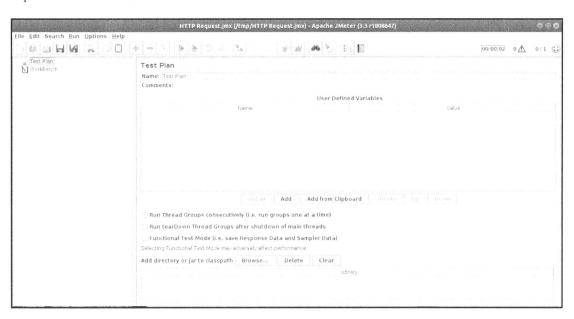

This interface is designed for building your test plans (scenarios); it allows you to create it without any configuration or deep knowledge of the tool. If you start the software from a command line, you will even have a warning message saying not to use it for actual load testing and to use the **command line interface** (**CLI**) for real runs.

Then, once you have started JMeter, you will build a *Test Plan* composed of steps. It will allow you to configure the threads and the way the number of *clients* is defined, add some assertions (validations of the output) to the scenario, and reuse variables between steps (for instance, a first step can get an OAuth2 token used to authenticate the next request or even handle the warm-up of your testing). In the elements you can add to the plan, there are some reports allowing you to get the figures you expect as output from a benchmark, such as the percentage of error, the min/max duration, the throughput, KB/sec, and so on:

Label	# Samples	Average	Median	90% Line	95% Line	99% Line	Min	Max	Error %	Throughput	Received K...	Sent KB/sec
Login page	8	1	0	1	12	12	0	12	100.00%	32.0/sec	59.25	0.00
Authentica...	1	1	1	1	1	1	1	1	100.00%	1000.0/sec	1851.56	0.00
TOTAL	9	1	1	1	12	12	0	12	100.00%	36.0/sec	66.66	0.00

This screenshot represents the *aggregated report* of JMeter which contains statistics about the plan execution—or a subpart of it. What is interesting here is the error rate (100% in the previous example) which allows you also to validate that the execution was *good enough*, that is, there were not too many errors saying we didn't test anything.

Once your plan is defined, you can save it in a .jmx file (JMeter default extension), which will allow you to replay it. At that point, you should be able to *locally* test your scenario (changing the URL of the plan a bit to adjust it to your local instance), but you can't yet test a cluster.

Finally, for real load testing, you will need to use the *remote testing* solution of JMeter. It will allow you to orchestrate multiple client nodes (often called *injectors* since they will *inject* requests into the system). The big advantages are:

- You don't rely on your local machine anymore
- You control which networks are used by the client (it can be the same as the server or not)
- You can horizontally scale, using N client machines instead of one

The last point is very important because of the network usage. When doing HTTP requests, you will use the machine network, and one of the most limiting criteria will be the number of clients per nodes. The more clients you have, the slower they will globally be as they add noise for other clients. That is to say, before launching a full run, make sure to size your injector correctly to establish how many clients you can use per injector node, without being limited by the infrastructure. You will rarely have tons of clients for a single machine in a real deployment. Thus, it is acceptable to have only one or two clients per machine, in some cases.

If you want to download JMeter, you can go to its download page (`http://jmeter.apache.org/download_jmeter.cgi`) on the Apache website.

Gatling

Gatling (`https://gatling.io/`) is an alternative to JMeter. You will find the same features as in JMeter (of course, there are some differences, but we will not list them here). The main difference is that you script your scenarios instead of configuring them, either in an XML file, or visually in a nice UI.

The scripting is based on a **Domain Specific Language** (**DSL**) and relies on the Scala language. This can sound like a **blocker** for a Java developer, since Scala is not very friendly if you have never done any Scala development. However, it is the strength of Gatling compared to JMeter; it is an Akka-Netty-based load testing solution. This means it is coded with technologies trying to be lock-free in their own backbone and enabling the injector code to scale. JMeter was known to be self-limiting in the way it was designed if you were requesting it to scale to too many users. In reality, this is not a huge limitation since, as we saw in the previous section, you will often also scale in terms of infrastructure to test your application reliably. Yet, it is interesting in development and in some highly scaling applications as you will not need so many machines to reach the same level of scalability of the injector.

 This is often a point we forget during a benchmark, and this is why it is important to prepare it before; to ensure the injector does not throttle the benchmark. Otherwise, you are testing the client/injector instead of the server/application.

Just to give you an idea, here is a simple Gatling script:

```
package packt

import io.gatling.core.Predef._
import io.gatling.http.Predef._
import scala.concurrent.duration._

class QuotesSimulation extends Simulation {
  val httpConf = http.baseURL("http://benchmark.test.app.quote
  -manager.io")

  val quotesScenario = scenario("QuotesScenario")
    .exec(http("quotes")
      .get("/quote-manager/api/quote"))
```

```
    setUp(
        quotesScenario.inject(rampUsers(64) over (60 seconds))
        ).protocols(httpConf)
    }
```

This simple script defines a scenario named `QuotesScenario`. It will request our `findAll` quote endpoint.

If you put this script in `$GATLING_HOME/user-files/simulations/packt/QuotesSimulation.scala`, be careful, as Scala uses the concept of packages as in Java, so you need the right nested folder compared to the `simulations` folder. Then you can run `$GATLING_HOME/bin/gatling.sh`, which will scan and compile the files inside the previous folder to find the simulations and ask you to select the one you want to launch:

```
$ ./bin/gatling.sh
GATLING_HOME is set to /home/rmannibucau/softwares/gatling-charts-
highcharts-bundle-2.3.0
18:12:52.364 [WARN ] i.g.c.ZincCompiler$ - Pruning sources from previous
analysis, due to incompatible CompileSetup.
Choose a simulation number:
     [0] computerdatabase.BasicSimulation
     [1] computerdatabase.advanced.AdvancedSimulationStep01
     [2] computerdatabase.advanced.AdvancedSimulationStep02
     [3] computerdatabase.advanced.AdvancedSimulationStep03
     [4] computerdatabase.advanced.AdvancedSimulationStep04
     [5] computerdatabase.advanced.AdvancedSimulationStep05
     [6] packt.QuotesSimulation
6
Select simulation id (default is 'quotessimulation'). Accepted characters
are a-z, A-Z, 0-9, - and _
quotessimulation
Select run description (optional)
Test our quotes endpoint
Simulation packt.QuotesSimulation started...
```

The `computerdatabase` simulations are the default ones; our simulation is the last one. Once selected, Gatling requests some metadata about the simulation, such as its `id` and `description`.

 The first time you launch Gatling, the startup can be lengthy as it will compile the simulation—there are some samples with the default distribution.

When the simulation runs, you will get some progress in the console (whereas with JMeter, you were able to get it in the UI for your tests and see the reports in real time):

```
==========================================================================
=====
2017-11-01 18:14:49 50s elapsed
---- Requests ------------------------------------------------------------
-----
> Global  (OK=54  KO=0 )
> quotes  (OK=54  KO=0 )

---- QuotesScenario ------------------------------------------------------
-----
[############################################################### ] 84%
          waiting: 10 / active: 0 / done:54
==========================================================================
=====
```

These small reports show the progress of the test. We can identify that we are at 84% of the simulation we configured, representing the 54/64 requests (users) we requested and that 50 seconds has elapsed already.

Once the test is finished, a small report is generated in the console:

```
Simulation packt.QuotesSimulation completed in 59 seconds
Parsing log file(s)...
Parsing log file(s) done
Generating reports...


==========================================================================
=====
---- Global Information --------------------------------------------------
-----
> request count 64 (OK=64 KO=0 )
> min response time 20 (OK=20 KO=- )
> max response time 538 (OK=538 KO=- )
> mean response time 63 (OK=63 KO=- )
> std deviation 63 (OK=63 KO=- )
> response time 50th percentile 53 (OK=53 KO=- )
> response time 75th percentile 69 (OK=69 KO=- )
> response time 95th percentile 98 (OK=98 KO=- )
> response time 99th percentile 280 (OK=280 KO=- )
> mean requests/sec 1.067 (OK=1.067 KO=- )
---- Response Time Distribution ------------------------------------------
-----
> t < 800 ms 64 (100%)
> 800 ms < t < 1200 ms 0 ( 0%)
```

```
> t > 1200 ms 0 ( 0%)
> failed 0 ( 0%)
================================================================
=====
```

This report contains the statistics about the execution and the response time distribution.

Finally, Gatling generates an HTML report (by default). Its location is logged at the very end of the program, just before it exits. You can open it with any browser and here is what it looks like:

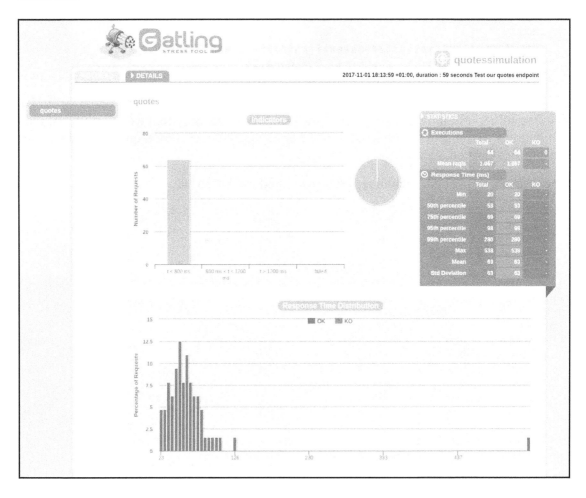

Back on the report, we find the statistics (on the left, in orange) and some detailed indicators in the center of the page. Between them, you have the number of requests, the response time distribution (allowing you to see if the response time is in an acceptable range or if the response time is constant enough for your target users), and so on. You can see, in the previous screenshot, that there are two tabs: **GLOBAL** and **DETAILS**. The **DETAILS** tab has this small menu on the left (with **quotes** on our screenshot), allowing you to drill down the details, per step, of the simulation/scenario. The **quotes** references the name we gave to the `http` request we defined in our simulation.

Gatling has a lot more features and ways to compose scenarios, and since it is code, it is also quite flexible. This is not the topic of the book, but don't hesitate to have a deeper look.

Again, don't forget the injector machines (the machines where you put the processes simulating the clients, that is, the Gatling process here) may not be powerful enough or may have not enough bandwidth to scale very highly. For that reason, you will need to distribute your injectors across several machines to reach the right amount of users in general.

Gatling, like JMeter, supports this mode even if it requires more work. The procedure is explained on their website (`https://gatling.io/docs/2.3/cookbook/scaling_out/`), but at a high level you will run the simulation on several nodes then grab all their outputs and aggregate them post-execution.

Other tools

There are many other tools you can use to define your scenarios; even some DIY solutions can be used. In all cases, you should ensure it scales well enough to not limit your benchmark since you want to test your application and not your benchmark tooling.

Ensuring you have support

When you start benchmarking, you will probably encounter some issues, such as:

- A network setup not correctly done
- A bug in a framework/a library/your application/the injector
- A remote service or database not absorbing enough load, and so on

In all potential cases you may encounter—given any *brick* of your software can have an issue—you should be able to have somebody you can call to help you fix the issue, or at least evaluate it quickly. This is particularly crucial if part of the benchmark costs *some* money (if you are renting some machines, consulting, and so on). The idea here is to be able to get rid of any blocker as fast as possible to not waste time on details.

Time boxing your optimization benchmark

An evaluation benchmark is time boxed by design; you run the benchmark and report the figures. Although, an optimization benchmark is more blurry. Concretely, you can spend a whole year optimizing a simple web service just because of the layers it uses and all the small tuning options you can test, from the network configuration, through the JVM memory, to the caching solutions.

Thus, it is crucial before starting to benchmark an application and optimizing it to define how long you will spend benchmarking your application. It can also be linked to a renting period and may require an estimation phase to work with the operation and development teams. But if you don't do it, the risk is that you will spend a lot of time on the details and not make the best of the benchmark.

Even if it is a high-level approximation, the Pareto principle can be used here to try to optimize the benchmark time. Concretely, try to do 20% of the optimization, which will give you 80% of the boost for your application. Then, if you have time, you can work on the remaining 20%.

Installing and resetting procedures

It may sound obvious, but before starting the benchmark, you must know how to properly install your application and inter connect it with other systems (databases, other applications, and so on). This part should be written down in a document to make sure it is easy to find when needed, and that it has been tested at least once before the benchmark.

The part we forget more often is the reset part, and it would be ideal if this part is automatized as well in the scenarios. This is mainly about ensuring each execution is repeatable, and executions are comparable.

Benchmark iterations

In the previous section, we prepared all we needed to start a benchmark in an efficient way. Now we need to see how we will work during the benchmark.

The first important thing is to establish that we only deal with optimization iterations here and not evaluation ones, which are straightforward—you run the scenarios and gather the reports.

Iterating

It is probably natural, but you will iterate with your optimizations. This means that you will run the same test again and again to measure the result of a change—for instance, increasing the pool size.

The direct implication of such a work structure is that you need to prepare yourself to store lots of reports in an organized way. There are many solutions for that and it mainly depends on the tools you are used to relying on. But at a very high level, you need to, at least, store:

- The benchmark report.
- The benchmark date (to be able to sort them, it is often useful to replay the iterations done afterwards).
- The benchmark configuration (you can store the full configuration or just write it in a file, named `CHANGES.txt`, for instance, where you list what you changed from the previous run). Note that it is important here to include the changes of external systems—such as databases—since they can directly impact your performance.

In terms of storage, you can just use a `benchmark` folder on your hard drive and create a folder per iteration containing the previous information. The folder name can contain the date. A common pattern is `<iteration number>_<date>_<short description>`, for instance `001_2017-11-14_increasing-pool-size`. Using a number (padded with *0)* will allow you to use your operating system sorting to sort the folder. The date gives you another entry point—when somebody tells you *yesterday, it was working better*, for instance. Finally, the small description allows you to more easily identify the reports to compare them.

It is not mandatory, but if you have a small tool (like a script or a small Java program) parsing the reports and configuration to store them in an index, you can more easily find the data and you will get a more powerful search. In the same way, if you already did the work to parse the data, you can easily implement a small `diff` tool to compare two reports, which will allow you to show the configuration changes and the impact on the performance—the reports. Generally, the reports are visual. Thus, being able to merge two reports allows you to compare them more efficiently (visually) than using two windows.

Changing a single setting at a time

While you are tuning the application, it is important to identify if a setting is the factor enhancing the performance or not, and thus identify it as important or not.

If you change multiple settings for a single run, you will not be able to say which setting triggered a change, or you can even neutralize a good setting by using another bad one and missing an optimization factor.

Resist the temptation to change everything at the same time, and try to keep a *scientific* approach, changing a single setting at a time.

Resetting any state between runs

We saw, in the previous section, that you must prepare as much data as the production database will work with, but also don't forget to reset the database state between each run.

If you don't do it, the risk is you will slow down the execution between each run and make the optimizations you do completely invisible. This is because databases have a sort of size limit (quite huge), but while you benchmark, you will generally insert a lot of data very quickly so it wouldn't be surprising to reach that limit. Once you reach this size limit, the database is less efficient and performance degrades. To ensure you can compare the runs and validate some tuning options, you must run in the same conditions. So, you should ensure the database has the same data between each run.

This explanation used the database as the main illustration because it is the most common pitfall, but it is true for any part of your system.

Warming up your system

Another crucial step to doing a benchmark is to not measure the data on a *cold* system. The reason is that a Java EE application generally intends to be long-running software; for that reason, it is common to have a *hot* system which already got optimizations after having ran during weeks or hours. These optimizations can be in action:

- The **JVM Just-In-Time (JIT)** compilation: This will optimize some common code paths. You can also investigate the `-XX:-TieredCompilation` option of the JVM to *pre-compile* the code, but you can encounter some issues with it on some servers.
- You can use some caching and therefore the application will be faster once the cache has all the data you test.
- If you use some external system you may need to do some expensive connections you will reuse later on (SSL connections are slow, secured connections are slow, and so on).

Having some warm-up iterations before the actual measures start is very important to hide all these initializations and just measure the *final* performance of your application.

After your benchmark

Once you have done your benchmark, you should have a *database* of your runs (the folder we talked about earlier with the reports, configuration, and so on). Now, to ensure you did the benchmark for a reason, there are few actions you should take.

In this section, we assume that you will do these steps after the benchmark, but you can do them during the benchmark itself. It is presented this way because it is something you can do *offline*, and if you have some costs associated with the benchmark, these are tasks you can postpone easily.

Writing a report

Normally, at this point, you have collected all the data corresponding to the hard work you did during the benchmark. It is quite important to aggregate this in a report. The report will mainly explain the investigation (why you changed some settings and so on) and expose the results of the runs.

You can, of course, ignore the useless runs (no significant change in the performance), but it is always interesting to integrate the ones corresponding to a performance boost or degradation.

The last part of the report should explain how to properly configure the server for production. It can be done inline in the report or point to another document such as a reference guide if it is about a product or a white book for an application.

Here is a high-level structure for a report:

- Application description: What the application does.
- Metrics: If you have some not so obvious or specific metrics, explain them here (before the next part).
- Scenarios: What your test did.
- Infrastructure/environment: How you deployed machines and external systems, how you set up the monitoring, and so on.
- Injection: How you stimulated the application (you can explain that you had N JMeter nodes, for instance).
- Runs: All the relevant iterations you did and their results.
- Conclusions: What do you keep from the benchmark? Which configuration should be used? You can also mention some tests you didn't get time to run.

Updating your default configurations

Even if, as shown in the previous section, the *final* configuration is part of the report, it will not prevent you from propagating all the good practices you deduced from the benchmark in the code base. The goal is to reduce the mandatory configuration.

For instance, if you identified that you need a timeout of 1 second instead of the default 30 seconds to have a good performance, updating your defaults to 1 second directly in the code base will avoid having a bad performance if the configuration is forgotten. This part is a trade-off between default usability and performance, but generally you can still enhance the default user/operation team experience by doing it.

 If you have some provisioning recipes or a Dockerfile, don't forget to update them as well, if relevant.

Reviewing the conclusions

Depending on your conclusions, you may need to cross-check, with developers or other members, that the outcome of the benchmark is valid.

For instance, if you deduced on our quote-manager that you needed to cache the quotes, then you may desire to validate:

- If it is OK to cache them business-wise (you can check it with your product owner or manager)
- How long you can cache them for, as you will probably want some updates on the prices at some point

Another common example is to validate that you can bypass or change the way you secured some part of the application because the security layer was too slow (switching from OAuth2 to HTTP signature, or some authentication mechanism to network security, for instance).

Once the conclusions are validated, you can also extract the part of the report related to the original SLA and make them validated by your customers, or the people you report to.

Enriching your project backlog

In some cases, you may have identified some issues in the code. They may or may not impact the performance, but in any case you need to create corresponding tasks to fix them upstream.

 If you used some hotfix or patch during the benchmark, don't forget to mention it and reference it inside the report to let people track whether it is actually fixed or not. Note that it can also be related to external libraries or containers and not only your application.

The more you work across teams, the more this phase is important. Otherwise, you get a report where the SLA is reached, and a product is never able to respect that because the enhancements are never integrated into the mainstream source code.

Summary

In this chapter, we saw that a benchmark is something you need to prepare before ensuring you can benefit the most from the benchmark time, and that it requires some organization. We also saw that to be useful you need to extract, from the work done, the conclusions it implies. This is really a scientific procedure—but an easy one—and you need to respect it if you want to optimize your time.

The next and last chapter will go one step further and look at how to reduce the distance between the development and the benchmark to reach a continuous performance evaluation, making your benchmark no longer harmful, since everything is already prepared and under control.

10
Continuous Performance Evaluation

We saw in the previous chapter that driving a benchmark requires work and is not a small operation. However, it doesn't solve all the needs of software development, since you only do it from time to time. Moreover, between two benchmarks, you can have huge performance regression not captured by the unit tests validating the features and behavior of your application.

To solve that, it is a good idea to try to add dedicated tests for performance. This is what this chapter is about. Thus, we will learn:

- Which tools you can use to *test* the performance
- How you can set up some continuous integration for performance
- How to write tests for the performance in such a context

Writing performance tests – the pitfalls

Performance tests have some challenges you need to take into account when you write your tests to avoid having a lot of false positive results (not passing tests where the performance is actually acceptable).

The most common issues you will encounter are:

- How to manage the external systems: We know that external systems are very important in applications today, but it is not always trivial to have them during tests.
- How to be deterministic: Continuous integration/test platforms are often shared. How do you ensure you have the resources needed in order to have a deterministic execution time and to not be slown down, as another build is using all the available resources?
- How to handle the infrastructure: To do an end-to-end test, you need multiple injectors (clients) and probably multiple backend servers. How do you ensure you have them available without them being too expensive if you use cloud platforms such as **Amazon Web Services** (**AWS**)?

You can see the setup of performance tests as a benchmark preparation phase. The main difference will be that you should not rely on external consulting in the long-term, and you will ensure the benchmark iterations are almost completely automatic—*almost* because you will still need to take some actions if the tests fail, otherwise there is no point having a continuous system.

Writing performance tests

Performance tests are present at all stages in a Java EE application, and so, there are several ways to write a performance test. In this section, we will go through a few main ones, starting with the simplest one (algorithm validation).

JMH – the OpenJDK tool

Java Microbenchmark Harness (**JMH**) is a small library developed by the OpenJDK team—yes, the same one doing the JVM—which enables you to easily develop microbenchmarks.

A microbenchmark designs a benchmark on a very small part of an application. Most of the time, you can see it as a *unit benchmark*, using the analogy with unit tests.

Yet, it is something important when setting up performance tests as it will allow you to quickly identify a critical performance regression introduced by a recent change. The idea is to associate each benchmark with a small part of code, whereas a benchmark will include several layers. So, if the benchmark fails, you will spend a lot of time identifying why, instead of simply checking the related code part.

Writing a benchmark with JMH

Before being able to write code with JMH, you need to add it as a dependency of your project. We will use Maven syntax in the following example, but it has equivalents for Gradle, and so on.

The first thing to do is to add into your pom.xml the following dependencies; we will use the scope test since the dependencies are only needed for our performance tests and not the "main" code:

```
<dependencies>
  <!-- your other dependencies -->

  <dependency>
    <groupId>org.openjdk.jmh</groupId>
    <artifactId>jmh-core</artifactId>
    <version>${jmh.version}</version>
    <scope>test</scope>
  </dependency>
  <dependency>
    <groupId>org.openjdk.jmh</groupId>
    <artifactId>jmh-generator-annprocess</artifactId>
    <version>${jmh.version}</version>
    <scope>test</scope> <!-- should be provided but for tests only this
    is more accurate -->
  </dependency>
</dependencies>
```

As of writing this book, the jmh.version property can take the 1.19 value. The jmh-core dependency will bring you JMH itself with its annotation-based API, and the jmh-generator-annprocess brings an annotation processor backbone—used when compiling the test classes/benchmarks—which will generate some sort of index file(s) used by the runtime to execute the benchmarks and the benchmark classes themselves.

The state

Once you have the right dependencies, you can develop your benchmarks. The API is quite straightforward. It uses the notion of a *state* and a state has a life cycle and (volatile) storage associated with the benchmark. The life cycle of a state is defined by marking methods with:

- `@Setup` to execute an initialization task
- `@Teardown` to release any created resource in the setup method

State classes can also contain fields decorated with `@Param` to make them contextualized and configurable (such as enabling them to get a different target URL depending on the execution for example).

A state class is marked with `@State`, which takes, as parameter, the scope of the state instance for a benchmark:

- `Benchmark` means the state will be a singleton in the scope of the JVM.
- `Group` defines the state as a singleton per group. A group is a way to put multiple benchmark methods (scenarii) in the same thread bucket during the execution.
- `Thread` defines the state as a singleton per thread (a bit like `@RequestScoped` for CDI).

Note that you can change how the life cycle is managed a bit by passing the runtime to `@Setup` and `@Teardown` to a different `Level`:

- `Trial`: This is the default, and as we just explained, the benchmark is seen as a whole
- `Iteration`: The life cycle is executed per iteration (warmup or measurement)
- `Invocation`: The life cycle of the state instance is executed per method; this is not recommended in practice to avoid some measurement errors

So, once you have your state object, you define the class containing your benchmarks which are nothing other than methods marked with `@Benchmark`. Then, you have several annotations you can add to the method to customize the benchmark execution:

- `@Measurement`: To customize the number of iterations or the duration of the benchmark.
- `@Warmup` : The same as `@Measurement`, but for the warmup (which is a sort of pre-execution of the benchmark not taken into account for the measurement, the goal being to only measure metrics on a hot JVM).

- @OuputTimeUnit: To customize the unit used for the metrics.
- @Threads: To customize the number of threads used for the benchmark. You can see it as the number of *users*.
- @Fork: The benchmark will be executed in another JVM to avoid test side effects. This annotation allows you to add custom parameters to the forked JVM.
- @OperationsPerInvocation: If you have a loop in your benchmark method, this option (a number) will normalize the measurement. For instance, if you execute five times the same operation in your benchmark and set this value to five, then the execution time will be divided by five.
- @Timeout: It lets you define a maximum duration for the benchmark execution. JMH will interrupt the threads if overpassed.
- @CompilerControl: To customize the way the annotation processor generates the code. For our use case, you rarely need this option, but while tuning some code portions, it can be interesting to test it.

Creating your first JMH benchmark

After all that theory, here is a basic benchmark developed with JMH:

```
public class QuoteMicrobenchmark {
    @Benchmark
    public void compute() {
        //
    }
}
```

In this case, we have a single benchmark scenario called compute. It doesn't use any states and didn't customize any thread or fork count.

In practice, this will not be enough and you will often need a state to get a service. So, it will more look like this:

```
public class QuoteMicrobenchmark {
    @Benchmark
    public void compute(final QuoteState quoteState) {
        quoteState.service.findByName("test");
    }

    @State(Scope.Benchmark)
    public static class QuoteState {
        private QuoteService service;

        @Setup
```

```
        public void setup() {
            service = new QuoteService();
        }
    }
}
```

Here, we created a nested `QuoteState` instance which will be responsible for getting us a service, and we injected it to the benchmark method (`compute`) and used it to get our service instance. This avoids creating an instance per iteration, and thus, avoids taking into account the container startup duration.

This sort of implementation works well until you need an actual container. But when you need a container, it will require some mocking which is absolutely something you should get rid of—even for unit testing—as it will not represent anything close to the real deployment until your code doesn't use Java EE at all (which also means you don't need to mock anything if that is the case).

If you use a CDI 2.0 implementation supporting standalone API—and your application doesn't need more for what you want to test—then you can change the state to start/stop the CDI container and look up the services you need with the new CDI standalone API:

```
@State(Scope.Benchmark)
public class QuoteState {
    private QuoteService service;
    private SeContainer container;

    @Setup
    public void setup() {
        container = SeContainerInitializer.newInstance().initialize();
        service = container.select(QuoteService.class).get();
    }

    @TearDown
    public void tearDown() {
        container.close();
    }
}
```

Here, the setup starts the `container`—you can customize the classes to deploy before calling `initialize()`—and then looks up the `QuoteService` using the `container` instance API. The `tearDown` method just closes the container properly.

Though, in GlassFish, you can't use that new API. But there is the `EJBContainer`, coming from Java EE 6, allowing you to do the same thing combined with the `CDI` class:

```
@State(Scope.Benchmark)
public class QuoteState {
    private QuoteService service;
    private EJBContainer container;

    @Setup
    public void setup() {
        container = EJBContainer.createEJBContainer(new HashMap<>());
        service = CDI.current().select(QuoteService.class).get();
    }

    @TearDown
    public void tearDown() {
        container.close();
    }
}
```

This uses exactly the same logic as before, except the `container` is started based on the `EJBContainer` API. This looks great, but it will not always work with all containers. One pitfall is that if you don't have any EJB, some containers will just not even try to deploy the application.

You can find several workarounds, but the saner solution is to check if you really need the full container or just a subset—such as just CDI—and in this case, you just start this subset (Weld or OpenWebBeans only for a CDI using a previous state). If you really need a full container and your vendor doesn't support any of the two previous ways of starting a container, you can also use a vendor-specific API, mock the container (but take care, you will bypass some execution time *cost*), use another vendor if close enough to your final container, or implement it with a third-party container manager such as the `arquillian` container API.

BlackHole to be a star

JMH provides a particular class—`org.openjdk.jmh.infra.Blackhole`—that can seem weird as it mainly only allows you to `consume` an instance. It is retrieved by injecting it into the parameters of the benchmark:

```
public void compute(final QuoteState quoteState, final Blackhole blackhole)
{
    blackhole.consume(quoteState.service.findByName("test"));
}
```

Why consume the returned value of a method if we do nothing about it? Remember that the Oracle JVM has what is called the **just in time compilation** (**JIT**) which optimizes the code at runtime depending on the statistics of the code paths. If you don't call that `consume` method, you can end up not measuring the actual code you want, but some very optimized flavors of this code, since, most of the time, in your benchmark methods, you will ignore part of the returned values which can, hence, be optimized with the *dead-code elimination* rule.

Running the benchmarks

JMH provides a main-friendly API to run the benchmarks. It is based on defining the execution options which are more or less the options you can associate with a benchmark method (the one we saw in previous section with annotations) and a list of includes/excludes to select the classes/methods to run. Then, you pass these options to a runner and call its `run()` method:

```
final Collection<RunResult> results = new Runner(
    new OptionsBuilder()
        .include("com.packt.MyBenchmark")
        .build())
  .run();
```

Here, we build a simple `Options` instance from the `OptionsBuilder` by including a benchmark class we want to include. Finally, we run it through the method with the same name as the runner, and collect the benchmark's results in a collection.

Integrating JMH with JUnit

There is no official JUnit integration of JMH. In spite of that, it is not that hard to do it yourself. There are lots of possible designs, but in the context of this book we will do the following:

- Our integration will go through a JUnit runner
- The benchmark classes will be identified by extracting the nested classes of the test class which will avoid using any scanning to find the benchmark classes or explicit listing
- We will introduce an `@ExpectedPerformances` annotation to be able to add assertions based on the execution

Structurally, a microbenchmark test using this structure will look like this:

```
@RunWith(JMHRunner.class)
public class QuoteMicrobenchmarkTest {
    @ExpectedPerformances(score = 2668993660.)
    public static class QuoteMicrobenchmark {
        @Benchmark
        @Fork(1) @Threads(2)
        @Warmup(iterations = 5) @Measurement(iterations = 50)
        @ExpectedPerformances(score = 350000.)
        public void findById(final QuoteState quoteState, final
        Blackhole blackhole) {
            blackhole.consume(quoteState.service.findById("test"));
        }

        // other benchmark methods
    }

    public static class CustomerMicrobenchmark {
        // benchmark methods
    }
}
```

Once you have the overall test structure, you just need to add the benchmarks themselves in the right nested class. Concretely, a benchmark class can look like this:

```
public static/*it is a nested class*/ class QuoteMicrobenchmark {
    @Benchmark
    @Fork(1) @Threads(2)
    @Warmup(iterations = 5) @Measurement(iterations = 50)
    @ExpectedPerformances(score = 350000.)
    public void findById(final QuoteState quoteState, final Blackhole
    blackhole) {
```

```
        blackhole.consume(quoteState.service.findById("test"));
    }

    @Benchmark
    @Fork(1) @Threads(2) @Warmup(iterations = 10)
    @Measurement(iterations = 100)
    @ExpectedPerformances(score = 2660000.)
    public void findByName(final QuoteState quoteState, final Blackhole
    blackhole) {
        blackhole.consume(quoteState.service.findByName("test"));
    }

    @State(Scope.Benchmark)
    public static class QuoteState {
        private QuoteService service;

        @Setup public void setup() { service = new QuoteService(); }
    }
}
```

In this test class, we have two benchmark classes using a different state (a different service in our EE application) and each of them can have a different benchmark method counts. The execution is handled by the runner set with @RunWith, using the standard JUnit (4) API. We will note the @ExpectedPerformances usage on all benchmarks.

> If you have already migrated to JUnit 5, or are using TestNG, the same sort of integration is possible but you will use extensions for JUnit 5 and probably an abstract class or a listener for TestNG.

Before seeing how to implement that runner, we must have this @ExpectedPerformances annotation. It is the one allowing us to assert the performance of our benchmark. So, we at least need:

- A score (duration but without specifying the unit, since JMH supports customizing the report unit)
- A tolerance on the score as there is no way you get exactly the same score twice

To do that, we can use this simple definition:

```
@Target(METHOD)
@Retention(RUNTIME)
public @interface ExpectedPerformances {
    double score();
    double scoreTolerance() default 0.1;
}
```

As you can see, we tell the user to define a score, but we use a default score tolerance of `0.1`. In our implementation, we will consider it as being a percentage (10%). This will avoid frequent failure if the machine load is not very stable when running your job. Don't hesitate to decrease that value or even make it configurable through a system property.

To make our previous snippet work, we need to implement a JUnit runner. This is a design choice, but you can also use a rule, exposing some programmatic API or not. To keep it simple, we will not do it here and just consider the whole benchmark setup as done through the annotations. However, for a real-life project, it can be handy to enable the environment (system properties) to customize the annotation values a bit. A common implementation is to use them as a template and multiple all numeric values by a configured ratio on the JVM to let the tests run on any machine.

Our runner will have these four roles:

- Find the benchmark classes
- Validate the model of these classes—typically, validate that each benchmark has an `@ExpectedPerformances`
- Run each benchmark
- Validate the expectations to make the test fail if we have a regression

It is simpler for us to extend `ParentRunner<Class<?>>`. We could use `BlockJUnit4ClassRunner`, but it is based on methods and JMH only supports filtering the executions per class. So, let's stick to it for now. If you put a single benchmark per nested class, then you can simulate a run per method behavior.

The first thing we need to do is to find our benchmark classes. With the JUnit runner API, you can access the test class with `getTestClass()`. To find our benchmark, we just need to check the nested classes of that class through `getClasses()` and make sure the class has at least one `@Benchmark` on a method to validate that it is a JMH class:

```
children = Stream.of(getTestClass().getJavaClass().getClasses())
        .filter(benchmarkClass ->
        Stream.of(benchmarkClass.getMethods())
        .anyMatch(m -> m.isAnnotationPresent(Benchmark.class)))
        .collect(toList());
```

We go through all nested classes of the test class, then keep (or filter) only the ones with a benchmark method at the least. Note that we store the result as we will need multiple times in our runner.

Then, the validation is as simple as going over these classes and their benchmark methods to validate they have the `@ExpectedPerformances` annotation:

```
errors.addAll(children.stream()
        .flatMap(c -> Stream.of(c.getMethods()).filter(m ->
        m.isAnnotationPresent(Benchmark.class)))
        .filter(m ->
        !m.isAnnotationPresent(ExpectedPerformances.class))
        .map(m -> new IllegalArgumentException("No
        @ExpectedPerformances on " + m))
        .collect(toList()));
```

Here, to list the errors of the JUnit validation, we add an exception per method annotated with `@Benchmark` but without an `@ExpectedPerformances`. We do it first by converting the classes to a stream of benchmark methods, then keeping only the ones without the `@ExpectedPerformances` annotation to keep the *set vision*.

Finally, the last key part of the runner code is to convert a class to an actual execution:

```
final Collection<RunResult> results;
try {
    results = new Runner(buildOptions(benchmarkClass)).run();
} catch (final RunnerException e) {
    throw new IllegalStateException(e);
}

// for all benchmarks assert the performances from the results
final List<AssertionError> errors = Stream.of(benchmarkClass.getMethods())
        .filter(m -> m.isAnnotationPresent(Benchmark.class))
        .map(m -> {
            final Optional<RunResult> methodResult = results.stream()
```

```
                    .filter(r ->
                    m.getName().equals(r.getPrimaryResult().getLabel()))
                    .findFirst();
                    assertTrue(m + " didn't get any result",
                    methodResult.isPresent());

                final ExpectedPerformances expectations =
                m.getAnnotation(ExpectedPerformances.class);
                final RunResult result = results.iterator().next();
                final BenchmarkResult aggregatedResult =
                result.getAggregatedResult();

                final double actualScore =
                aggregatedResult.getPrimaryResult().getScore();
                final double expectedScore = expectations.score();
                final double acceptedError = expectedScore *
                expectations.scoreTolerance();
                try { // use assert to get a common formatting for errors
                    assertEquals(m.getDeclaringClass().getSimpleName() +
                    "#" + m.getName(), expectedScore, actualScore,
                    acceptedError);
                    return null;
                } catch (final AssertionError ae) {
                    return ae;
                }
            }).filter(Objects::nonNull).collect(toList());
    if (!errors.isEmpty()) {
        throw new AssertionError(errors.stream()
            .map(Throwable::getMessage)
            .collect(Collectors.joining("\n")));
    }
}
```

First, we execute the benchmark holder class and collect the results. Then, we iterate over the benchmark methods and for each of them, we extract the result (primary result label is the method name). Finally, we extract our @ExpectedPerformances constraint and compare it with the primary result of the test. The little trick here is to catch the AssertionError the assert can throw, and collect them all in a list to convert them in another AssertionError. You can just format the message the way you want, but doing it this way keeps standard JUnit formatting of the errors. The other tip here is to put the benchmark class and method in the error message to make sure you can identify which benchmark failed. The alternative way can be to introduce another annotation to use a custom name for each benchmark.

Now that we have looked at all the small technical points, let's put it all together. To start, we will define that our runner will use `Class` children, which will represent each of our nested classes:

```
public class JMHRunner extends ParentRunner<Class<?>> {
  private List<Class<?>> children;

  public JMHRunner(final Class<?> klass) throws InitializationError {
    super(klass);
  }

  @Override
  protected List<Class<?>> getChildren() {
    return children;
  }

  @Override
  protected Description describeChild(final Class<?> child) {
    return Description.createTestDescription(getTestClass().getJavaClass(),
child.getSimpleName());
  }
```

In the code executed by the parent constructor (`super(klass)`), JUnit will trigger a test validation where we compute the children we previously saw to be able to return them in `getChildren()` and to let JUnit handle all our nested classes. We implement `describeChild` to let JUnit associate a `Description` with each nested class and to have smoother integration with IDE (the goal is to show them in a tree when you run the tests). To compute the children and validate them, we can use this JUnit implementation of `collectInitializationErrors`—using this hook avoids computing it multiple times per test class:

```
  @Override
  protected void collectInitializationErrors(final List<Throwable>
errors) {
    super.collectInitializationErrors(errors);

    children = Stream.of(getTestClass().getJavaClass().getClasses())
      .filter(benchmarkClass -> Stream.of(benchmarkClass.getMethods())
        .anyMatch(m -> m.isAnnotationPresent(Benchmark.class)))
      .collect(toList());

    errors.addAll(children.stream()
        .flatMap(c -> Stream.of(c.getMethods())
        .filter(m -> m.isAnnotationPresent(Benchmark.class)))
        .filter(m ->
        !m.isAnnotationPresent(ExpectedPerformances.class))
```

```
      .map(m -> new IllegalArgumentException("No
    @ExpectedPerformances on " + m))
      .collect(toList()));
}
```

Then, we need to ensure we can run our children (benchmarks) properly. To do that, we extend another JUnit hook which is designed to run each child. The only thing we take care of is mainly ensuring JUnit @Ignored is supported for our children:

```
@Override
protected boolean isIgnored(final Class<?> child) {
  return child.isAnnotationPresent(Ignore.class);
}

@Override
protected void runChild(final Class<?> child, final RunNotifier
notifier) {
  final Description description = describeChild(child);
  if (isIgnored(child)) {
    notifier.fireTestIgnored(description);
  } else {
    runLeaf(benchmarkStatement(child), description, notifier);
  }
}
```

In runChild(), we delegate the execution to the JUnit engine by adding, as an implementation of our test execution, the code we saw just before based on JMH runner but wrapped in a JUnit Statement to let it be integrated with JUnit notifiers. Now, we just need this execution implementation (benchmarkStatement). This is done by completing the class with the following code:

```
private Statement benchmarkStatement(final Class<?> benchmarkClass) {
  return new Statement() {
    @Override
    public void evaluate() throws Throwable {
      final Collection<RunResult> results;
      try {
        results = new Runner(buildOptions(benchmarkClass)).run();
      } catch (final RunnerException e) {
        throw new IllegalStateException(e);
      }

      assertResults(benchmarkClass, results);
    }
  };
}
```

```
// all options will use JMH annotations so just
include the class to run
private Options buildOptions(final Class<?> test) {
  return new OptionsBuilder()
      .include(test.getName().replace('$', '.'))
      .build();
}
```

This reuses everything we previously saw; the `buildOptions` method will force the JMH runner to use the annotations on the benchmark for the execution configuration and we just include a single test at a time. Finally, we implement the `assertResults` method as we explained before:

```
public void assertResults(final Class<?> benchmarkClass, final
Collection<RunResult> results) {
  // for all benchmarks assert the performances from the results
  final List<AssertionError> errors =
  Stream.of(benchmarkClass.getMethods())
      .filter(m -> m.isAnnotationPresent(Benchmark.class))
      .map(m -> {
        final Optional<RunResult> methodResult = results.stream()
            .filter(r ->
            m.getName().equals(r.getPrimaryResult().getLabel())))
            .findFirst();
        assertTrue(m + " didn't get any result",
        methodResult.isPresent());

        final ExpectedPerformances expectations =
        m.getAnnotation(ExpectedPerformances.class);
        final RunResult result = results.iterator().next();
        final BenchmarkResult aggregatedResult =
        result.getAggregatedResult();

        final double actualScore =
        aggregatedResult.getPrimaryResult().getScore();
        final double expectedScore = expectations.score();
        final double acceptedError = expectedScore *
        expectations.scoreTolerance();
        try { // use assert to get a common formatting for errors
          assertEquals(m.getDeclaringClass().getSimpleName() + "#" +
          m.getName(), expectedScore, actualScore, acceptedError);
          return null;
        } catch (final AssertionError ae) {
          return ae;
        }
      }).filter(Objects::nonNull).collect(toList());
  if (!errors.isEmpty()) {
```

```
        throw new AssertionError(errors.stream()
            .map(Throwable::getMessage)
            .collect(Collectors.joining("\n")));
    }
  }
}
```

Now, with this runner, you can execute the test in the main build with surefire or failsafe and ensure your build will not pass if you have huge performance regression.

 This is a simple implementation and you can enrich it in several ways, such as by simulating one child per benchmark to gain a nicer report in the IDE and surefire report (just run it the first time you encounter the enclosing class, then store the result and do the assertion per method). You can also assert more results, such as the secondary results or the iteration results (for example, no iteration is slower than X). Finally, you can implement some `living documentation` features, adding an @Documentation annotation which will be used by the runner to create a report file (in asciidoctor, for instance).

ContiPerf

An alternative to JMH, which is a bit less advanced but much easier to use, is ContiPerf. You can add it to your project with this dependency:

```
<dependency>
    <groupId>org.databene</groupId>
    <artifactId>contiperf</artifactId>
    <version>2.3.4</version>
    <scope>test</scope>
</dependency>
```

We will not detail it completely in this book as we spent a lot of time on JMH already. But in a few words, it is based on a JUnit 4 rule. Thus, it can be combined with other rules and sorted thanks to the JUnit `RuleChain`, which makes it very powerful, with all light EE containers having a JUnit-based testing stack such as TomEE or Meecrowave, for instance.

The very big advantage of ContiPerf is that it is aligned with the JUnit model:

- It is based on the standard JUnit `@Test` method marker
- You can reuse the JUnit standard life cycle (`@BeforeClass`, `@Before`, and so on)
- You can combine it with other JUnit features (runners, rules, and so on)

Here is what a test can look like in terms of structure:

```
public class QuoteMicrobenchmarkTest {
    private static QuoteService service;

    @Rule
    public final ContiPerfRule rule = new ContiPerfRule();

    @BeforeClass
    public static void init() {
        service = new QuoteService();
    }

    @Test
    @Required(throughput = 7000000)
    @PerfTest(rampUp = 100, duration = 10000, threads = 10, warmUp =
    10000)
    public void test() {
        service.findByName("test").orElse(null);
    }
}
```

We immediately identify a JUnit structure, with an `@BeforeClass` initializing the test (you can start a container here and close it in an `@AfterClass` if needed), and a `@Test` that is our benchmark/scenario. The only difference with a JUnit test is the `ContiPerfRule` and the `@Required` and `@PerfTest` annotations.

The `@PerfTest` describes the test environment—how many threads, how long, how many iterations, the duration for the warmup, and so on.

The `@Required`, on another side, describes the assertions (validations) to do. It is equivalent to our `@ExpectedPerformances` in our JMH integration. It supports most of the common validations such as the throughoutput, the average, the total time, and so on.

Arquillian and ContiPerf – the diabolic pair

In the JMH section, we got the issue that starting a container was sometimes hard and really not straightforward. As ContiPerf is a rule, it is compatible with `Arquillian`, which can do all that work for you.

`Arquillian` is a project created by JBoss (Red Hat, now) for abstracting the containers behind a **service provider interface** (**SPI**) and integrating it with JUnit or TestNG. The idea is to run a test from your IDE as usual, without having to care about needing a container.

At a high level, it requires you to define what you deploy into the container and to use the `Arquillian` runner with JUnit (or an abstract class with TestNG). Thanks to a mechanism of extensions and enrichers, you can inject most of what you need into the test class, such as CDI beans, which is really handy for writing tests. Here is a sample:

```
@RunWith(Arquillian.class)
public class QuoteServicePerformanceTest {
    @Deployment
    public static Archive<?> quoteServiceApp() {
        return ShrinkWrap.create(WebArchive.class, "quote-manager.war")
                .addClasses(QuoteService.class,
                InMemoryTestDatabaseConfiguration.class)
                .addAsWebResource(new ClassLoaderAsset("META
                -INF/beans.xml"), "WEB-INF/classes/META-INF/beans.xml")
                .addAsWebResource(new ClassLoaderAsset("META-
                INF/persistence.xml"), "WEB-INF/classes/META-
                INF/persistence.xml");
    }

    @Inject
    private QuoteService service;

    @Before
    public void before() {
        final Quote quote = new Quote();
        quote.setName("TEST");
        quote.setValue(10.);
        service.create(quote);
    }

    @After
    public void after() {
        service.deleteByName("TEST");
    }

    @Test
    public void findByName() {
        assertTrues(service.findByName("TEST").orElse(false));
    }
}
```

This snippet illustrates `Arquillian` usage with its common characteristics:

- The `Arquillian` runner is in use; it is the magic that will start the container (once), deploy the application (per test class by default), execute the tests (inherited from JUnit default behavior), undeploy the application when all tests of the class were executed, and shut down the container once the tests have been executed.
- The static `@Deployment` method returns an `Archive<?>` describing what to deploy into the container (the application). You don't have to deploy the full application and you can change it per test if you want. For instance, in our sample, we didn't deploy our `DataSourceConfiguration`, which is pointing to MySQL, but instead, a `InMemoryDatabaseConfiguration`, which we can assume uses an embedded database such as derby or h2.
- We have a CDI injected into the test directly, our `QuoteService`.
- The rest of the test is a standard JUnit test with its life cycle (`@Before`/`@After`) and its test methods (`@Test`).

> If you find the construction of the archive too complicated, there are some projects such as the TomEE `ziplock` module that simplify it by reusing the *current* project metadata (such as the `pom.xml` and compiled classes), which allows you to create the archive with a single method invocation: `Mvn.war()`. Some containers, including TomEE, allow you to deploy each archive a single time. But if your container doesn't support it, you can use the `Arquillian` suite extension to achieve almost the same result. The overall goal is to group your tests to deploy a single time your application and save precious minutes on your tests execution duration.

`Arquillian` also allows us to go further and execute the test either from inside the container—as the previous example—or from a client perspective using the `@RunAsClient` annotation. In this case, your test is no longer executed inside the container but in JUnit JVM (which can be the same or not, depending on whether your container uses another JVM or not). In any case, coupling `Arquillian` with ContiPerf allows you to validate the performance without many headaches. You just have to add the ContiPerf rule and annotations on the methods you want to validate:

```
@RunWith(Arquillian.class)
public class QuoteServicePerformanceTest {
    @Deployment
    public static Archive<?> quoteServiceApp() {
        final WebArchive baseArchive =
        ShrinkWrap.create(WebArchive.class, "quote-manager.war")
```

```
            .addClasses(QuoteService.class)
            .addAsWebResource(new ClassLoaderAsset("META
            -INF/beans.xml"), "WEB-INF/classes/META-INF/beans.xml")
            .addAsWebResource(new ClassLoaderAsset("META
            -INF/persistence.xml"), "WEB-INF/classes/META
            -INF/persistence.xml");
        if (Boolean.getBoolean("test.performance." +
        QuoteService.class.getSimpleName() + ".database.mysql")) {
            baseArchive.addClasses(DataSourceConfiguration.class);
        } else {
            baseArchive.addClasses(InMemoryDatabase.class);
        }
        return baseArchive;
    }

    @Rule
    public final ContiPerfRule rule = new ContiPerfRule();

    @Inject
    private QuoteService service;

    private final Collection<Long> id = new ArrayList<Long>();

    @Before
    public void before() {
        IntStream.range(0, 1000000).forEach(i -> insertQuote("Q" + i));
        insertQuote("TEST");
    }

    @After
    public void after() {
        id.forEach(service::delete);
    }

    @Test
    @Required(max = 40)
    @PerfTest(duration = 500000, warmUp = 200000)
    public void findByName() {
        service.findByName("TEST");
    }

    private void insertQuote(final String name) {
        final Quote entity = new Quote();
        entity.setName(name);
        entity.setValue(Math.random() * 100);
        id.add(service.create(entity).getId());
    }
}
```

This is almost the same test as before, but we added more data to ensure the dataset size doesn't affect our performance much in the `@Before` method used to initialize the database. To integrate the test with ContiPerf, we added the ContiPerf annotations to our method and the ContiPerf rule. The last trick you can see is a system property in the archive creation, able to switch databases depending on the JVM configuration. It can be used to test against several databases or environments and validates you are compliant with all your target platforms.

To be able to run this example, you need to add these dependencies into your pom—considering that you will test it against GlassFish 5.0, you need to change the container dependency and `arquillian` container integration:

```
<dependency>
  <groupId>junit</groupId>
  <artifactId>junit</artifactId>
  <version>4.12</version>
  <scope>test</scope>
</dependency>
<dependency>
  <groupId>org.jboss.arquillian.junit</groupId>
  <artifactId>arquillian-junit-container</artifactId>
  <version>1.1.13.Final</version>
  <scope>test</scope>
</dependency>
<dependency>
  <groupId>org.jboss.arquillian.container</groupId>
  <artifactId>arquillian-glassfish-embedded-3.1</artifactId>
  <version>1.0.1</version>
  <scope>test</scope>
</dependency>
<dependency>
  <groupId>org.glassfish.main.extras</groupId>
  <artifactId>glassfish-embedded-all</artifactId>
  <version>5.0</version>
  <scope>test</scope>
</dependency>
```

JUnit is the test framework we use and we import its Arquillian integration (`arquillian-junit-container`). Then, we import our `arquillian` container integration (`arquillian-glassfish-embedded-3.1`) and Java EE container, as we use an embedded mode (`glassfish-embedded-all`). Don't forget to add a ContiPerf dependency too if you plan to use it.

JMeter and build integration

We learned in a previous section that JMeter can be used to build scenarii you execute against your application. It can also be programmatically executed—it is Java-based, after all—or executed through some of its Maven integrations.

If you use its Maven plugin from lazerycode (`https://github.com/jmeter-maven-plugin/jmeter-maven-plugin`), you can even configure the remote mode to have real stress testing:

```
<plugin>
  <groupId>com.lazerycode.jmeter</groupId>
  <artifactId>jmeter-maven-plugin</artifactId>
  <version>2.2.0</version>
  <executions>
    <execution>
      <id>jmeter-tests</id>
      <goals>
        <goal>jmeter</goal>
      </goals>
    </execution>
  </executions>
  <configuration>
    <remoteConfig>
      <startServersBeforeTests>true</startServersBeforeTests>
      <serverList>jmeter1.company.com,jmeter2.company.com</serverList>
      <stopServersAfterTests>true</stopServersAfterTests>
    </remoteConfig>
  </configuration>
</plugin>
```

This snippet defines the `jmeter` plugin to use `jmeter1.company.com` and `jmeter2.company.com` for the load testing. Servers will be initialized and destroyed before/after running the plans.

Without entering into the deep details of the plugin—you can find them on the related GitHub wiki—the plugin uses configurations stored in the project in `src/test/jmeter` by default. This is where you can put your scenarii (`.jmx` files).

The challenge with this solution is to provide `jmeter[1,2].company.com` machines. Of course, you can create some machines and let them run, though, this is not a very good way to manage the AWS machines and it would be better to start them with the build (allowing you to have concurrent builds, if needed, on multiple branches at the same time).

There are several solutions for that need, but the simplest is probably to install on the CI platform an AWS client (or plugin) and launch it before/after the Maven builds the corresponding commands to provision the machine, set the machine hosts in a build property, and pass it to the Maven build. It requires you to variabilize the plugin configuration, but nothing fancy, as Maven supports placeholders and system property input. Nonetheless, running the tests from your machine can be hard as you will need to provision yourself with the machine you will use. Thus, this reduces the shareable side of the project.

Don't forget to ensure the task of shutting down the instance is always executed, even when the tests fail, or else you could leak some machines and have a billing surprise at the end of the month.

Finally, as JMeter is a mainstream solution, you can easily find platforms supporting it natively and handling the infrastructure for you. The main ones are:

- BlazeMeter (`https://www.blazemeter.com/`)
- Flood.IO (`https://flood.io/`)
- Redline.13 (`https://www.redline13.com/`)

Don't hesitate to have a look at their websites, their prices, and compare them to what you can build yourself directly with AWS if you don't have dedicated machines on your CI. This can allow you to solve the environment and infrastructure issues performance tests often encounter.

Gatling and continuous integration

Like JMeter, Gatling has its own Maven plugin, but it also has some companion AWS integration (`https://github.com/electronicarts/gatling-aws-maven-plugin`) natively integrated with Maven.

Here is what the official Gatling Maven plugin declaration can look like in your `pom.xml`:

```
<plugin>
  <groupId>io.gatling</groupId>
  <artifactId>gatling-maven-plugin</artifactId>
  <version>${gatling-plugin.version}</version>
  <executions>
    <execution>
      <phase>test</phase>
      <goals>
```

```
      <goal>execute</goal>
    </goals>
  </execution>
</executions>
</plugin>
```

The first plugin (1) defines how to run Gatling. The default configuration will look for simulations in `src/test/scala`.

This setup will locally run your simulations. So, you will likely migrate to the non-official plugin, yet integrated with AWS, to be able to control the injectors. Here is what the declaration can look like:

```
<plugin>
  <groupId>com.ea.gatling</groupId>
  <artifactId>gatling-aws-maven-plugin</artifactId>
  <version>1.0.11</version>
  <executions>
    <execution>
      <phase>test</phase>
      <goals>
        <goal>execute</goal>
      </goals>
    </execution>
  </executions>
</plugin>
```

This plugin will integrate Gatling on AWS. It requires some AWS configuration (like your keys), but you will generally configure them outside the `pom.xml` so as not to put your credentials in a public place—properties in a profile in your `settings.xml` is a good place to start. Here are the properties you will need to define:

```
<properties>
  <ssh.private.key>${gatling.ssh.private.key}</ssh.private.key>
  <ec2.key.pair.name>loadtest-keypair</ec2.key.pair.name>
  <ec2.security.group>default</ec2.security.group>
  <ec2.instance.count>3</ec2.instance.count>

  <gatling.local.home>${project.build.directory}/gatling-charts
  -highcharts-bundle-2.2.4/bin/gatling.sh</gatling.local.home>
   <gatling.install.script>${project.basedir}/src/test/resources/install-
  gatling.sh</gatling.install.script>
  <gatling.root>gatling-charts-highcharts-bundle-2.2.4</gatling.root>
  <gatling.java.opts>-Xms1g -Xmx16g -Xss4M
  -XX:+CMSClassUnloadingEnabled -
  XX:MaxPermSize=512M</gatling.java.opts>
```

```
    <!-- Fully qualified name of the Gatling simulation and a name
    describing the test -->
    <gatling.simulation>com.FooTest</gatling.simulation>
    <gatling.test.name>LoadTest</gatling.test.name>

    <!-- (3) -->
    <s3.upload.enabled>true</s3.upload.enabled>
    <s3.bucket>loadtest-results</s3.bucket>
    <s3.subfolder>my-loadtest</s3.subfolder>
  </properties>
```

Defining all these properties doesn't prevent you from changing the values through a system property. For instance, setting `-Dec2.instance.count=9` will allow you to change the number of injectors (nine instead of three). The first group of properties (ec2 ones) define how to create the AWS instances and how many to create. The second group (Gatling one) defines where Gatling is and how to run it. The third group defines the simulation to run. Finally, the last group (s3 one) defines where to upload the results of the test.

This configuration is not yet functional, as it is not yet self-sufficient:

- It relies on Gatling distribution, which is not yet installed (`gatling.local.home`)
- It relies on a script we didn't create yet (`install-gatling.sh`)

To be able to not depend on a local Gatling installation, we can use Maven to download it. To do so, we just need the dependency plugin of Maven:

```
<plugin>
  <groupId>org.apache.maven.plugins</groupId>
  <artifactId>maven-dependency-plugin</artifactId>
  <version>3.0.2</version>
  <executions>
    <execution>
      <id>download-gatling-distribution</id>
      <phase>generate-test-resources</phase>
      <goals>
        <goal>unpack</goal>
      </goals>
      <configuration>
        <artifactItems>
          <artifactItem>
            <groupId>io.gatling.highcharts</groupId>
            <artifactId>gatling-charts-highcharts-bundle</artifactId>
            <version>2.2.4</version>
            <classifier>bundle</classifier>
            <type>zip</type>
```

```
                <overWrite>false</overWrite>
<outputDirectory>${project.build.directory}/gatling</outputDirectory>
                <destFileName>gatling-charts-highcharts-bundle
                -2.2.4.jar</destFileName>
            </artifactItem>
        </artifactItems>
        <outputDirectory>${project.build.directory}/wars</outputDirectory>
        <overWriteReleases>false</overWriteReleases>
        <overWriteSnapshots>true</overWriteSnapshots>
      </configuration>
    </execution>
  </executions>
</plugin>
```

This configuration will extract the Gatling distribution into the
`target/gatling/gatling-charts-highcharts-bundle-2.2.4` folder and let the
plugin use it when it runs.

For the script, you can use this one, which is for Fedora. However, it is easy to adapt to any
distribution if you pick another image on EC2:

```
#!/bin/sh
# Increase the maximum number of open files
sudo ulimit -n 65536
echo "* soft nofile 65535" | sudo tee --append /etc/security/limits.conf
echo "* hard nofile 65535" | sudo tee --append /etc/security/limits.conf

sudo yum install --quiet --assumeyes java-1.8.0-openjdk-devel.x86_64 htop
screen

# Install Gatling
GATLING_VERSION=2.2.4
URL=https://repo.maven.apache.org/maven2/io/gatling/highcharts/gatling-char
ts-highcharts-bundle/${GATLING_VERSION}/gatling-charts-highcharts-bundle-
${GATLING_VERSION}-bundle.zip
GATLING_ARCHIVE=gatling-charts-highcharts-bundle-${GATLING_VERSION}-
bundle.zip

wget --quiet ${URL} -O ${GATLING_ARCHIVE}
unzip -q -o ${GATLING_ARCHIVE}

# Remove example code to reduce Scala compilation time at the beginning of
load test
rm -rf gatling-charts-highcharts-bundle-${GATLING_VERSION}/user-
files/simulations/computerdatabase/
```

This script does three main things:

- Increases `ulimit` to make sure the injector can use enough file handlers and not be limited by the OS configuration
- Installs Java
- Downloads Gatling from Maven centra, extracts the archive (like we did with the previous Maven plugin), but on the injector machines which don't have to use Maven, and finally cleans up the extracted archive (removing sample simulations)

> If you need any dependencies, you will need to create a shade (and use the default `jar-with-dependencies` as a classifier). You can do that using `maven-assembly-plugin` and the `single` goal.

Deploying your (benchmark) application

In the two previous sections, we learned how to handle the injectors, but you will also need to deploy the application to test, if possible, on a dedicated instance for the test. This doesn't mean you need to forget what we looked at in the previous chapter, such as ensuring the machine is used in production and other potentially impacting services are running. Instead, you must ensure the machine(s) does what you think it does and not something unexpected that will impact the figures/tests.

Here, again, using cloud services to deploy your application can be the easiest solution. The simplest solution will likely rely on some cloud CLI (such as AWS CLI or `aws` command) or a small `main(String[])` you can write using the cloud provider client API or SDK.

Depending on if you code the deployment yourself (or not), it will be more or less easy to integrate with the Maven (or Gradle) build. As part of your project, an `exec-maven-plugin` can enable you to integrate it exactly where you need to in the Maven life cycle. Most of the time, this will be done before the performance test but after test compilation, or even after packaging the application (if you keep the performance test in the same module, which is feasible).

If you don't code the deployment yourself, you will need to define the stages of your performance build:

1. Compile/package the project and tests.
2. Deploy the application (and don't forget to reset the environment too if needed, including cleaning a database or JMS queue).
3. Start the performance test.
4. Undeploy the application/shut down the created server (if relevant).

With Maven or Gradle, it is easy to skip some of the tasks, either with a flag or a profile, and consequently, you will end up with commands like this:

```
mvn clean install # (1)
mvn exec:java@deploy-application # (2)
mvn test -Pperf-tests # (3)
mvn exec:java@undeploy-application #(4)
```

The first command, `(1)`, will build the full project but bypass the performance tests as we don't activate the `perf-tests` profile by default. The second command will deploy the application on the target environment using a custom implementation based on AWS SDK, for instance, potentially creating it from scratch. Don't forget to log what you do, even if you are waiting for something, or else you—or others —may think the process is hanging. Then, we run the performance test `(3)` and finally we undeploy the application with a command symmetric to `(2)`.

With such a solution, you need to ensure `(4)` is executed as soon as `(2)` is executed. In general, you will enforce it to always be executed and handle a quick exit condition if the expected environment to destroy doesnt exist.

To orchestrate the steps, you can have a look at the Jenkins pipeline feature: it will give you a lot of flexibility to implement this type of logic in a straightforward manner.

Going further overpasses the scope of this book, but to give you some pointers, the deployments can rely on Docker-based tools which makes it really easy to deploy on cloud platforms in general. Nevertheless, don't forget Docker is not a provisioning tool. And if your *recipe* (the steps for creating your instance) is not simple (installing software from the repository, copying/downloading your application, and starting it), then you can invest in a provisioning tool such as chef or puppet to be more flexible, powerful, and to avoid hacks.

Continuous integration platform and performance

Jenkins is the most commonly used continuous integration platform. There are alternatives, such as Travis, but the ecosystem of Jenkins and the easiness to extend it makes it the clear leader for Java and enterprises applications.

The first thing we want to solve on the build/test execution platform for performance is the isolation of the builds, the goal being obviously to ensure the obtained figures are not affected by other builds.

To do that, Jenkins provides several plugins:

- Amazon EC2 Container Service Plugin (`https://wiki.jenkins.io/display/JENKINS/Amazon+EC2+Container+Service+Plugin`): Allows you to run the builds (tests) in a dedicated machine created based on a Docker image.
- Throttle Concurrent Build Plugin (`https://github.com/jenkinsci/throttle-concurrent-builds-plugin/blob/master/README.md`): Allows you to control how many concurrent builds can be executed per project. Concretely, for performance, we want to ensure it is one per project.

In terms of configuration, you will need to make sure the performance tests are executed with an accurate configuration:

- Regularly, using Jenkins scheduling, but probably not each time there is a commit or a pull-request. Depending on the criticity, the stability of your project, and the duration of your performance tests, it can be once a day or once a week.
- The previous plugins—or equivalent—are in use and correctly configured.
- The build notifies the correct channels if they fail (mail, Slack, IRC, and so on).

It will also be important to ensure you store the history of the runs to be able to compare them, in particular if you don't run the performance test with each commit, which would give you the exact commit, introducing a regression. To do that, you can use another Jenkins plugin which is exactly intended to store the history of common performance tools: the Performance Plugin (`https://wiki.jenkins.io/display/JENKINS/Performance+Plugin`). This plugin supports Gatling and JMeter, as well as a few other tools. It is a nice plugin, allowing you to visualize the reports directly from Jenkins, which is very handy when investigating some changes. What's more, it is compatible with Jenkins pipeline scripts.

Summary

In this chapter, we went through some common ways to ensure the performance of your application is under control and to limit the risk of getting unexpected bad surprises when you go into a benchmark phase, or worse, in production! Setting up simple tests or complete environments for a volatile (temporary) benchmark each week (or even each day) are very feasible steps, enabling a product to be delivered with a better quality level once the entry cost has been paid.

After having understood how Java EE instruments your application to let you focus on your business, how to monitor and instrument your application to optimize your application, and how to boost your application with some tuning or caching, we now know how to automatically control performance regressions to be able to fix them as soon as possible.

As a result, you have now covered all the parts of product—or library—creation related to performance, and you are able to deliver highly performant software. You've got this!

Another Book You May Enjoy

If you enjoyed this book, you may be interested in another book by Packt:

Architecting Modern Java EE Applications
Sebastian Daschner

ISBN: 978-1-78839-385-0

- What enterprise software engineers should focus on
- Implement applications, packages, and components in a modern way
- Design and structure application architectures
- Discover how to realize technical and cross-cutting aspects
- Get to grips with containers and container orchestration technology
- Realize zero-dependency, 12-factor, and Cloud-native applications
- Implement automated, fast, reliable, and maintainable software tests
- Discover distributed system architectures and their requirements

Leave a review - let other readers know what you think

Please share your thoughts on this book with others by leaving a review on the site that you bought it from. If you purchased the book from Amazon, please leave us an honest review on this book's Amazon page. This is vital so that other potential readers can see and use your unbiased opinion to make purchasing decisions, we can understand what our customers think about our products, and our authors can see your feedback on the title that they have worked with Packt to create. It will only take a few minutes of your time, but is valuable to other potential customers, our authors, and Packt. Thank you!

Index

www.ingramcontent.com/pod-product-compliance
Lightning Source LLC
Chambersburg PA
CBHW080618060326
40690CB00021B/4735